CHRISTIAN MISSION
IN RECONSTRUCTION:
AN ASIAN ANALYSIS

Choan-Seng Song

ORBIS BOOKS

Maryknoll, New York 10545

1977

To my colleagues and friends
at the offices of
The Reformed Church in America
with whom I shared
A Heritage of Mission
and
A Mission of Hope.

Library of Congress Cataloging in Publication Data

Song, Choan-Seng, 1929–
    Christian mission in reconstruction—an Asian analysis.

Reprint of the ed. published by the Christian Litera-
ture Society, Madras.
    Includes bibliographical references.
    1.   Missions—Asia.   I.   Title.
BV3151.S66   1977   266'.0095   77-23237
ISBN 0-88344-073-3
ISBN 0-88344-074-1 pbk.

Foreword

I feel privileged to have been asked to provide a short Foreword for this book, as I shall be able to say an introductory word concerning Dr. C. S. Song, who is a friend and colleague of mine of long standing and comes from the same Island of Taiwan. At Tainan Theological College he first taught the Old Testament and later moved to the field of Systematic Theology. In 1965 he was made my successor as Principal, and so he is well known among the theological community in both North East and South East Asia, both as a theological educator and as a theologian.

I welcome this publication for three reasons. First, as C. S. Song points out, we have come to the end of an era and it is urgent—in fact, imperative—for us to reflect theologically and, perhaps even more important, missiologically, on what the end of an era means and what the new era is to be like. This is a painful process which may.raise many new questions and even embarrassing ones for which we have no ready answer, but which we all have to face—we church people and theologians in Asia especially.

Secondly, in this rigorous reflection we have to face the ongoing as well as the radically changing contexts of Asia. Of course, to follow the contemporary jargon, Asia is part of the Third World, which is sometimes described as the Two-Thirds World. The vastness of Asia is such that it forms two-thirds of the Two-Thirds World both in terms of its geographical extent, the size of its population, and also in terms of its poverty and hunger, its search for liberation. Practically half of Asia is now ideologically in the communist world and this fact has enormous implications for the search for a new society in Asia today. Side by side with this contemporary Asia which is undergoing not only a radical but a revolutionary change, there is also that on-going, old Asia, with its ancient cultures and age-old religions. Anyone wrestling with the Christian mission today has to take this double context of Asia, both old and new, seriously. C. S. Song's book is tremendously interesting and challenging precisely because he is trying to wrestle with these questions.

Thirdly, since it is the *Christian* mission with which we are dealing, we must be faithful to the biblical message and here C. S. Song, as an Old Testament scholar as well as a systematic theologian, has rightly emphasized that the Christ-centred mission should take equally seriously the biblical affirmation of creation and liberation, the two major themes right through his book.

It is fascinating, as we read the book, to see how the context of Asia and the biblical text interact, as Dr Song tries to help us understand the end of one era and the beginning of another. All this has been interwoven into one concern for the Christian Mission in Asia in the contemporary world.

I hope this book will be read and discussed not only among ourselves, the Christian leaders in Asia, but also by our colleagues in other parts of the world, so that the debate may go on, constructively and fruitfully, in the search for the new era in Christ's mission.

SHOKI COE

Preface

CHRISTIAN mission in Asia is undergoing a painful transition. It endeavours to become relevant and viable to Asian contexts. It begins to shape its own identity. It also strives to relate the destiny of Asia to the message of the Gospel.

Understanding of the nature and meaning of this transition is essential to the missionary task of the church in Asia. Christian mission can no longer be conducted as if the world would eventually accommodate itself to Christianity. The assumption that spiritual forces other than that of Christianity would wane and decline and lose hold on millions of people on account of inherent weaknesses has proved to be false. Furthermore, we are forced to admit that secular forces, no less spiritual in nature and essence, have been putting into rigorous question the premises of Christian faith advocated by the church both in the East and in the West. It is, therefore, to be expected that there will inevitably be some radical change in the theology and structure of Christian mission in Asia. This is especially so as Western influences through personnel and finance become less and less ponderous and significant.

Increasingly those of us who hold the Christian faith have to learn to view Christian mission in relational contexts. After all, the heart of the Gospel is that God relates Himself to man in Jesus Christ completely. It is in God's total relatedness to man in Jesus Christ that man is redeemed as well as judged. God has not imposed Himself on man in such a way that man becomes deprived of his integrity within his historical and cultural contexts. God in Jesus Christ enables man to be what he should be in the contexts of the temporal and spatial framework to which he is ordained.

Thus, I have attempted in this book to reconsider Christian mission in the relational contexts of Asia. I began with the affirmation that the biblical concept of the creation should be taken seriously in our treatment of revelation and redemption. When salvation gets divorced from the creation, it is bound to lose its universal dimension and significance. This inevitably leads to the impoverishment of Christian understanding of history and culture. Christian mission premised on such impoverished understanding of history and culture has proved to be detrimental to the wholesome appreciation of Asian history and culture in God's revelation. It is on the basis of such theological assumption that I have tried to deal with Christian mission in the relational contexts of Asian religions and cultures.

Related to what has been said above is the imperative for Christian mission to become ruthlessly contemporary. Differently stated, Christian mission cannot be conceived and conducted in abstraction. If Christian mission is to be relevant and viable at all, it must become related to what is happening in Asia today. For this reason, I have dealt at great length with the now celebrated concept of liberation. In many ways, the people in Asia need to be liberated at the very root of their being. Liberation may take place in politics, economics, cultural traditions or in religious beliefs. It is the liberation of man from both external and internal forces to become man as he is created in the image of God. It is, therefore, the responsibility of Christian mission not to teach and advocate, in the particularism of Asia which has suffered much under colonialism and political dictatorship, submission and passive obedience as Christian virtue.

I am quite aware of the fact that, in treating the subject matter of Christian mission in this way, I may have raised more questions than answers. But it has not been, in the first place, my intention to provide answers for the questions that are being raised with regard to the nature and role of the Christian church in mission. And secondly, it is my conviction that the future of Christian mission, humanly speaking, consists in our willingness to raise and face more and more questions, even embarrassing ones. The weakness of our human nature forces us to avoid difficult and awkward questions and to resort to easy and uncomplicated answers. But our salvation often comes from those brave ones who dare to ask tough questions for which no ready-made answer is available. What I have intended in this book is to invite my fellow seekers of the truth to press towards mutual enlightenment under the guidance of the Spirit of God who manifests Himself in the realities of our contemporary world.

Another point which I would like to make clear in this connection is this: I have not pretended to speak for Asian Christians as a whole. Speaking on behalf of Asian Christians as a whole is an audacity I do not dare to commit. When I speak of the church in Asia, Asian Christians, or Asian culture, it must be understood that I do so merely for convenience sake. In no way is Asia a homogeneous entity. To ignore this factor in treatment of subjects and themes related to Asia, including that of the Christian church and Christian mission, is to invite disaster. What I have set out to do here in this book is to put forward my own personal perception of and reflection on Christian mission as I know it, experience it and theologize about it. And since I happen to be an Asian, I believe I am entitled to add the descriptive phrase, 'an Asian Attempt' to the title of this book. However, it is my hope that some theological implications of this treatise on Christian mission may be found to have some bearings on diverse situations in different parts of Asia. It is, moreover, my modest and humble expectation that the views expressed in this book will serve the purpose of stimulating dialogues, conversations and discussions between Western Christians and the Christians in the so-called Third World. It will be very rewarding indeed, as well as exciting, if we can get our brothers and sisters outside the normal boundary of the Christian church into deliberations on the redemptive mission of God in the world.

The original form of this book was a series of five lectures I was invited to give at the Inter-denominational Furlough Missionary Conference held at Mt. Beulah, Mississippi, in the summer of 1971. The conference was sponsored by the Overseas Personnel Section of the Division of Overseas Ministries, National Council of Churches of Christ in the U.S.A., under the leadership of Reverend Herbert O. Muenstermann. I am grateful to him for extending to me the privilege of lecturing at the conference. Subsequently, I have completely re-written those five lectures.

My experience at Mt. Beulah, Mississippi, made a deep and lasting impression on me and on my theological thinking. For the first time in my life, I saw for myself what it was like to be a black in the deep south of the United States. I began to understand the anger, agony and desperation of black brothers and sisters. And the contention of black leaders, especially that of black theologians, began to make sense to me. This experience of mine is reflected in no small measure in some sections of this book.

Since I have dedicated this book to my colleagues at the offices of the Reformed Church in America located at 475 Riverside Drive in New York City, an explanation seems to be in order. From January 1971 to August 1973, I served the General Programme Council of the Reformed Church in America as Secretary for Asian Ministries. It did not take me long to realize that I was working with a team of dedicated persons intensely engaged in the ministries of the church. Besides their dedication to the tasks and responsibilities with which they are entrusted by the church, they are creative and forward looking. They dare to dream. The team work, therefore, was exciting. Each member had something to contribute and also always had something to learn from others. There was no dogmatism or doctrinarianism. The gifts of each individual were thus used to the fullest. It was an enriching experience to be part of such a team. I must however confess, that, as a mission executive I was somewhat of an anomaly, because I could not stop theologizing even while being involved in administrative responsibilities. In fact, it was their tolerance, understanding and encouragement that enabled me to divide my time between my office and libraries, and complete the writing.

My particular thanks, therefore, go to Marion de Velder, General Secretary of the Reformed Church in America, Arie R. Brouwer, Executive Secretary, John E. Buteyn, Isaac Rottenberg, Alvin Poppen, Marvin Hoff, Leonard De Beer, William Howard, Arthur Van Eck, and others. In them I was fortunate to have colleagues, friends and, above all, brothers in Christ.

I must also mention my three other close friends: Shoki Coe, Director of the Theological Education Fund, George Todd, Secretary for Urban Industrial Missions, Commission on World Mission and Evangelism, and Harry Daniel, Associate General Secretary, Christian Conference of Asia. They read the entire manuscript, made many useful and insightful comments, and made arrangements for its publication. I am deeply grateful to them for the interest they have shown in my book and for the reassuring words they have expressed with regard to the ideas propounded in it.

Further, I am immensely indebted to Diane Gubas, who worked with me at the Reformed Church in America. She made a number of useful comments and suggestions regarding contents and language. She undertook the typing with great patience and skill from my hand-written manuscript. And above all, her gentle urging contributed no less in enabling this book to see the light of day.

Finally, I cannot conclude this preface without expressing my gratitude to my wife and our two small daughters. We are pilgrims on earth together for better or for worse. On October 31, 1970, we arrived in New York from Formosa, greatly concerned about the future of our homeland. But our stay in that fascinating and agonizing metropolis was not going to be of permanent nature. At the end of August, 1973, we once again struck the temporary tent we had pitched there for three years to move to the next station of our earthly pilgrimage. We have since been in Geneva, Switzerland, where I am on the staff of the Commission on Faith and Order of the World Council of Churches. Indeed, as the writer of Hebrews says, here on earth we have no lasting city. Trusting, therefore, in the faithfulness of God, we shall continue our journey into the future which is ours because it is first and foremost God's.

Contents

[Biblical quotations in this book are taken from the
New English Bible unless otherwise indicated.]

CHAPTER ONE

Celebration

Our missionary efforts fail when they are based on
pity rather than true compassion. Instead of seeking
to do something *with* the Africans and Asian peoples,
we have too often sought to do something *for* them.
—MARTIN LUTHER KING, *Strength to Love*, p. 21.

1. At Last the End of an Old Era!

IT seems appropriate to begin this treatise on Christian Mission
with a note of celebration. But to celebrate what? To celebrate
the glorious history of Christian Mission? To celebrate its great
success? Not exactly. What we propose to celebrate here is the
end of the foreign missions of the church in the West!

Celebration primarily has to do with *fait accompli*. It is what
happened in the past that needs celebrating. By celebrating the
end of the foreign missions of the church in the West, we formally
bring to a close the era of Western foreign missions. It marks
the conclusion of a play, so to speak. The curtain is down never
to rise again. There will be no response to shouts for *encore* from
the audience. It is literally *finis*. This is all there is to it.

Furthermore, celebration has to do with joy and whole-hearted
joy at that. It should take place in the midst of rejoicing—
rejoicing that the church in the Third World has at long last come
of age, rejoicing that she is now bold enough to declare that the
final chapter of Western foreign missions has been written.

And there is something more important. This celebration
will in fact be a manifesto of liberation from the missions largely
shaped, conditioned and carried out by the churches in the West.
How can the church in the Third World preach the Gospel of
liberation when she is fettered in the traditions and practices of
Western Christian missions? When she is considered as a part
and parcel of Western religious and cultural phenomena? Hence,
if she is still haunted by the apparition of Western foreign missions,
let us drive it away with firecrackers. If she is still afraid of the

ghost of the Western missionary past, let us scare it away with beating of drums and of cymbals.

Indeed, the celebration signals radical change within the church in the Third World. She makes demands for entirely new relationships with the church in the West. She lets it be known that man does not live by bread alone, that she is awakened to the truth that the freedom of spirit is far more essential than the abundance of financial aid. She refuses to be judged and evaluated by ethical, cultural and religious standards and values prevailing in the West. Moreover, she is confronted with the need to probe into the depth of the mystery of God's salvation in her own social, cultural and political contexts. The continuous presence of Western foreign missions in their traditional garbs has only proved to be an obstacle, a hindrance, to all such efforts. For a new era of Christian mission, a Copernican revolution of ideas and practices related to mission is necessary.

In retrospect, it is true to say that the term 'foreign missions' has enjoyed a time-honoured status in the history of modern Christianity. For more than a century, Christian mission has been known to the Christians in the West solely as foreign missions. It must be pointed out that the understanding of Christian mission as foreign missions is a misinterpretation of the missionary message of the Bible. For in the common usage, the term 'foreign missions' hides behind it the idea that our 'Western home' has totally come under the saving grace of God, that it is those foreign lands in Asia and Africa inhabited by uncivilized peoples that need our mission. Needless to say, a value judgment is implied in an affirmation such as this. This is shown in the fact that in the minds of many Western Christians, 'uncivilized' and 'unevangelized' were almost regarded as synonymous. This subtle identification of the Gospel and the Western way of life contributed much to the misconception and belittlement of Asian and African cultures. Missionaries were thus viewed quite naturally not only as heralds of the Good News but also as bringers of the 'civilized' way of life. It is no wonder that foreign missions easily became by-products of the so-called Western Christendom.

The surprising fact is that it is only very slowly and belatedly that the people in Asia, Africa and Latin America came to realize Western Christendom was a myth. Neither Hiroshima nor

Auschwitz succeeded in demythologizing the myth. It persisted through World War II and continued even after the war. The confrontation of brutal naked powers between the West and the East resulting in the victory of the Western allies only seemed to have enhanced the credibility of the myth. For this, we must admit, Western Christian mission deserves some credit. But the irony is that Western foreign missions fell, knowingly or unknowingly, into the trap of untruthfulness at this point. Through foreign missions, the West was presented to the East as the Kingdom of God on earth, whereas the East was pictured in the West as everything standing for God-forsakenness.

What proved to be fatal to the myth was the sudden outburst of secularism in the West in the so-called post-Christian era. The religious curtain was lifted, and through direct contacts or through mass media, the people in Asia, Africa and Latin America began to see and experience for themselves the 'secular' nature of the 'Christian' West. It dawned on them that the Western society is as pagan as their own society. Secular forces, be it economic, ideological or cultural, are seen to be hard at work to tear down the religious facade of the Western world, which is bent on worldly gain even at the expense of those living in the non-Western world. For Western foreign missions, this is all very embarrassing. But if one cares to look at the realities of the post-Christian West more deeply, one may realize that these secular forces are in fact a blessing in disguise for Western missionaries who can at last be divested of what is called the 'White man's burden'. Theirs can no longer be a mission of expanding the mythological entity called Western Christendom. They no longer owe to their fellow human beings in Asia, Africa and Latin America the sharing of the highly questionable commodity labeled as Christian cultural heritages. They are now compelled to face the teeming humanity in Asia, Africa and Latin America not as the object of evangelizing but as fellow creatures, among whom God has never ceased to be present since the foundation of the world. From the standpoint of mission in its truly Christian perspective, this is a phenomenal change. This demands a new interpretation of the Biblical message with its focus on the acts of God. This also will entail a new theology of Christian mission. And consequently, a new chapter in the history of Christian mission will begin.

It has to be conceded that what has been put forward above is not something entirely new. It must be pointed out that during the past decade the term 'foreign missions' has been more than once challenged, and with each challenge it becomes less and less respectable until it has practically ceased to be used by most mission agencies. To illustrate what has just been said, some farsighted mission thinkers can be cited as making daring pronouncements in the sixties that the institution called foreign missions has become obsolete. In 1960, for example, William Hogg wrote:

> Being in ecumenical mission means part of a trans-national and trans-denominational world wide mission. For North American missionary agencies, being in ecumenical mission means acknowledging that a denominational foreign mission board sending White missionaries to Asia, Africa and Latin America in the traditional way, and thinking solely or primarily of extending its own denomination, is obsolete. The day for racially and denominationally limited mission has passed.[1]

The pronouncement of the end of Western based foreign missions in 1960, however, did little to change the actual practice of mission. Christian mission continued to be essentially 'White' Christian mission administered by Western mission boards. Asia, Africa and Latin America continued to be the theaters of operation for missionaries and mission executives from North America and Europe. It was primarily the mission *for* the 'underdeveloped' peoples and not mission *with* those who, in their own way, are no less mature culturally and spiritually than those in the 'developed' countries.

Many things have since changed, of course. There was more recognition of local leadership. There was more willingness on the part of missionaries to become interested in that which is indigenous, including non-Christian religious and socio-political issues and problems. Mission boards too became more sensitive to the rapidly changing situations on 'mission fields'. But it is fair to say that for the church in the West in general, the exploitation of what we may call the 'romance of foreign missions' continued without much change. As far as the Christians in the pews are concerned, their church was still engaged in romance with the unevangelized peoples beyond their Western borders. Missionaries were sent and welcomed home by them as those fulfilling on their behalf their desire for such spiritual romance. Most of mission money, if not all, was the most visible expression of their psychological and emotional satisfaction derived from their substitute involvement in the romance of Christian mission. It therefore seldom occurred to them that

> More White missionaries symbolize dependence upon the West. They suggest a continuing colonial situation. Their presence seems to give substance to the taunts of the non-Christians that Christianity is, after all, a Western religion.[2]

It is no wonder that the expansion of Christianity outside the Western world took an entirely different course from, say, Buddhism. No sooner did it leave the land of its birth than Buddhism became *Chinese* Buddhism and further *Japanese* Buddhism. Perhaps this is an extreme case not to be emulated by Christianity. But is it not true to say that Christianity has gone to the other extreme of non-conformism?

There is another factor which needs to be mentioned. Rightly or wrongly, the Western mission agencies were intent on giving growth to the churches which they had brought into existence. The often used word, 'paternalism' is too mild a term to describe the situation. Practically this amounted to the establishment of the structure of authority within what is called the younger church. Even today one may still come across the residual structure of ecclesiastical authority in which missionaries still exercise a subdued but subtle authority. The myth of Western Christendom may have been dissolved, yet the myth of the Western man blessed with the long history of cultural and political influence of the West on the rest of the world still plays some role in the subconsciousness of the non-Western man.

Be that as it may, it is more important to point out that Western mission agencies were, in the person of omnipresent missionaries, usurping the work which, according to Paul, belongs to God and to Him alone. The words of Paul to the young Christian congregation at Corinth are just as pungently relevant to the history of modern Christian mission.

> What then is Apollos? What is Paul? Servants through whom you believed, as the Lord assigned to him. I planted,

> Apollos watered, but God gave the growth. So neither he
> who plants nor he who waters is anything, but only God
> who gives the growth.[3]

Paul is rightly regarded as the greatest pioneer missionary, but
unfortunately, this most fundamental mission theology of his did
not always constitute the basic guiding principle of modern
Western Christian mission.

To be sure, adventures in mission are not possible without the
urging of the Holy Spirit, but in due course mission agencies
began to regulate the course the Holy Spirit should take. Protestant mission agencies catering for as many as 42,952 missionaries in 1963 throughout the world could not but become a mam-
moth machinery arresting the spontaneous indigenous and independent growth of Christian communities in Asia, Africa and
Latin America. Hence the indictment from a man like Kenneth
Cragg:

> It is, in perspective, one of the sorest liabilities of modern
> Christian mission that it has been so exclusively pursued
> by White humanity and served by White institutions.[4]

These are hard words to swallow, especially for those who have
laboured tirelessly and unreservedly as missionaries in the non-
Western lands. But all sentiments apart, there is no denying the
truth of this statement. The so-called indigenous church is often
no more than an extension of the denominational or sectarian
church of which the Western missionary happens to be a member.

The rapid growth of Christian sects in Africa in recent years,
for example, provides a striking contrast to the church brought
into being by Western missionaries. According to recent statistics,
the independent Christian sects in Africa are estimated to number
five thousand and to have nine million adherents. These sects
are far from being static or 'established,' for

> they are also said to be increasing at the rate of about 100 a
> year and have firmly established as a 'fourth force' in African
> Christianity along side Roman Catholics (45 million),
> Protestants (29 million) and Orthodox and Coptic churches
> (14 million).[5]

Taken by itself, this is an alarming phenomenon, posing a threat
to the 'established' church which often has more ties with her

'mother' church in the West than with the culture in which she is situated. But in the long run, the movement of these independent groups may prove to be a blessing in disguise. For among other things, the movement should surely stimulate the established church in search of a way of life more relevant to local culture and ethos. Confronted with a new phenomenon such as this, both Western mission agencies and the leadership of the established church in the non-Western world should humbly and repentantly accept the verdict that

> the emergence of the new churches has been the inability of missionary founded churches to integrate themselves with African cultural forms.[6]

But repentance alone is not enough. There should be the will and courage to break away from the bondage to the missionary ecclesiology developed in the West and transplanted to the East. The treatise on Christian mission presented in this book is a humble contribution to such an end. At the same time it seeks to give encouragement to those who may be working along a similar line.

In short, Western mission agencies have not been satisfied with the role of planting and giving water to Christian communities in the non-Western lands. They have shaped these Christian communities, moulded them and forced them to grow into 'White' churches in 'Black' Africa or 'Yellow' Asia. Thus, despite denominational differences and sectarian idiosyncrasies a great uniformity was achieved. It looked as if the non-Western world would soon be evangelized and Westernized. And in due course, many a devout Christian in the West even naively began to think that the Western Christendom came very close to being in possession of these non-Western lands. It is, therefore, no wonder that when the great debacle came to China in 1949 caused by the irrevocable political change, many Christians in America were chagrined and mourned, saying: 'We have lost China!' In reality they did not lose China because they had never owned China. What they lost were the church buildings, educational and medical institutions and sizeable property that they had helped to establish and run.[7] In one respect, the communist take-over of the whole of China dealt a serious blow to the Western missionary dream of Whitenizing China through Western foreign missions.

In this connection, we want to point out that there are certain secular factors which are contributing to drastic changes in the relationship between the churches in the West and in the East. One of these factors has to do with politics. International politics has changed so drastically in the last decade or two that the involvement of Western powers in the non-Western nations can no longer be taken for granted. The tide of the Western dominance of the world has definitely changed. Those nations in Asia, Africa and Latin America can no longer submit themselves to the whims of Western powers. That is why the Vietnam war is so utterly tragic. It is also entirely anachronistic because it would have been more comprehensible had it happened half a century ago. This being the generally accepted principle of international politics, Western foreign missions cannot but be affected. The Western Christians simply have to realize that the dogged pursuit of whitenizing non-White Christian communities would only lead to disaster. Therefore,

> The thrust of mission in Asia must be now in Asian hands, no longer in the West. The context of mission in Asia is now the Asian church and the whole human community. The primary responsibility of the Christian community in Asia, in co-operation with the Christian community in all six continents, is to discern and carry out the church's mission with resources and structures consistent with church selfhood, with the ecumenical imperative and with the pluralism of life in contemporary Asia.[8]

The significance of this statement in the *Kuala Lumpur Report* consists in the fact that Christian mission in Asia has at last come to the decision to become *conformed* to the political realities in Asia in the post-colonial era.

Another factor which forces Western mission agencies to take a sober look at their work overseas is related to the ever-shrinking financial resources from which they can draw. For various reasons most Western mission boards and most ironically those boards in affluent America have been suffering from unprecedented financial setbacks. This is no place to go into any detail into this peculiar misfortune which has befallen the Western mission boards. For our purpose here, we only have to mention that as a result of this financial set-back, Western mission agencies are forced to cut back substantially both the budget and the number of missionary personnel.[9] On the part of the church in the West, this may be regarded as lack of faith, loss of nerves, or the beating of retreat for Christian soldiers. For the churches in the non-Western world, which have been heavily dependent on Western personnel and cash, this new situation cannot help causing confusion and consternation. But surely there must be a positive side to the retrenchment of Western Christian mission. In my opinion, through the present crisis in mission, God is calling the churches both in the West and in the East to a new obedience of faith—obedience to the diverse ways in which God wishes to accomplish His purpose in the world. Thus, we are standing at the threshold of a new era of Christian mission. On account of this, it is only right and proper that we rejoice and celebrate the end of Western foreign missions. Let us not boast in what we have done. Let us not be self-indulgent in our own accomplishments. Instead, let us boast in God who is, after all, the Lord of history.

2. The Mission of One for Many

Biblically, the term foreign missions with emphasis on the word foreign is a mistaken concept. Johannes Blauw, a Dutch mission executive, rightly observed some years ago in his *Missionary Nature of the Church:*

> The emphasis in the New Testament is always on the 'going,' but this indicates a crossing of the boundary between Israel and the Gentiles rather than geographical boundaries, though the first naturally does not exclude the second. We are concerned with emphases, but these may become very important, as is the case with the expression 'uttermost parts of the earth'. I think this is why the latter has received so much emphasis—because in missionary circles the phrase echoes the idea of 'far-away places,' particularly in Asia and Africa.[10]

Hence, quite naturally Christian mission became entirely a one-way traffic affair. Foreign missions came to be regarded as a means by which the church in the West was taking part in the hastening of the second coming of Christ. The intensity with which conversion of individual pagan souls is still aimed at by the missionaries of conservative orientation is due largely to this geographical understanding of Christ's command on mission. Intent on gaining quick results, they showed little patience and appreciation for non-Western cultures and religions. Certainly it was not without reason that Western foreign missions was to become almost synonymous with spiritual imperialism.

It is well for us to remember that the main trends of Biblical thinking related to God's acts require us to view the whole creation, or the whole world inhabited by man, as one great unity. The complexities reflected in diversity of race, history, culture, religion or geography are not witness against this unity. To the contrary, the richness of God's creation is exhibited in these complexities. This surely is one of the great contributions which the Bible has made to man's understanding and experience of the profound mystery of God's creation. And this divine mystery is unfolded, sometimes partially and sometimes more than partially, in the dramas that are acted out in the course of the history of mankind. The Bible attempts to bring to a focus God's diverse dealings with man through intense concentration on the historical entities called Israel and the Christian communities. In Jesus Christ the divine-human drama is intensified almost to a breaking point. It is, however, in this fragile point culminated in the event of the cross that the whole wealth and richness of God's love is disclosed fully. Viewed from this Biblical perspective, many scattered and disconnected pieces in the Bible begin to come together like a jigsaw puzzle to make a coherent picture.

The basis of this coherent picture has to do with the Biblical witness stressing that a nation or individuals are chosen by God for the sake of other nations and individuals as well as for their own sake. This is clearly the emphasis made on the election of Abraham. Through him, it is said, 'all the families of the earth shall bless themselves' (Genesis 12:3).[11] Thus, the missionary message of the Old Testament centers on Israel being faithful to the covenant which God has made with them. As soon as they deviate from their covenantal relationship with God and fall short of being right with God, they bring down on themselves the stern warnings from the prophets. Why is this? The answer is that here is something beyond Israel at stake. As long as Israel is faithful in her relations with God, all the families on earth may be blessed by God. On the contrary, when she allows herself to become unfaithful and corrupt her relations with God, all the families on earth will be in danger of forfeiting God's blessings. This is a terrible responsibility that goes with the privilege of being chosen by God.

It seems to me that this will explain the attitude Jesus took with regard to the men and women outside his own race by birth. In the region of Tyre and Sidon, he was approached by a Canaanite woman who begged him to heal her daughter tormented by a devil. In reply he said: 'I was sent to the lost sheep of the house of Israel, and to them alone' (Mat. 15:24). Surely to give such a reply to someone in dire need is uncharacteristic of him. But why should he say it? Is there not a better way of saying no to the woman without causing misunderstanding? Why should her urgent need be set aside for the sake of the house of Israel, an abstract entity in contrast to the particular human being kneeling in front of him with her heart crying out for her daughter?

This is not all. In sending out his disciples on evangelistic mission, Jesus categorically forbids them to have anything to do with the Gentiles. They are dispatched with this specific instruction:

> Do not take the road to the gentile lands, and do not enter any Samaritan town; but go rather to the lost sheep of the house of Israel. And as you go proclaim the message: 'The kingdom of heaven is upon you.'[12]

A saying such as this is very baffling, to say the least. Why does Jesus try to limit his ministry to the house of Israel? Why does he seem to be excluding the lost sheep of the gentile world from hearing the Good News about the Kingdom of Heaven? The clue to these questions is to be found in the remark we made above about the election of Abraham. He was elected so that not only he and his family would be blessed but all the nations and peoples on earth would come to share the blessings of God. This is one of the dominant themes of the Bible as a whole, namely, the theme of one for many.

We have a telling illustration of this in the intercession of Abraham on behalf of Sodom recorded in Genesis 18:16-23. When Abraham was told what God was intending to do to the wicked city, Sodom, he was quickly on his knees pleading God to spare it. The tension of the drama thus acted out before us is not heightened by the increase in the number of the righteous people in order for Sodom to be spared, but rather in the steady decrease of the number of righteous people from fifty down to ten. The tension became almost unbearable when Abraham ventured his plea for the last time. In fact, he was frightened, but still pressed his plea saying:

> I pray thee not to be angry, O Lord, if I speak just once more: suppose ten can be found there?[13]

To this God replied: 'For the sake of the ten I will not destroy it.

The drama of this unusual confrontation of God and Abraham on account of Sodom ends there, but the whole drama of God's saving love for mankind does not end there. It goes on throughout the Bible and comes to a climactic expression in Jesus' mission. With the whole world in his vision, Jesus endeavours to make his own nation this 'ten' in order that the rest may be saved. That is why he tried to concentrate his ministry on the house of Israel. That is why he considered it his primary responsibility to seek the lost sheep of Israel. He made every effort to restore in his own people the consciousness of having been chosen for the sake of all the families on earth. He was consistent in his aim. But the house of Israel had already spent itself. They held on to the securities they had built around their religion. Even Jesus' vituperation against the Pharisees and lawyers, calling them hypocrites, snakes and vipers, did not wake them up to a new realization of their unique responsibility towards their fellow creatures. Finally, it was Jesus Christ, himself, who came to stand for the entire house of Israel and carried out the divine mission of being a blessing to all the families on earth. He became this 'ten,' carrying under his arms the whole world on the cross. He was the chosen nation, the chosen race, the chosen servant and the chosen man. He gave his life as a ransom for many (Mark 10:45).

This is Christ's mission. This must be the essence of the Christian mission also. In the last analysis, Christian mission does not consist solely in converting pagans to Christianity. Western foreign missions have been operated on the assumption that Christian mission must find its expression in physical extension and numerical expansion. This is not to say that growth in number and in structure has no place at all in Christian mission.

But when these are regarded as the primary purpose of Christian mission, expansionism tends to be the guiding principle of missionary activities. And this in turn constitutes much of the evil related to denominationalism. Is it not true that denominational jealousy and competition was much to be seen in foreign missions?

Essentially, Christian mission is the mission of suffering. And inasmuch as it is the mission of suffering, it becomes the mission of healing and reconciling. That is to say, the essence of Christian mission consists in the manifestation of healing through suffering. Through the suffering of the few, the nations will be healed. Those Servant Songs of *The Second Isaiah* in the Old Testament, the magnificence of which can never be surpassed by any literary hand, are the supreme witness to the essence of Christian mission. The following verse, for example, expresses exactly and pointedly what is said here:

> The chastisement he bore is health for us and by his scourging we are healed.[14]

It is not our intention to suggest here that suffering has a meritorious effect on the person who undergoes suffering. Nor can we make a virtue out of suffering. It is a means by which God's purpose for man is accomplished. As has been pointed out:

> whereas prophets like Jeremiah suffered in the course of, or as a result of, their witness, for both the Servant and Jesus suffering is the means whereby they fulfil their mission and bring it to a triumphant conclusion.[15]

This is a very important insight which goes right to the heart of the Christian Gospel. This is, in fact, another way of saying that without the cross there is no resurrection. To by-pass the cross is to forfeit the resurrection. The church of the resurrection can only be founded on the church of the cross.

It may be observed that this central element of Christ's mission is notably lacking in modern Christian missions. The church in the West launched into foreign missions with formidable manpower and economic strength. She was far from being the church of suffering. Perhaps it should be said that the church in the West ceased to be the suffering church since 311 A.D., the year in which the emperor Constantine's edict declared Christianity a legitimate religion. From then on, the history of the Christian church was partially the history of internal struggles for eminence and power. And in the emergence of the Holy Roman Empire, the church became the *ecclesia gloriae*. It was the church not with divine glory but with human and thus vain glory.

There are at least two things which have served as redeeming factors for this *ecclesia gloriae*. One factor is the spirit of reformation which challenges the introverted church not to seek her own earthly glory but to bear the cross for the world. It is this *ecclesia semper reformanda* within the institutionalized church that is the true church of God. In the Old Testament, the prophets represent this reforming spirit against fearful odds. They feel constrained to speak against social and political evils of their days. Above all they see the root of all these evils in the apotheosis of human authorities and institutions. Thus, the prophets pose themselves against the apostasy of their people and their nation. It is no less true with the history of the Christian church. The *ecclesia gloriae* is more often than not the church of apostasy. The struggles of reformers at every period of the history of the church are the struggles against the apostasy of the *ecclesia gloriae*.

On the other hand, the missionary churches in Asia, Africa and Latin America have served as another redeeming factor for the church in the West especially in the 19th and 20th centuries. Through foreign missions, the Christians in the West were thus enabled to divert from their preoccupations with their own churches to become interested in success stories in 'mission fields'. The appeals for funds and personnel for foreign missions helped to raise their morale and fill their spiritual vacuum. Hence, is there not some truth in saying that the missionary churches in the non-Western lands were serving to give a lease of life for the church in the West? Cannon Burgess Carr said somewhat cynically:

> If there is one single thing I have learned about the church
> during these seven years that I have lived and worked in
> Europe and Africa, it is this. You here in the North
> Atlantic world need us in Africa. This has been a revela-
> tion to me, since all along I have been led to believe that
> the situation was just the reverse.[16]

As if this is still not candid enough, he went on in the same address to advance his criticism in words that might sound blasphemous to the ears of the well-meaning Christians:

Your churches are deceived into believing that you are strong
and alive, because on occasion you can raise sums of money
and recruit large numbers of volunteers for emergency
service. Regrettably, you have in Africa, as well as elsewhere in the world, built-in systems which guarantee that
these emergencies will erupt with predictable regularity.[17]

Statements such as this will arouse resentment. One may be
prompted to dismiss it as the height of ingratitude. But let us
not be too hasty in our judgment. We, East and West alike, are
caught in the enormous ambiguities of this complex world.
Certainly it would be too naive for us to claim that what we have
done in the name of Christian mission has been done with nothing but the purest possible motivations. For who can deny that
the massive aid that flowed from the church in the West to the
church in the East through the pipelines called foreign missions
was partly political in nature and in reality?

It has to be admitted that the systems called Western Christian
missions are increasingly viewed by enlightened men and women
in the non-Western lands as part of the exploitation machinery
employed to the full by the colonial rulers. This must not be put
aside lightly as a case of extreme nationalism corrupting the fellowship of world wide Christianity. Rather this is a sober recognition of the fact that no action undertaken by a group or body of
people, even if that group or that body happens to be Christian
in character, can be apolitical. Much appraisal of Western foreign
missions is being done from this perspective. This will result in
a very different assessment of Western foreign missions such as
pointed out above. We do not mean to say that, by such appraisal,
we are trying to write off Western foreign missions with one sweep-
ing stroke. It is, however, my contention that Western foreign
mission of the past century has been more the undertaking of the
ecclesia gloriae than that of the *ecclesia crucis*. And precisely
because of this, much has to be undone in order for the church
in the Third World to emerge as a new creature for this new age.

Writing from a prison cell where he underwent sufferings and
agonies with his own German nation which had opted for the
Führer rather than God, Bonhoeffer has this to say about the
church:

The church is her true self only when she exists for humanity. As a fresh start she should give away all her endowments to the poor and needy.[18]

What a challenge to the church which has grown rich and pompous! And what a challenge to foreign missions which have become elaborate operations by which affluent Western churches keep the churches in Asia, Africa and Latin America to have some semblance of affluence in the midst of poverty and suffering!

All in all, one important lesson which the history of the Western foreign missions seems to be teaching us is this: there should be an honest and critical re-evaluation of value systems and styles of life which have been built into Christian communities in East and West. We have regarded and enjoyed these value systems and styles of life as part and parcel of being members of the church. But there are abundant signs telling us that in order for a new church to come into existence these value systems and life-styles must either go or be radically modified. At the Asian Ecumenical Conference for Development in 1970 in Tokyo, Japan, this was expressed with forcefulness and clarity. The conference message said, among other things, that

> Churches and Christian organizations should take a firm stand on the side of the poor and the oppressed and they should, together with others, especially with the socially concerned youth, evolve concrete measures to bring about revolutionary changes in the socio-economic and political structures characterized by discrimination, exploitation and corruption.[19]

This is a demanding task indeed, which can be undertaken only after the church has denied much of her value systems and life-styles geared primarily to the Western consumer society and after the church has begun to build new value systems and life styles more in keeping with the new age and mission of Jesus Christ.

And so, we celebrate and rejoice in the end of Western foreign missions. We have painfully come to the end of an old era. A new era of Christian mission is yet to be born. It is demanded of us to press on and see what implications the mission of Christ may have for the Christian mission of today and tomorrow.

REFERENCES

1. William Hogg, *One World, One Mission*, New York: Friendship Press, 1960, p. 177.

2. *Ibid.*, p. 113.

3. I Corinthians 3:5-7.

4. Kenneth Cragg, *Christianity in World Perspective*, New York: Oxford University, Press, 1968, p. 24.

5. *The New York Times*, May 31, 1971, pp. 1-2. 'There are 249 million non-Christians among Africa's total population of 346 million. These include 145 million Muslims. The remaining 104 million include animistic, semi-Christian and uncommitted groups.'

6. *Ibid.*, cf. also David B. Barrett, *Schism and Renewal in Africa*. Eastern Africa: Oxford University Press, 1968, pp. 83 ff.

7. 'By the 1920's missionary schools were a central feature of the missionary effort (in China) with almost as much personnel and as great an investment as the more direct evangelical missionary work. In 1927 there were sixteen universities and colleges; ten Christian professional schools of collegiate rank; four schools of theology and six schools of medicine–some 4,000 students enrolled. These schools represented a total property investment of $ 19,000,000. Their current expenses amounted to $ 3,250,000 annually.' (Paul A. Vaag, 'A Survey of Changing Mission Goals and Methods,' in *Christian Missions in China—Evangelists of What?* edited with an introduction by Jessie G. Lutz, Boston: D. C. Heath and Company, 1965, p. 6.)

8. *Missionary Service in Asia Today*, A report on a consultation held by the Asia Methodist Advisory Committee at Kuala Lumpur, February 18-23, 1971, p. 10.

9. If statistics offer any guide at all, we may note that in 1963 there were 42,952 Protestant missionaries working in various parts of the non-Western world (cf. above p. 8). In 1969 the number was reduced to 33,289. (cf. *North American Protestant Ministries Overseas Directory*, 9th Edition, compiled and written for the Missionary Research Library by Missions Advanced Research and Communication Center, 1970, pp. 2-4. The current number would certainly be further reduced due to increasing financial difficulties that are facing mission boards.

10. Johannes Blauw, *Op. cit.*, New York: McGraw Hill Book Company, 1962, p. 111.

11. The Revised Standard Version.

12. Matthew 10:5-7. This is no easy saying to understand. *Interpreter's Bible*, vol. 7, p. 364, for instance, attempts an explanation in the following way: 'Would it have been necessary for Jesus to give this command? The presence of this saying in the tradition helps to explain why a Gentile mission developed so late. There is a tradition in the second century preaching of Peter that Jesus told the disciples to wait twelve years before going to the Gentiles (James, *Apocryphal N. T.*, p. 17)'. This still does not explain why Jesus gave that command if the command did come from Jesus.

13. Genesis 18:32.

14. Isaiah 53:5.

15. C.R. North, 'The Suffering Servant in Deutero-Isaiah', pp. 208–9. Quoted by Alan Richardson in his *A Theological Word Book of the Bible,* p. 251, under the heading 'suffer.'

16. Cf. his papers entitled 'The Churches and the Development of Peoples—the African Experience,' which he read at U.S. Conference Meeting at Albany, April, 1971.

17. *Ibid.*

18. Bonhoeffer, *Letters and Papers from Prison*, p. 180.

19. Workshop Reports and Recommendations, Asian Ecumenical Conference for Development, Tokyo, Japan, July, 1970, p. 3.

CHAPTER TWO

The Divine Mission of Creation

The heavens tell out the glory of God,
  the vault of heaven reveals his handiwork.
One day speaks to another,
  night with night shares its knowledge.
And this without speech or language
  or sound of any voice.
Their music goes out through all the earth,
  their words reach to the end of the world.

—Psalm 19:1-4

1. Creation and Christian Mission

WHAT I propose to do in this chapter is to discuss the meaning of the story of creation in the first chapter of Genesis in the Old Testament for the Christian mission in the post-Western missionary era. I am conscious of the fact that this may immediately provoke some questions: What, one may ask, has the story of creation to do with Christian mission? Isn't the main burden of Christian mission related to redemption and not to creation? Is it not true to say that in the Bible accounts are chiefly given of those men and women who have come to experience the wonderful love of God in many different ways? In other words, does the Bible not deal with God's salvation and that alone?

It goes without saying that our answer to these questions is yes. From beginning to end, one basic theme which runs through the Bible is the theme of God's personal dealings with man and the world *redemptively*. God, as the Bible tells us over and over again, does not deal with man without specific aim and purpose. He does not relate Himself to man and his world in a general sort of way. Whenever He acts, He acts personally, directly and concretely. He does not act in a vacuum. He addresses Himself to man with particular concern, needs or interests. At every turn the Bible tries to communicate this, and it is really remarkable that it succeeds in doing so. Just read a few psalms in the Old Testament, and you will be so impressed with the personal and intimate tone in which psalmists pour out their hearts to God and the way in which God listens to them and participates in the agonies of their hearts. To give just one example:

> Hear my cry, O God, listen to my prayer.
> From the end of the earth I call to thee with fainting
> heart; lift me up and set me upon a rock.
> For thou hast been my shelter,
> a tower for refuge from the enemy![1]

The Bible thus gives us insight into the divine-human drama unfolding itself before our eyes around the theme of redemption.

Furthermore, God's dealing with man is radical in the sense that He goes to the root of man's need, namely, the need of being right with God and with his fellow creatures. Thus, God's timely act of redemption brings about new relationships in the ordering of the whole of creation. As a result, a new creation comes into being. In this way, the experience of redemption is an experience ultimately related to the experience of creation. Can we not, therefore, relate the story of creation in the book of Genesis to the experience of God's saving acts on the part of the Jewish people in exile? As we shall see presently, for them to be able to relate redemption to the entire process of God's creation serves to liberate them from their religious isolationism and spiritual provincialism. They find themselves staring at the unfathomable depth of God's mystery in creation and redemption. They are led to the beginning of all things, which is their present suffering and liberation. They realize that the darkness had to be there, that chaos seemed to be gaining the upper hand, that the order of the cosmos and the being of man were threatened. Can we not, therefore, conclude that the story of creation in Genesis 1 has not so much to do with the primeval history of the universe? Rather it seeks to express the joy of redemption from the tyranny of chaos. It tries to convey the exuberance of being which is set free from the sinister power of destruction. In Karl Barth's words:

> But what makes non-being a menace, an enemy which is
> superior to created being, a threatened destroyer, is obvi-
> ously not its mere character as non-being, but the fact that
> it is not elected and willed by God the creator but rather

rejected and excluded. It is that to which God said No when He said Yes to the creative. And that is chaos according to the biblical term and concept.[2]

In short, in the first creation story in Genesis 1:1-2:4a, redemption is seen in the perspective of creation.

We may reinforce what we have just said by referring to the circumstances in which the first story of creation gets to be written. As we all know, the creation story is the production of the religiously creative mind of the Jewish people taken captive to Babylonia by King Nebuchadnezzar in 587 B.C. The Babylonian captivity seems first to put an end to Israel as a political and religious entity distinct from other nations. It is reasonable to assume that her spiritual force must have eroded from its very foundation. But through this traumatic experience of national disaster, she learns to perceive another dimension to the faith she has inherited from the past. As John Bright observes:

> When one considers the magnitude of the calamity that overtook her, one marvels that Israel was not sucked down into the vortex of history along with other little nations of Western Asia to lose forever her identity as a people. And if one asks why she was not, the answer lies in her faith. . . Yet this answer is not to be given glibly, for the exile tested Israel's faith to the utmost. That it won through was not something that transpired automatically, but only with much heart-searching and after profound re-adjustment.[3]

Perhaps one of the most profound readjustments they have had to make is related to their understanding of Yahweh, their God. An infinitely rich dimension of God's relation with the world has been revealed to them in the totally new situation. They have begun to take a fresh look at the saving acts of God in the context of the whole of creation. A new understanding of the place and mission of Israel among the nations thus becomes possible.

To be sure, there are those among the exiled in Babylonia who find it difficult to sing 'the Lord's song in a foreign land' (Psalm 137). Nationalism is not discarded as an old garment. The nostalgia for the land of promise is not buried out of sight. There is still strong inclination to interpret the nature and acts of God exclusively in favour of Israel as a privileged nation. But the deepened perception of the redemptive works of God under the form of creation affected their spirituality in such a way that fundamental change cannot but take place in their orientation towards the purpose of God for the nations. The culmination of this spiritual reorientation is to be seen in the great missionary called the Suffering Servant in the *Second Isaiah*. He is not chosen only for Israel in exile. He is to live and die even for those beyond the boundary of his own race and nation. This is why he, in accepting the divine call, proclaims:

> Listen to me, you coasts and islands.
> Pay heed, you peoples far away:
> From birth the Lord called me,
> He named me from my mother's womb.[4]

The election of the Servant is thus an 'ecumenical' event, which must be acknowledged and celebrated by all nations. No one can afford to be indifferent to it, for the mission of the Servant is of ecumenical significance. There is already a distant echo of this in the call of Abraham. It is through Abraham and his house that 'all the families of the earth shall bless themselves' (Genesis 12:3).[5] In the person and work of the Suffering Servant, this distant echo becomes a clear and loud proclamation; it has become a reality which will have a profound impact on the spirituality of mankind.

The Biblical faith is, in the last analysis, the faith which transcends the boundaries of race, nationality, culture and even religion. The creator-redeemer God is not to be captured by and crystallized into one particular racial and cultural texture. On account of this, we can only speak of a national or state church with great caution. A state church tends to become so closely related to the political and cultural interests of the nation that she begins to identify the cause of her nation as the cause of God. The faith in the creator-redeemer God permits no such nationalization of God. A nationalized God ceases to be relevant for other nations and peoples. It is, therefore, understandable that the people of the Third World[6] have become extremely restless with what they call the 'White' God who comes armed with everything which the white West stands for. They have begun an earnest search for 'black' God or 'yellow' God. Is God coloured? Yes and No. Yes. because God seems to make Himself known in different ways to different peoples in different places. Consequently, responses to this God must also take different forms and expressions. But at the same time we must say No, because God is not to be identified *simply* and *solely* with a particular form of His manifestation and with a particular expression of man's response. God has the whole of creation to deal with. He cannot be bound by any nation or any culture. God is the God of freedom. Much of the agitation against 'white' Christianity in the Third World springs from the perception that the white West has imprisoned God and thus deprived God of His freedom. That is why God is preached and presented everywhere as the 'white' God.

After a century of expansion from its Western base, Christianity is said to have failed in no small degree in crossing the self-imposed boundaries of Western culture. To be sure, Western missionaries have had to cross the geographical boundaries. Beyerhaus, Professor of Missiology at the University of Tubingen, pointedly says:

> It must in fact be questioned how many missionaries today really do cross any decisive frontier. For it is a dreadful possibility that they have traversed continents and oceans and still never left their home, because in their mission stations in Bangkok or Botswana they busily reconstruct their little Bielefeld, Birmingham or Boras. In this way they prevent themselves from achieving that which is the real mark of having crossed the frontier: the missionary identification.[7]

This is a severe criticism with much justification, particularly when directed to the life-style of missionaries. The question of the missionary identification is the question of life-style. But if we press the question further, we will realize that there is something much deeper and much more fundamental than just a matter of life-style. It is the question of whether missionaries ever think deeply about the meaning of God and what He does in a different cultural context, whether they have seen the necessity of correcting and even discarding some basic elements in their faith in the light of their new experience. In short, it is the question of whether their faith is shaken to its foundation. Only after this shaking of the foundation, a reconstruction of Christian faith can begin.

And the reconstruction may take place at least in the four areas of culture, history, society and politics corresponding to the four aspects related to God's creation. In the following discussion we shall endeavour to see what implications the consideration of these areas of creation may have for the reconstruction of the Christian faith in the non-Western lands.

2. Cultural Dynamic of Creation

The concept of culture is not easy to define. What you mean by culture depends very much on the world view in which you believe. If you are a staunch materialist, you may look upon culture as visible and tangible forms through which man's endless pursuit for a reconstruction of the physical world is given expression. On the other hand, if you happen to be a consistent idealist, you may regard culture as a bundle of ideas projected in terms of the spacio-temporal framework. Or you may try to understand culture from the point of view of psychology, anthropology or sociology. In the contemporary world, which is fashioned very much by the progress in science and technology, culture tends to be interpreted in relation to the process of modernization. It is clear that no matter what definition you may give to the concept of culture, you have to realize that no definition can exhaust the meaning of the concept, that each definition will have both merits and demerits. Fortunately, for our purpose here we are not required to side with one particular definition of culture to the exclusion of all other definitions. Nor is it necessary for us to come up with a supposedly new definition in order to proceed with our discussion. All we have to do here is to look upon culture as comprehensive expressions of the creative dynamic released from its origin. In the human realm, the release of the creative dynamic takes forms in painting, sculpture, music, architecture, technology, and so on. This power to create becomes imprisoned, so to speak, in the multi-dimensional structure which serves as media for man's self-expression. Thus, tension develops between man's creative dynamic and the structure through which his dynamic has to be expressed. The tension testifies both to the greatness of man and to his finiteness.

The above consideration leads us to speak of the cultural dynamic of God's creation from which man's creative power is derived. Culture as a whole is none other than the manifestation of God's creative power translated into actual forms and events. Thus, creation may be regarded as God's culture in its totality. The writers of the first creation story present us with a superb picture of God's power of creation becoming a cultural dynamic giving forms, order, and above all, life to that which is formless, chaotic and without life. That is why each creational act of God is punctuated with the exclamation that God saw the work of His hand as good. This is the unqualified affirmation of what God has done. The 'good' here does not imply moral judgment passed on God's work. Good in this particular context should not be contrasted with bad or evil. Even a genuine work of art fashioned out of man's mind and hand may transcend the boundary of good and evil. Is it not true then to say that evil loses its power over the creative dynamic of the truly artistic mind? If this is the case with man's work of art and culture, how much more so with God's creation! Creation may become corrupted and may decay, but it never comes under the dominium of evil. It remains God's creation no matter what. Bonhoeffer is therefore right when he says:

> That God's work is good in no way means that the world is the best of all conceivable worlds. It means that the world lives completely in the presence of God, that it begins and ends in Him, and that He is its Lord. Here is meant the goodness which is undifferentiated from evil, whose goodness consists in its being under the dominion of God.[8]

This is an insight which very often got lost in the course of the development of Christian thought in the West. And a re-introduction of this insight into Christian theology by theologians such as Bonhoeffer becomes a starting point for many new movements in contemporary western theology laying emphases on secularization, the immanence of God, Christian responsibility for the world and so on.[9]

This affirmation of creation being under God's dominion is very important for our understanding and appreciation of culture, especially when we find ourselves confronted with cultural expressions and activities different from those to which we are accustomed. This provides the basis on which we may enter into meaningful, inter-cultural experiences. Let us face the fact that each and every one of us is tainted with cultural provincialism. Can we call this cultural chauvinism? A story is told of a man who had grown up and lived in a country whose traffic law required its citizens to keep to the right and who happened to be in another country for the first time where different traffic regulations were practised. As soon as he saw people driving on the left side of the road, he exclaimed: 'They are driving on the *wrong* side of the road!' Needless to say, this was a judgment passed on a different set of traffic regulations on the basis of his own. This kind of cultural confrontation will never pass into fruitful experience of inter-cultural exchange. Basically, this is the hopeless and at the same time harmful, 'my country, right or wrong' attitude.

The more intense a form the cultural dynamic of man's spiritual activities takes, the more dangerous and futile cultural confrontation becomes. Here we are especially referring to religion. We can agree that in religion we have the intense concentration of man's cultural dynamic and creative energy. Religion is in a true sense a synthesis of culture. In religion the communion between the divine and the human gets expressed in visible and audible forms in an extremely heightened degree. Can we therefore not say that it is man's religious genius that gives birth to culture? In other words, is the source and origin of man's cultural dynamic not to be found in man's communion with the cultural dynamic of God become embodied in His creation? Gerardus van der Leeuw, great phenomenologist of religion, puts it beautifully when he speaks of Bach's *Mass in B Minor* in the following words:

> In Bach's *Mass in B Minor*, the Credo is a glorious piece of music, an expression of beauty and an expression of holiness. All the voices speak, one after another: 'Credo. . .' It is as though all the stops of human piety and human sense of beauty were released. We fear a letdown immediately. Then the violins begin, high and radiant, the old intonation of the liturgy. Now it is as though the mystery were revealed; here God speaks.[10]

That is why van der Leeuw finds it possible to speak of the holy in art. In the holy, God's speech and man's response are joined together for the communion of spirit. With uncontestable eloquence, van der Leeuw muses:

The dance reflects the movement of God, which also moves us upon the earth. The drama presupposes the holy play between God and man. Verbal art is the hymn of praise in which the eternal and his works are represented. Architecture reveals to us the lines of the well-built city of God's creation. Music is the echo of the eternal *Gloria*.[11]

What seems to happen in culture is that the divine Spirit of creation makes impact on the spirit of man to translate the heavenly into the earthly.

This last statement, it seems to us, has universal validity, for if Christian expressions of cultural dynamic are the end results of spiritual interactions between heaven and earth, how can one deny such spiritual quality to expressions of cultural dynamic working in other contexts, Buddhist for example? It is said that 'the minds of the mediaeval Japanese artists have always been trained in the nature-mysticism of Buddhism.'[12] Without this basic perception, it will be difficult for anyone, especially those from different cultural backgrounds, to appreciate the beauty and genius of culture brought into being in predominantly Buddhist Asian countries. But once one is able to identify and appreciate this spiritual quality deep rooted in the being of the Asian, one begins to understand the hopes and meanings in which the spiritual quality concerned come to expression. Japanese architecture, for instance,

> is utterly unlike the Gothic. Its chief beauty consists in the long, curving, horizontal lines of the eaves, and in the gentle slope of the roofs. Such forms harmonize well with the hills and trees, and such buildings become a part of the landscape instead of appearing like gigantic and laborious constructions built in defiance of nature.[13]

To a considerable degree this is true of most of the expressions of Asian cultural dynamic. The unfortunate thing is that western missionaries have never truly grasped this basic quality of the Asian mind. They have endeavoured to establish Gothic theology, that is Gothic understanding and interpretation of Christian faith, in lands where the shape of spirituality is not only foreign to it but entirely incompatible with it.

Thus, we must speak of the cultural task of Christian mission. It consists in an effort to search for and appreciate different shapes which the cultural dynamic of creation takes in different cultural and historical contexts. Christian mission goes about this cultural task with the basic assumption that diversity in shapes of culture is not witness against the unity and sovereignty of God's creation. Rather it is an affirmation of the richness of God's nature and His relation to the world He has brought into existence. It follows that there is no justification whatsoever for Christian mission to work and operate with the dichotomy of Christian and non-Christian cultures. The message of the Bible, particularly that of God's overarching relationship to every aspect of His creation and His dominion over it, tends to be distorted on account of such a dichotomy. It simply will not do for Christian mission to pose itself as the guardian of the so-called Christian culture against what is often carelessly labelled as non-Christian culture.

Christian mission must therefore be first of all a critique of cultures. If the word critique sounds a little too judgmental in connotation, we may call it theology of cultures. It is a theological perception and interpretation of the spirituality of a particular culture in the light of the Biblical faith in God as the creator. This ought to be a theological task vigorously pursued by those engaged in Christian mission. It is a task that requires an open mind and cheerful willingness to let new light shine into the citadel of the Christian faith. At the same time through such an effort the Christian and the people of other faiths are ultimately drawn into the question of truth. And in so far as it is the question of truth, it has to be stressed that no one possesses the final answer. Those who are primarily concerned with Christian mission must be humble enough to acknowledge this. They have to present their case for Christian faith with conviction and assurance, but they must do this without claiming to have sole access to the whole truth of God. Such an attitude is required of them by the very nature of the truth they seek to serve and witness. The truth of God does not permit man's total penetration. The attempt to defy his basic human limitation and trespass this boundary of man's knowledge causes man to fall from the truth.

It follows that we must be content with speaking of 'degrees of truth.' At most all we can say is that in and through Jesus

Christ we believe we are given access to considerable degrees of God's truth, particularly when it is made known to us in the form of God's love for the world in creation and in redemption. A perception such as this will not lead us into the temptation of putting Christian religion on top of all other religions, and it will keep us from confusing the Christian way of life as the embodiment of the whole truth of God.

Christian mission as a theological task related to the search of truth in cultures is thus entrusted with a two-fold responsibility. On one hand there is the negative responsibility of bringing into light how the love of God for man and the world is misapprehended, distorted and even corrupted in cultures. But to stop at this negative aspect is to make caricature of God's lordship over His creation. This would tacitly mean that finally evil is a viable form of being, posing as a threat to God's being. If we believe in the 'goodness' of God's creation, we cannot regard this as the final word. There should be at the same time a positive responsibility on the part of Christian mission to fathom how this same love of God is reflected in the life and work of those who live in different contexts of culture and ethos. To use the analogy of architecture again, Christian mission in the non-Western lands, especially in Asia, should not emulate the defiant spirit of Gothic architecture with emphasis on contradiction and incompatibility. Christian mission should be more like Asian architecture which seeks to express the spiritual yearning for harmony in the midst of agony and pain. For centuries Asian peoples have continued to live and experience great turbulence of history. Their lot has not been an easy one. Disorder in society, disruption of family life, dislocation of people, caused by war and natural disaster have been and still are order of the day rather than exception. In the midst of this all, Asian cultural and religious genius has never ceased to search for inner tranquillity and harmony of nature. It is to this kind of situation that Christian mission has to address itself. Thus, only in developing empathy for different cultural dynamics manifested in non-Christian contexts are Christians enabled to come to grips with the mystery of the divine cultural dynamic at work in creation. This, I believe, is the pre-requisite of Christian mission. Is this not basically the reason why the Bible begins with the story of creation and ends with a vision of

a new creation? Let us remember: new creation is not to be the
total destruction of the old creation, but fulfilment or completion
of it. This is the divine mission of creation and redemption,
Christians are called to take part in this divine mission. And this
essentially is Christian mission.

3. Histories as Continuation of Creation

Increasingly, Christian mission finds itself faced with impacts
of historical pluralism and is forced to take them seriously. This
is significant when we consider that in this day and age there
seems to be emerging a world culture built on science and technology. The language of science and technology is cut and dry. It
permits little equivocation. Consequently, its symbolic character
is reduced to a minimum. Particularly in contrast to poetic
language, the language of science and technology is factual and
not emotive language. Thus, probability of misunderstanding is
greatly reduced. At last in this language, modern man seems to
have achieved what those unfortunate builders of the Tower of
Babel failed to achieve, namely, one world with one language,
one history and one culture.

But the fact remains that this is a short-lived dream of modern
man. After all, we in this age of science and technology do not
seem to fare any better than the builders of the Tower of Babel.
The fact that use of electricity, for example, is now almost
universally a routine matter for most of the inhabitants of the
earth does not automatically mean that they can communicate
with one another without difficulty. Nor does the shortening of
geographical distance by modern means of transportation and communication at once result in the coming into being of a world
community with some historical uniformity. The truth of the
matter seems just the opposite. Nationalism is certainly not a
by-product of science and technology, but without the challenges
posed by scientifically and technologically advanced nations,
nationalism would not have been stimulated into assuming a prominent role in Third World politics. And as people find themselves more and more in international contexts, the problem of
their historical identity becomes very much sharpened. Especially
when issues of justice and human rights increasingly become the
focus of men and women striving for their own destiny, the ques-

tion of historical identity inevitably comes more and more to the
fore. Therefore it is extremely doubtful whether the concept
such as one world culture has any substantial meaning. In fact,
we live in the world of pluralism. It is this reality of historical
pluralism that needs to be taken into consideration when we face
the world of our present day.

The church in the West has, through her theology and practice
of Christian mission during the past century, failed to do justice
to the reality of historical pluralism. Her aim consists in
'Christianizing' the non-Western lands with a hope to creating
one historical entity which can be identified as Christian. Simply
put, the planting of the Kingdom of God in other parts of the
world is understood as an extension of the western Christendom.
What constitutes the theological basis of such western Christian
mission is the highly monolithic interpretation of the relation
between revelation and history. Most western theologians will,
with a few exceptions, find themselves in full agreement with
Christopher Dawson when he says:

> . . . it is very difficult, perhaps even impossible to explain the
> Christian view of history to a non-Christian, since it is
> necessary to accept the Christian faith in order to under-
> stand the Christian view of history, and those who reject
> the idea of a divine revelation are necessarily obliged to
> reject the Christian view of history as well.[14]

In accordance with this statement, revelation, faith and history
are set in a well-defined logical order. A certain way of responding to revelation, which is Christian faith in this case, is made a
sine qua non for the understanding of the meaning of history.

To press such a theological assumption to its logical conclusion,
we shall be driven to assert that from the Christian point of view
communication on the meaning of history between the Christian
and the people of other faiths has to be suspended. All discussion
on this important subject among the Christian thinkers becomes
intermural conversation. This has largely been the case in the
past; and it is likely to continue, if the apprehension of the meaning of history is conditional to the embracing of the Christian
faith. This is to limit the faith in Christ as the bearer of God's
love to the narrow confine of the religious phenomenon called

Christianity and the institutionalized religion called the Christian Church. Against such a view, I would like to argue that faith in Christ does not serve as the point of departure in inter-religious encounter but as the focal point through which the meaning of history is understood and interpreted in the contexts of historical pluralism. It is, therefore, more correct perhaps to say *meanings* of history instead of meaning of history. There is no reason why Christ should provide only one way of looking at the unfolding of the mystery of God's dealings with man in different spacio-temporal contexts.

The truth of the matter seems that the presence of Christ opens up the real possibility of men and women responding to God in different historical contexts. Far from suppressing these responses as having little to do with God whom He represents, Jesus Christ commends them. He, for example, is astonished at the faith exhibited by the Roman centurion by saying that he did not find it even in Israel.[15] This is the faith that cannot be explained by the norms of religion accepted by Israel. It has its origin outside the confines of the Jewish religion. Throughout His ministry, Christ more than once uncovers this latent faith which comes to sudden manifestation in His presence. Does this not indicate that there is apprehension of the meaning of history outside the realm of Christianity not unrelated to the work of God in Jesus Christ? It is true that the name of Jesus Christ is unidentified, but the reality of His presence in and through the Spirit cannot be denied.

By a stroke of religious genius, John, the author of the fourth Gospel, gives us insight into the mystery of the relation between creation and incarnation. This is an eloquent testimony of how the interpretation of the meaning of history gets broken away from a narrow religious background and set in the wider context of creation. According to the prologue in John's Gospel, the Word of God becoming flesh is not an isolated moment in the history of the interaction between God and man. This event of the incarnation reaches far back to the very beginning of time. Not only this, the Word that became flesh was neither something that resulted from the divine act of creation nor a silent and passive spectator of the creation. As John's testimony has it, the Word was actively involved in the process through which the creation

came into being. It is this Word, it is this Christ who at the
appropriate moment in the history of the world 'became flesh . . .
came to dwell among us.'[16] If we acknowledge as we must do
the profound meaning of such a statement, we can no longer say
like Christopher Dawson did that it is not possible to explain
the Christian view of history to the people of other faiths. It
becomes impossible to do so when the incarnation is seen in separation from creation, and history is viewed as essentially unrelated
to God's act of creation in the beginning of time. When the
event of Christ is divorced from the total process of creation,
Christianity becomes armed with historical particularism bent on
claiming universal validity for its particular view on history. In
this way the church fails to realize that different particulars in
different historical contexts may have inherent meaning derived
from the common denominator which is the whole complex reality
of creation-incarnation. Historical particularism advocated by the
expanding Christian Church thus easily takes on a militant attitude
towards other historical entities.

We must stress that the intrinsic meaning of each historical
entity has its origin in God the Creator. In so far as this is true,
evaluation and judgment of that historical entity has to be based
on this dimension of the divine creation as well as on the particular
view of history formulated within the tradition of Christianity.
Take for instance the traditional Chinese concept of the imperial
ruler as the son of Heaven. The emperor is called son of Heaven
because his sovereign power is granted him by virtue of the decree
of Heaven. He sums up in himself all people and all things in
his domain and even beyond. China is thus regarded as the Middle
Kingdom occupying the place of centrality and eminence in terms
not only of geography but also of culture and religion. The well-
being of all nations depends largely on the degree in which they
come into beneficial relation with China. This is a magnificent
picture of heaven and earth converging on the person of the son
of Heaven. He is chosen and elevated to this awesome height of
power and sovereignty to execute the will of Heaven. He is
thus expected to go about his duty in fear and trepidation. He is
to rule and govern with human-heartedness, justice and wisdom
lest he should forfeit the decree of Heaven. When he misuses his
power and departs from the royal virtues such as human-hearted-

ness and justice, Heaven discloses its displeasure by inflicting natural disasters and social unrest within his domain. Then the people under some other charismatic leader rise to overthrow him. This is the revolution which signals the transfer of the decree of Heaven from one ruler to another. Revolution is therefore a religious as well as a political event. Through it, the decree of Heaven continues to be administered without interruption. This ancient Chinese ideal of a ruler as the son of Heaven reflects to some degree the Biblical picture of man as one who is given the responsibility of carrying out the will of the Creator.

The will of the Creator for the human creature is given in unambiguous terms in the creation story. Man is to be the maker of civilizations and histories in accordance with the purpose of God's creation. As Stauffer puts it:

> God's will is carried out in and through the will of the creative. The creative act of God was continued in a history for which man's will was the responsible agent. It was man's duty to fill the earth and subdue it; he had to care for God's garden and give names to the animals; he had to subject land and sea to himself as farmer and worker and king. . . This makes very clear what the divine conditioning of history originally was. History is the continuation of the work of the creation put into the hands of man who is possessed of a will.[17]

This is a very important statement, particularly the last sentence regarding the nature of history. On account of over-emphasis on Jesus Christ as a particular historical event in the history of the Jewish nation, history both personal and of the world as a whole tends to be thought of as having its point of departure in that calendar year marking the end of B.C. and the beginning of A.D. The massive concentration of western theologians on the history of Israel and the history of the Christian Church in their interpretation of the acts of God in the world has thus made it difficult for them to allot a positive place to the histories of nations in their theological systems. Western Christian mission during the last hundred years or so is this highly segmented theology of history in action. This is by no means to say that Jesus Christ should be given a more qualified place in the Christian understanding of history or in the carrying out of the mission of the church. On

the contrary, Jesus Christ should be released from the captivity of
the so-called *Heilsgeschichte*[18] and set in the process of history as
the continuation of the work of the creation.

It is, therefore, urgent that this dimension of creation be
restored to the mission of the Christian church. Through the
theological movement towards secularization in the contemporary
theological scene, creation, the incarnation and history at last get
related again in a very vital way. This new theological movement
which claims its origin in Bonhoeffer's concept of 'religionless
Christianity' and is given tremendous impetus by Harvey Cox's
The Secular City[19] will continue to mold and remold Christian
understanding of the creation and history. It goes without saying
that the missions of the church cannot remain unaffected by this
current opening up of new theological frontiers. It is not simply
the geographical frontiers that we are dealing with here. It is
the frontiers of meanings with regard to the histories as the continuation of the creation that should occupy the theologians in the
non-Western nations. The task of the mission of the church,
among other things, is thus to extend continually the frontiers
of meanings in the histories of nations as witnesses to the acts of
God in creation and redemption. When these two foci of creation and redemption are brought to bear at the same time on the
histories of the nations, the articifical distinction and the arbitrary
separation of the Christian and the non-Christian, the sacred and
the profane, the Jew and the Gentile, will lose its meaning and
validity. We may call this the secularization of the Christian
mission. This will be the subject of our discussion in a later
chapter.

4. The Impacts of Social Change

In stressing the importance of a theology of social change for
any understanding of the nature and the task of the church in the
present day world, Harvey Cox writes:

> The starting point for any theology of the church today must
> be a theology of social change. The church is first of all
> a responding community, a people whose task it is to discern
> the action of God in the world and to join in His work.[20]

Social change as such is, of course, not to be identified as the
action of God. The point which Cox stresses here is that in and

through social change God is working His purpose out for the salvation of mankind. Precisely for this reason social change poses a direct challenge to the church as she seeks to fulfil her mission.

Despite the fact that what was said above is true, the church on the whole is slow in meeting the challenge of social change. In fact, she tends to regard social change with great suspicion and to react to it in a negative way. It is only fair to say that not Christianity alone falls into this *via negativa*. Religions all have this tendency to be the guardian of the old traditions and conventions in opposition to new changes. The reason is self-evident. New changes call into question the validity of the old norms of beliefs and practices for a new day. They pose as threats to the well-established systems of authority represented by religions. New changes also often mean impatience with security which religious systems jealously promise to provide for their adherents. As a matter of fact, social change in today's world has brought about and continues to bring about collapse of the religious securities with which people surrounded themselves in the past. Instead of security, we must face the fact that in matters related to moral judgments and value systems we are beset with uncertainty and ambiguity. The time has long past when the church can offer unequivocal answers and solutions to many issues and problems that affect our daily lives. The issue of abortion can be cited as a case in point here. Should the church say an outright yes or no to abortion? Does the church have unambiguous reasons, moral, religious or even medical to substantiate the affirmative or the negative attitude she may take towards abortion? The truth of the matter is that the church in today's world simply does not find herself in a position to produce clear-cut answers to an issue such as this. Part of Christian obedience to God consists in acknowledging uncertainties in many crucial areas of our lives. With Paul we must confess we only see things through the mirror darkly.

I believe faith with which we live with uncertainties of life must thus leave room for doubt and incompleteness. Helmut Thielicke, German theologian, in addressing himself to the problem of abortion, has this to say:

> I, for example, am professionally engaged with ethical questions all the time. But this does not mean that I have

all the answers in a matter such as this . . . the very nature of the borderline questions with which we are here confronted precludes the possibility of any final answers: the questions must remain open.[21]

Is this ethical agnosticism? Is this the confession of incompetence on the part of the church in the face of complex issues in modern society?

Nothing could be farther from the truth. The church is not called upon to provide ready-made solutions to the baffling complexities of life like a multiplication chart which makes answers readily available to lazy pupils. The church which bears the marks of the agony and ambiguity of the cross simply does not function in this way. Faith is not to be regarded as a mechanical process which expects certain conclusions to follow from certain axioms. There is some beauty in such neatness. But this is an abstract beauty which simplifies the complex drama of life to the point of absurdity. It takes life out of life, as it were, for what sign of life is still there when life is reduced to precepts, axioms and laws? There is no joy in such living. Words such as hope or expectation could be scratched out of one's vocabulary. Life would become an entirely colourless and weary tour of duty fulfilling one obligation to another in a well-defined and closed system of life.

In the course of her history, the Christian Church has often represented such a closed view on life and the world. She has more than once responded to change in various areas of life with sheer irrationality. She waged futile war against scientists such as Galileo Galilei. She pursued those who tried to differ from her in matters of faith to the bitter end. And by building life on endless 'thou shalt nots', she made life miserable for masses of people who were powerless against the formidable power wielded by her. One cannot help recoiling in fear and in disgust when one is told that all this was done in the name of Christian love and out of concern for the salvation of those poor souls who dared to demur from the authority of the church.

With great relief, however, we have been witnessing the disintegration of this high-handed posture of the church in recent years. The collapse of the systems of beliefs and behavior held tenaciously by the church has fortunately been taking place with accelerated speed. Once again the church can become open for this exciting new world of science and technology. She can become part of the process through which modern man explores mysteries of the universe without inhibitions. But more importantly she is becoming ready to echo sympathy and empathy to the tunes welling out of the depths of human hearts regardless of where they come from. Without this new openness to the world and to the future, the Christian mission is at most a long midsummer dream better forgotten if the challenge of the realities of this new day is to be met seriously. Increasing numbers of Christians both in the West and in the East are now finding it possible to experience the joy of standing side by side with their fellow creatures in search of the truth which its divine Author has mysteriously scattered around throughout His creation. The age of the monopoly of truth by anyone, even by the Christian, is gone. The sense of togetherness in pursuit of the truth will therefore bring men and women of different cultural, racial and religious backgrounds to greater appreciation of one another and to the realization of the majesty of God's love in the creation and the incarnation.

We want, therefore, to assert that God's creation, especially with regard to the developmental possibility and responsibility of its resources by man, is essentially incomplete. The creation story, both in its priestly version and the older J version, does not seem to be interested in depicting the creation as a completed system leaving practically no room for further cultivation and progress. As these writers of the story of creation see it, God is intensely interested in man's participation in the work of creation which continues always with new possibilities for the future. God has called the creation into existence. He has provided the framework of time and space which would prevent the creation from relapsing into chaos and darkness. But this same God has made man to have dominion over other creatures and to 'till the ground' (Genesis 2:5). The meaning of such a statement is far more profound than we usually think it to be. Karl Barth has some penetrating observations to make in relation to the second story of creation when he says:

> It is just because man, with God as his refuge and hope, can
> triumph over the earthiness of earth from which he comes

and to which he must return, that he is destined, within the totality of the creaturely world to serve the earth as a husband, man and a gardener. The hope of the arid, barren and dead earth is that it will bear the vegetation planted by God. According to the second account of creation, we must add that this is the hope of the whole creaturely world. It proceeds from death to life. But the realization of this hope waits for the being which, earthly by nature, will triumph over the aridity, barrenness and deadness of the earth because God is his refuge and hope, because God has constituted Himself as such. His existence will be the sign which will contradict the whole earthiness of earth. His act will be an act of release for the earth too, and for the whole creaturely world.[22]

What a great privilege for man this is! And what an awesome responsibility!

In creation we are confronted with the social change of a most fundamental nature. Creation brings about the social change of the deepest kind. It is not merely a structural or organizational change; it is the kind of change which affects the being of man and the world. Furthermore, through this kind of change, man together with the whole creation, fulfils the meaning of what it means to be created by God, namely, triumph over the powers that militate against life ordained by God. Thus, the impacts of social change intended and envisaged by God's creation go to the very root of man's being.

It is to the credit of western Christian mission that some social change was brought about for the betterment of the life of the people as individuals. In China, for example, missionaries were to be remembered and commended for their untiring campaign against the chronic habit of opium smoking. Considering that opium was contributing to the decay of the body, mind and spirit of an alarming number of the Chinese, we must admit that missionaries' efforts deserved nothing but praise and admiration. Lin Yutang, the noted Chinese writer who quit seminary training in rebellion against the western form of Christianity in China but returned to the Christian faith after a long detour, humorously described the struggle against opium as follows:

> The missionaries highly disapproved of the merchants (i.e.
> western traders in opium), and the merchants highly dis-
> approved of the missionaries, each thinking the others
> insane. As far as a Chinese could see the missionaries had
> taken care to save our souls so that when the gunboats
> blew our bodies to bits we were bound to go to heaven,
> and that made it 'quits,' of course.[23]

Although this was said half in earnest and half in jest, there was
no denying the fact that the Chinese Church with the help of
missionaries had a significant part to play against this decadent
habit prevailing in the Chinese society.

Be that as it may, it is also true to say that on the whole
Christian mission is not quick to grasp the impacts of social
change on the course of the destiny of men and women in Asia
and in other parts of the non-Western world. Perhaps it is more
accurate to say that somehow the urgent call to repentance and
earnest presentation of the need for redemption by missionaries
failed to get related to the impacts of social change. The Good
News was proclaimed outside the contexts of creation with the
result that Christian communities pretending to be immune to
the impacts of social change came into existence. It is no wonder
that the radical change that convulsed China in the middle of
the present century overtook the church in China completely by
surprise. In spite of many ominous signs forecasting the advent
of a complete social and ideological change, the church in China
doggedly pursued her course of action detached from the great
national upheaval. In retrospect we can say that what she needed
most was faith in the God of creation as well as trust in Jesus
Christ as the personal Saviour.

Let the history of the church in the non-Western world not
repeat the mistakes of their predecessors. As it is, the church is
still very much behind the social change which continues to transform our inhabited world both for better and for worse. In
contrast with the pace of change, she can only be seen as dragging
her feet overburdened with the heritage of the past. She needs
to break away from her past as each act related to God's creation
is the transformation of the past for the sake of the future. The
German word *aufheben* communicates aptly this dynamic of the
relation between the past and the future. The past which cannot

be made to live in the future must be abrogated, however high the cost may be. At the same time for man to have a future at all, he must be liberated from the tyranny of the past which has ceased to be relevant in a changed situation. The task of the Christian mission in a given situation is to serve the God of creation and redemption by reading meaning out of no-meaning, by making sense out of no-sense, and by giving witness to the presence and act of God in the midst of change. This leads us to the discussion of creation as the divine 'political' act in the next section.

5. Political Implications of God's Creation

As early as in the beginning of the fifties, Canon Max Warren, then General Secretary of the Church Missionary Society, hit the nail on the head when he pointed out the basic weakness of the missionary Christianity to be its schizophrenic tendency to shy away from the political implications of the nature and task of the church. To illustrate his point, he referred to a young Muganda woman studying at an English university who on some occasion said to her English audience:

> Many Africans are seeking answers to their questions but the Church is not playing its full part in helping young people to face the problems of society. To them God is the God of the Church; He is not the God of politics and social life. They need help to see Him as one God: to see that the Church is concerned with the whole of life.

Commenting on the above highly poignant remark, Canon Warren goes on to say: 'The God of the Church: He is not the God of politics—so, apparently they have learned Christ, these Africans, and discovered in Him not integration but divorce, not atonement but separation. A great gulf is fixed between the scripture lesson and education for career, between what happens in the church and "the high tumultuous lists of life".'[24]

The issue brought up here by Canon Warren is the issue which still causes the Christian community everywhere to be divided into two camps under the grossly misleading labels of 'liberal' and 'conservative'. Although there is much shadow boxing in this polarized state of the Christian community, the issue is serious enough to create a great gulf among the delegates to the Uppsala Assembly in 1968 in the section on Renewal in Mission. Lesslie Newbigin, sensing a great detriment here to the cause of Christian mission, issues a warning and a plea:

> . . . to establish communication across this gulf is surely one of the most urgent tasks of the ecumenical movement. So long as it remains unbridged, the call to mission will be heard—on both sides—as a call not to unity but to separation.[25]

It is lamentable that polarization does exist here at the heart of Christian mission. It has divided the Western Christian mission into two camps which vie for dominance in the non-Western lands. This is a divided mind of the church in the West coming to visible expression. It has vitiated much of the good cause of the Gospel in the eyes of 'pagans' whom Western missionaries want to reach. By becoming in this way a call to division and separation instead of a call to unity and solidarity, the Western Christian mission has betrayed its cause. It has preached a lie in place of truth. Bitter bickerings among Christians of different persuasions have made the love of God appear to be diminutive and hollow. To make the matter worse, converts in Asia and elsewhere are all too quickly processed into one camp or the other, thus perpetuating the practice of making the salvation of God a caricature.

We would like to assert that the choice between the God of politics and the God of the church is a false one. The fact is that the God of politics is the God of the church, that the God of the church is the God of politics. This implies that the church is a political existence. The church is part and parcel of this total political world. Political impacts between the church and the world are mutual. Neither the church nor the world can escape this mutuality in political involvement. The Bible itself is a perennial witness to this. The history of Israel was motivated politically as much as religiously. The Old Testament prophets constantly made trips between the temple and the palace. The mission of the prophets was thus in a true sense a political mission. It had to do not only with the order and worship within the religious community but also with the love and justice in social order. The famous exchange between Jesus and the pharisees on the question of paying taxes to Caesar is a very telling example of the tension

that exists with regard to the church and politics.[26]   The answer
of Jesus is often regarded as a clever way out of a difficult dilemma.
In that case the answer can only be regarded as a prevarication.
Then one would be prompted to press the question and ask what
should be the practical standard to make a distinction between
the things that belong to Caesar and the things that are God's.
It is precisely so difficult to make such a distinction that from the
Biblical and therefore theological point of view, it is wrong to try
to keep politics out of the church.   The answer of Jesus to the
questioning of the pharisees is no equivocation of the issue. Rather
it is more correct to say that Jesus by answering as he did threw
the question back at the questioners, challenging them to make
a decision in their own political-ecclesiastical contexts.   It was a
matter of decision of faith on a particular political issue. It follows,
therefore, that any decision to which one may come would be a
political as well as a religious decision.   This only goes to under-
line the obvious fact that the church is in the world and that the
world is in the church.   Any theological position which does not
do justice to this plain reality cannot be a guide to the church
in her efforts to serve God and man.

We can go back, I believe, to the very root of our faith in
God's creation to substantiate what has been said above.   The act
of creation, we may say, is a political act. Here we are using the
word political in a broad sense of having to do with power. Politics
cannot be divorced from power.   It is a manifestation, organization and mobilization of power for a certain definite purpose in
the ordering of human society. Obviously, this is a platitude. But
we need to be reminded of this again and again lest we forget it
or take it for granted.   When asked why he wanted to run for the
presidency of the United States, John F. Kennedy was reported
to have said that the White House was the place where the power
was.   And he was right.   Just think of the power released from
that massive citadel of power, both to construct the bridge of peace
in the world and to shatter it with demonic force! This in essence
is the demonic nature of power in the hands of man.   Each and
every government has, with differing degrees, power to build and
to destroy.   You simply cannot govern without power.   A government without power is a chimera.   This is equally true for individual persons.   Each and every person has some power accord-

ing to his status, wealth and occupation. The relation between the ruler and the ruled, the dominator and the dominated, the superior and the inferior, is determined on the basis of power. We may thus go so far as to say that the phenomena of politics, whether of international, national or social nature, is the phenomena of power. Can we not say then that in a very true sense politics is the phenomenology of power?

In this analogy we would like to stress that creation as the political act of God is the manifestation of the divine power. The creation stories in the first and the second chapters of Genesis are no other than the phenomenologies of the power of God. The creating power of God, taking the form of Word and Spirit, brings into existence the whole creation. And it is this same divine power which continues to become concretised into the ordering of the cosmos with all things and all beings in it. What a tremendous exhibition of the divine power this is! In traditional theology, the word omnipotence is used to describe the Creator-God. To coin a term, what we have here is a cosmic politics. This is the politics which affects the whole of the cosmos. Paul is very much aware of the cosmic dimension of God's creational activity. That is why for him salvation involves no less than the whole universe. In writing to the Christians in Rome, Paul cannot refrain from saying that 'the whole created universe groans in all its parts as if in the pang of childbirth,' and that 'the universe itself is to be freed from the shackles of mortality and enter upon the liberty and splendour of the children of God.'[27] In the same spirit, John, the elder of the earliest Christian communities, exiled to the island called Patmos, envisions the restoration of the creation in terms of a new heaven and a new earth taking the place of the first heaven and the first earth.[28] This grandiose picture of God's dealing with His creation is a powerful affirmation of God's politics of power in the universe.

To interpret the creation of God in terms of power is very timely and important especially for the churches in the Third World. Too long the stories of the creation have been understood by the Asians, for example, either literally as an eye-witness accounts of how the universe came into being, or simply as myth or legend. Seen as a literal record of the origin of the universe, they only serve as a defence-mechanism for the self-styled defenders of the faith against the 'impious' scientists. Treated as legend or myth, they are regarded as not more than a literary and religious device which has no substantial role to play in the unfolding of the history of Israel and the nations. But the truth of the matter is that creation as the manifestation of God's power plays a crucial role at each moment in history. History can be said to consist of events as witnesses either for or against God's power of creation. To put it differently, it is when the church is confronted with happenings in the world that she begins to know what it means to speak of God's revelation and acts in the world.

This leads us to examine further the concept of omnipotence mentioned earlier. According to John Macquarrie, God's omnipotence means

> that he, himself, not any factual situation, is the source and also the horizon of all possibilities and only those are excluded that are inconsistent with the structure and the dynamics of God himself.[29]

I think here is a clue to understanding the mission of the church as having to do with the politics of God and the politics of man.

First of all, there are possibilities in the course of history which can only be regarded as ambiguous. Any historical possibility is ambiguous because it turns into an actuality as the result of man acting on the power released by God. Once released, God's power comes, in a very real sense, to be disposed of by man. That is why man is supposed to have dominion over the earth and its creatures. To be sure, the power man has is a delegated power, and the authority he possesses is a delegated authority. He can only have limited use of that power and authority. Nevertheless, it is real power and real authority. For this reason ambiguity sets in and takes hold of the structures of power which man builds around himself. It is always an open question as to whether a particular structure of power is, to use Macquarrie's expression, consistent with the structure and dynamics of God.

To ask this question, to probe into the nature of the structures of power exhibited in different situations, is precisely the mission of the church. Perhaps we can call this the political mission of the church. The mission of the church is of a political nature not because she lets herself become part of the struggle for political power but because she is expected to direct critical questions to the use and forms of power in given human situations in the light of the structure and dynamics of God. This is the function performed by the prophets in the Old Testament with regard to their own nation and also other nations. And at critical turns in history, some astonishing judgments are made by the prophets. The Persian Cyrus, who made his entry into Babylon in 539 B.C. and put an end to the Neo-Babylonian empire by expelling its last King Nabonidus, is hailed as an instrument of God for the future destiny of Israel. Deutero-Isaiah actually regards him as God's shepherd who will fulfil all God's purpose.[30] In this particular instance, the political power exercised by Cyrus is an extension of the politics of God.

The political mission of the church, that is, the responsibility of the church to discern and interpret the will of God in and through political structures of powers that be, is faced with great difficulty when confronted with the powers that seem to pose themselves against God. Since all power comes from God and belongs to God, it follows that all political power, including that which is against God, ultimately has its source and origin in God. Jesus makes this clear when he is confronted with the political power and authority represented by Pilate. As a ruler over the defenceless, colonized Jews, Pilate is very much conscious of the power he has in determining the fate of his subjects. He, therefore, reminds Jesus somewhat sadistically that he has authority to release or crucify Jesus. But Jesus gives a startling answer. 'You would have no authority at all over me,' he said, 'if it had not been granted you from above.'[31] In the book of Revelation, the author seems to go so far as to suggest that the beast with its destructive power derives its authority from God Himself.[32]

It is Paul who has drawn a logical conclusion with regard to a Christian attitude towards political authorities in the famous thirteenth chapter of his letter to the Christians in Rome. His advice to them carries the air of conclusiveness. Every person, he exhorts,

> must submit to the supreme authorities. There is no authority but by act of God, and the existing authorities are instituted by Him; consequently, anyone who rebels against authority is resisting a divine institution, and those who so resist have themselves to thank for the punishment they will receive.[33]

Is Paul advocating unconditional civil obedience? Is he ruling out the possibility of rebellion against any political authorities? Is he denying Christians the right and responsibility to dissent under any circumstances? Unfortunately, it has sometimes been interpreted this way. This explains why some Christians, and especially these Christians in Asia constituting the minority of the population, tend to adopt a passive attitude towards state authorities. This is unfortunate because if we read Paul's letter a little further, we realize that Paul bases his argument on the assumption that the cause of right is the key to the whole question of state authorities and civil obedience. If you do right and good, so he seems to be arguing, state authorities as a divine institution would not wield their sword to intimidate and terrify you.

Paul does not go on to state the case on the reverse side. That is, supposing you do right and good, and state authorities wield their power and sword to crush and destroy you. Would Paul still exhort you to do nothing but obey? Probably not. When the powers that be come to stand for injustice, it is apparent that the power that comes from God is abused and thus becomes corrupted. Paul would be the last one to argue that Christians owe obedience and respect to the abuse and corruption of power.

The implication here for the mission of the church is this. On one hand, it is the joyous task of the church to make explicit the will and purpose of God in the powers of this world when they reflect the structure and dynamics of God, that is to say, when they reflect the love and justice of God. On the other hand, it is the responsibility of the church not to keep quiet when the powers of this world have fallen short of the structure and dynamics of God. Thus, the church lives in tension. She cannot be a partisan to any political power. She maintains creative tension with it in order that her prophetic vision is sharpened as events unfold themselves before her eyes to shape the destiny of men and women.

It has to be pointed out that there has been a tendency to identify democracy with divine sanction of power and to regard communism as total aberration of the divine power. That is why powerful nations can wage war against Communist countries in the name of democracy and by invoking the name of God. It becomes a religious war. Western Christian mission in Asia has, in the last two or three decades, echoed and given spiritual support to this Western political ideology. It has, therefore, failed its prophetic task. The church in Asia has to be set free from the contamination of this pseudo-interpretation of what God is doing in the world. She needs to become engaged in re-interpretation of political power systems and political history which have shaped and continue to shape the structures of politics in various countries in Asia. It should be stressed that we can no longer think of and practise the Christian mission in separation from this political mission of the church. In other words we have learned in Asia through painful experience that Christian mission understood and practised in the narrow sense of converting pagans to Christianity has isolated the Christians from the political life of the nation of which they are supposed to be responsible citizens. To use a very graphic expression of an Asian churchman addressing a group of his prominent American counterparts, Asian Christians in the midst of political uncertainty and economic depravity after the Second World War were given sleeping pills by the churches in the West to have a false sense of security and to get much needed sleep at night. By sleeping pills, he meant the aids from the Western churches. But now, he said, we no longer want these sleeping pills. We need to wake up from our sleep to become actively involved in the formation of the political destiny of our country.

He was utterly so right. Christian mission does not consist in counting the sleeping heads of converts in the security of mission compounds. This kind of what I would call mission-compound Christianity will do more harm than good to the cause of Christian faith. Within its boundary one can hardly perceive the creative dynamics of God at work. One also does not find the confrontation there with the power of this world that comes ultimately from the Creator-God.

But things are beginning to change. An increasing number of Christians in Asia are finding themselves thrust more and more into the vortex of actions in which the power of the Creator-God and the powers that be intersect and interact. Out of this involvement the church will learn to re-define her mission and re-shape her style of life. This will call forth a new chapter in the history of the Christian church in Asia and in other parts of the non-Western world.

REFERENCES

1. Psalm 61:1-3.

2. Karl Barth, *Church Dogmatics* II, 1, p. 76.

3. John Bright, *A History of Israel*, Philadelphia: The Westminster Press, 1959, p. 328.

4. Isaiah 49:1.

5. From the Revised Standard Version.

6. The term the Third World is used not only in a geographical sense. Nor is it used of the under-developed or developing nations from the economic standpoint. It also refers to the men and women, whether in the West or in the East, who are deprived of human rights and social justice.

7. 'The Ministry of Crossing Frontiers,' in *The Church Crossing the Frontiers*, Essays on the Nature of Mission, in honour of Bengt Sundkler, Uppsala, 1969, pp. 44f.

8. Bonhoeffer, *Creation and Fall*, A Theological Interpretation of Genesis 1-3, London: SCM Press Ltd., 1959, translated from *Schöpfung und Fall*, 1937, by John C. Fletcher, p. 22.

9. In summarizing Bonhoeffer's contribution to the radical understanding of the Christian faith, Goodsey accurately predicted saying: 'In the final period of his theology, Bonhoeffer was breaking fresh ground in his concept of "wordly" Christianity, and it is here that he is helping the church to a new understanding on the relation between God and the world. In the long run, this will undoubtedly be Bonhoeffer's greatest contribution and it is possible that his thought will lead to a significant revolution of the understanding of the Christian faith' (John D. Goodsey, *The Theology of Dietrich Bonhoeffer*, Philadelphia: Westminster Press, 1960, p. 281).

10. Gerardus van der Leeuw, *Sacred and Profane Beauty: the Holy in Art*, trans. by David E. Green, New York: Abingdon Press, 1963, pp. XII-XIII.

11. *Ibid.*, p. 265.

12. Masaharu Anesaki, *Art, Life and Nature in Japan*, Boston: Marshall Jones Company, 1933, p. 22.

13. *Ibid.*, p. 18.

14. Christopher Dawson, *The Dynamics of World History*, New York: Sheed and Ward, 1956, p. 235.

15. Matthew 8:5f.

16. John 1:14.

17. Ethelbert Stauffer, *New Testament Theology*, trans. John Marsh, New York: The Macmillan Company, 1955, p. 62.

18. The term *Heilsgeschichte*, in spite of its wide use, is not without some opponents, Richard Niebuhr among them. As Isaac Rottenberg points out, Richard Niebuhr attacks 'the concept of *Heilsgeschichte* because in his judgement it completely severs the ties between "regular history", the history of "objective occurrences" and "sacred history." ' (cf. Rottenberg, *Redemption and Historical Reality*, Philadelphia: The Westminster Press, 1964, p. 49).

19. New York: The Macmillan Company, 1965.

20. *The Secular City*, p. 105.

21. Thielicke, 'Ethics in Modern Medicine' in *Who Shall Live?* ed. by Kenneth Vaux, Philadelphia : Fortress Press, 1970, p. 147.

22. Barth, *Church Dogmatics* III. 1, p. 237.

23. Lin Yutang, *From Pagan to Christianity*, New York: The World Publishing Company, 1959, p. 36.

24. Max Warren, *The Christian Mission*, London: SCM Press, 1951, p. 9. Quoted by Paul Lehmann in *Ethics in a Christian Context*, New York: Harper and Row, p. 81.

25. Lesslie Newbigin, 'Call to Mission . . . A Call to Unity?' in *The Church Crossing the Frontiers*, p. 257.

26. Mark 12:15-17. Also Matthew 22:15-22; Luke 20:20-26.

27. Romans 8:20-22.

28. Revelation 21:1

29. John Macquarrie, *Principles of Christian Theology*, New York: Charles Scribner's Sons, 1966, p. 189.

30. Isaiah 44:28.

31. John 19:11.

32. Revelation 13:1-8.

33. Romans 13:1-25 cf., 1 Peter 2:14.

CHAPTER THREE

Mission of Enfleshment

He did not abhor the virgin's womb,
He became human flesh,
He was baptized with the baptism of sinners.
He was friend of all men,
He was numbered with the transgressors.
He was forasken on the cross.
Eloi, Eloi, Lama Sabachthani
My God, My God, Why hast thou forsaken me?
God has arrived, at least at the place of sinful man.

—D. T. NILES, *Upon the Earth*, p. 53.

1. From Creation to Incarnation

THE God of creation is the God of incarnation. As has been discussed in the preceding chapter, this is the basic thesis underlying the theology of the Prologue of the Fourth Gospel. There exists an intrinsic relation between creation and incarnation. The author of the Fourth Gospel is at pains to get at this mystery of God. By mere stretch of imagination one cannot even begin to comprehend what this is all about. Only through the gift of faith is one led to have some insight into the meaning of God's mystery which happens entirely outside man but is supremely concerned about him. In the words of John's Prologue, 'And the Word became flesh and dwelt among us, full of grace and truth.'[1] The little word 'and' at the beginning of this profound statement purports to link the act of the creation with God's being present in the world through Jesus Christ. This Word was the Word present at the creation. It was instrumental in the coming into being of those in the created world. And it was no other than this Word that became flesh. This activity of God called incarnation was, to use John Macquarrie's words, 'equiprimordial with creation itself'.[2]

Here John, the author of the Fourth Gospel, grasps the mystery of all mysteries, namely, God's mission of enfleshment. This is God going out of Himself to become embodied in particular historical persons and events. This activity of God from creation to incarnation has been going on since the beginning of time.

World history is part of the totality embraced by the framework of creation and incarnation. No event and no person is excluded from this creation-incarnation framework. This particularly gives man, yes, every man, a sense of belonging, the *raison d'être* of being in the world, and a consciousness of destiny. This is the contribution which the Christian faith has decisively made to humanity.

It follows that creation and incarnation are not to be regarded as two separate entities divided by a chronological gulf. Instead, they are intertwined, pushing the history of mankind and the universe towards completion. Creation and incarnation are thus two moments of one and the same act of God. To separate them is to make the work of God a torso. For creation detached from incarnation is equivalent to words unspoken. Words remain in the mind of the speaker and thus uncommunicated. But at the creation, words spoken by God were heard and transformed into deeds, events and concrete objects. 'And God said, "Let there be light;" and there was light.'[3] It was as straightforward as that. God remains God who was and is and ever shall be. The creation then means that this God become something other than Himself. Only an omnipotent God can do this. And in the terminology of the New Testament, especially that of John's Gospel, this is precisely what incarnation means. The Word became flesh. The verb 'became' (*egeneto*) expresses the movement from God's Word to man's flesh, from the divine essence to the human essence. Here the divine movement from creation to incarnation becomes complete. In this flesh, in this particular human being called Jesus Christ, creation and incarnation become one concrete historical event embodying the love of God for the whole world. God became a man. In a very true sense, the creation envisaged in the first two chapters of Genesis did not become complete until this historical moment when the Word became flesh in Jesus Christ. In the words of Kazoh Kitamori, the Japanese theologian of the pain of God:

> Jesus, the personification of the pain of God, assumed the 'flesh' of this historical world. Jesus 'in the flesh' was 'real man,' a historical person. God himself had to enter the world of real sin in order to bear the responsibility of real sin.[4]

God brought His creation-incarnation complex to its completion by entering the world Himself. This is what we earlier called the mission of enfleshment, namely, God the Creator became what He had created. The Creator became the Incarnator.

What has been said above regarding the act of God in creation and incarnation has much to illumine the nature and essence of Christian mission. Since God's mission in creation and incarnation is that of enfleshment, that of imparting Himself, Christian mission as witness to God's mission should be that of imparting to others one's own self as grasped by the love of God in Jesus Christ. In the last analysis, the mission of Christians is to *be with* this world, or more concretely, to be one with the agony and joy of this world with the transforming power of God's love. Jesus Christ is God's being with this world. He is the *presence* and *manifestation* of God's solidarity with man in the latter's sin and salvation. That is why Jesus Christ allowed himself to be baptized with the baptism of repentance. He permitted himself to be tempted. And finally he let himself be crucified between two thieves. Jesus Christ is God's imparting of himself to man. Paul puts this in words that can be easily understood not only by his fellow Christians in the first century but also by us in the twentieth century. He exhorts the Christians in the city of Rome saying, 'Rejoice with those who rejoice, weep with those who weep.'[5] Jesus Christ, himself, demonstrated this quality of being one with others during the course of his ministry. On hearing that Lazarus had died, 'Jesus wept'.[6] Through the parable of the lost sheep,[7] the lost coin,[8] and above all the prodigal son,[9] Jesus wanted His hearers to share not only with the overwhelming joy of God in having recovered the lost, but with the happiness of those who have experienced new hope in life.

To rejoice with those who rejoice and to weep with those who weep is to give oneself up for others. This is the essence of the mission and ministry of Jesus Christ. Unlike our preaching, his preaching is not mere verbal communication of some objective truth. In his preaching, he communicated himself. His preaching is, therefore, his very own life in action. I have just referred to the parable of the prodigal son. Joachim Jeremias has correctly observed that it should be called the parable of the father's love.[10] What we see in that parable is the love which constitutes the being of the father in action. What a contrast this love of God is to the pharisees and the scribes whose rigid and lifeless religiosity made it possible for them to complain and say that Jesus 'receives sinners and eats with them'![11]

Is it not true to say that the institutionalized Western Christian mission has come very close to ceasing to reflect, Christ's mission of impartation? The systems of Western Christian mission have made it almost impossible for those engaged in mission work to give themselves up for those they are sent to serve. Christian mission has degenerated into the display of the glory and richness of the 'Christian' West to the poor 'pagan' East. It is no wonder that the churches in the Third World established by missionary efforts from the West can only pay lip service to the mission of enfleshment. Often theirs is the mission of disembodiment. Let us frankly admit that this capitalist form of Western Christian mission has failed the test of time. That is why the once formidable missionary force in China crumbled without further ado at the Communist take-over of China in 1949. According to Richard Bush's study and analysis, T. C. Chao, Dean of the Yenching School of Religion and the most prominent Protestant theologian in China, seeing the Communist take-over of China,

> emphasized the weakness of the church and the power of God's judgment upon it, the need for repentance and reform, a new theology, new methods of evangelism and relevant social service. The Christian response to the new day (O time! O Day!) is to bear Christian witness to the communists. . . Communism is man's challenge to Christianity, but it is also God's judgment upon flabby churches.'[12]

Flabby Christian mission and flabby Christian church! How could this have stood the onslaught of the masses of downtrodden and poverty-stricken people? At the very height of missionary success in China, Christian mission was in reality losing one of the basic elements that constitutes its very nature, namely, the impartation of the very self of Christians, both missionary and national, for the cause of justice in society and liberation of those suffering from human tyranny. Indeed as T. C. Chao puts it, Communist rise to power in China was God's judgment upon the flabby church.

God's mission of enfleshment in Jesus Christ is, furthermore, God becoming what He is not. This entails the risk of God losing His own identity. How can God become no longer God? Will this not amount to God denying His own being? Jews just could not accept this God present in Jesus Christ and Greeks could not help ridiculing the whole idea as folly.[13] This miracle of enfleshment, however, does not result in God forfeiting His identity as Creator and Redeemer. On the contrary, by becoming other than what He is, namely, by becoming present and manifest in Jesus Christ, He has revealed Himself as what He truly is. This is the heart of the paradox of the Christian faith. It should also constitute the heart of Christian mission.

Christian mission, to apply the above argument, should be the mission of the church becoming what she is not in order to let the love and justice of God become visible among men. This sounds paradoxical, but this is the logical implication of what we understand to mean by the mission of enfleshment. This calls into question the meaning and practice of evangelism as it is usually understood by missionaries or evangelists, especially of conservative inclination. The process of evangelism is often that of converting people into the fold of the Christian community and integrating them into the religious structure of the church. Conversion is thus understood and practised as a religious action which enhances and expands the size and number of Christian communities. By and by, such Christian communities begin to find their identity by becoming enclosed circles. That is to say, they develop their own moral codes, rules of behaviour, idiosyncrasies of inner circle language, and, of course, their own sets of values. Their smile becomes a 'Christian' smile. The way they greet each other and look at each other have come to obtain the 'Christian' touch. The way Christians carry themselves will not fail to impress others as belonging to the community of people who call themselves 'Christian'. There was, in fact, much of this in Judaism at the time of Jesus Christ. The devout Jews, particularly the pharisees and scribes, 'love to say their prayers standing up in synagogues and at the street corners.'[14] When they fast, 'they make their faces unsightly so that other people may see that they are fasting'.[15] Faith in this way becomes ostentatious religiosity. Jesus called them hypocrites and urged His followers to go behind the closed doors when they wanted to pray and asked them to 'anoint their head and wash their face' when they were fasting. Nothing could be more against the mission of God in Jesus Christ than this self-conscious and morbid religiosity.

Western Christian mission to Asia has done much to establish a Christian identity of such religiosity, religiosity that reflects almost every trait and idiosyncrasy of the particular brand of Christianity and culture from which missionaries came. This has been done and perpetuated almost to the extent of absurdity. This is what I called earlier, 'compound Christianity'. On Sunday, the joyful day to celebrate the resurrection, dead silence used to prevail within mission compounds. All activities came to a sudden stop. One could intrude that sanctity at the risk of being thrown out. In tropical Asia it was not, and still is not, uncommon to hold afternoon worship services at the hottest hour of the day for no other reason than that was the time of worship service observed by the missionaries' home church in the frigid zone of the globe.

The first essential step which must be taken by Christian mission, therefore, consists in breaking out of its own Christian western identity, and becoming almost everything that the church has so far forbidden herself to become. I do not think the word 'indigenization' will adequately represent what is urged here. In one sense the word can be understood to encourage Christian churches in Asia to become rooted in Asian society as strongly organized and structured centers of Christian traditions from the past. This is precisely what Christian mission should not do. Therefore, the word incarnation, or enfleshment, is both Biblically and theologically more accurate and sound to describe the nature and task of the Christian mission. This amounts to Christians in Asia denying their inherited Christian values and becoming ready to let their Christian faith become flesh in their cultural and religious demands and aspirations. In the words of Van Leeuwen,

> . . . here are opportunities in inexhaustible abundance for the Christians to steep themselves no less completely than their non-Christian fellows and compatriots in the values, spiritual and material, social and individual, philosophical and psychological, political and economic, of the non-Western civilizations. In that way a Christian can make as vital a contribution to the renewal of Islamic or of Indian civilization as any Muslim or Hindu.[16]

This is a big order indeed and a revolutionary one too! What Van Leeuwen is advocating here and throughout this important book of his from which the above quotation was taken is that evangelism in the sense traditionally accepted and practised simply will not do. It is just not the business of Christian mission to defeat other religions, to invalidate their claims to truth, to snatch men and women out of the damnable snares of these pagan religions. The task of Christian mission is *not* to Christianize the world but make a contribution to 'the renewal' of civilizations deeply rooted in other religions. A shocking idea? Yes! A betrayal of Christian faith? No! Essentially this is to envision faith and culture in the perspective of creation and incarnation. As a matter of fact this was the main subject matter we argued and discussed in the previous chapter.

In so far as Christian mission regards it most essential to participate in God's mission of enfleshment, the Christians engaged in such a mission are required to have this revolutionary re-orientation. Let me reiterate: the chief task of Christian mission is to let the faith in Jesus Christ become the germinal element which enables civilizations to be renewed as witness to the glory of God's creation and manifestation of the presence of God as saviour in the world.

There is another point which follows from our discussion in the foregoing pages. By becoming other than what He is, God makes Himself available to man. God's mission of enfleshment means that God has now become available to man. Jesus Christ is this availability of God. On many an occasion, Jesus tries to put this across to his disciples and to those who followed him. To Philip who requested Him to show them the Father, this was Jesus' reply: 'Have I been with you so long, and yet you do not know me, Philip? He who has seen me has seen the Father.'[17] In Jesus Christ we are confronted with God. The tragedy is that most of the people whom Jesus met and taught either were unable to see this or refused to believe this. But the love of God does not easily allow us to get away with our unbelief. Often against our own will and in spite of ourselves, we are pulled towards God in Jesus Christ through the tumultuous sea of doubt, unbelief and self-centeredness. As D. T. Niles puts it:

> When God seems far away; when our eyes, dim with tears,
>   are unable to see His face; or when our souls burdened

with sin shrink from Him; then it is that we realize what Christ is able to do for us. We hold to Christ and, when the crisis is past, realize that in holding to Him we were all the time holding to God. In sober truth Jesus is Emmanuel—God with us (Matt. 1:23).[18]

Here is God going all the way to make Himself available and accessible to us.

We said 'all the way' because this is precisely what God has done in Jesus Christ. That is why Karl Barth can speak of the humanity of God.[19] To use our own terminology here, the humanity of God simply means the availability of God to man in Jesus Christ. In Jesus Christ, God stands where we stand. He is present at every critical moment in the course of our lives. He is our Partner, Brother, Friend and the One in whom we can confide ourselves without reservation. In Jesus Christ, the barrier between God and man on account of man's sin is broken. A new God-man relationship emerges. Jesus Christ is this new God-man relationship. All this is what we mean by the availability of God to man in Jesus Christ.

There is something terribly unconventional about all this. Certainly for God to assume humanity in Jesus Christ cannot be explained by the logic of this conventional society in which we live. On account of this, the ministry of Jesus Christ is characterized by radical unconventionality. It is through this unconventionality that He was able to make God available to the poor, the oppressed, tax collectors or prostitutes. In striking contrast, the conventionality of Jewish religion was making God unavailable to the masses of people in the street. Ironically, religion becomes the barrier for people to approach God. These harsh words of Jesus to the pharisees are excruciatingly to the point. He says: 'Alas, alas for you, lawyers and pharisees, hypocrites that you are! You shut the door of the Kingdom of Heaven in men's faces; you do not enter yourselves, and when others are entering, you stop them. Alas for you, lawyers and pharisees, hypocrites! You travel over sea and land to win one convert; and when you have won him you make him twice as fit for hell as you are yourselves!'[20]

Here is a very serious warning to the church and her mission. In order to make God available to men and women in need,

Christian mission has an imperative duty to become unconventional. When we ponder a little more deeply, this is not so difficult to understand. Most of our social conventions and religious performances do serve to suppress the spontaneous expressions of man's deep-seated agonies and sufferings. In church and in society we are expected to behave in accordance with some prescribed norms of respectability and acceptability. These norms refuse to let people face the humanity in each and every person at the crossroads. Those people who cannot accept these norms or feel they are not qualified for these standards because of what they are and because of what they do are driven to places where they are less shackled by the codes of decency and respectability. To reach these people, Jesus went so far as to violate religious codes of his day. He ate with sinners. He healed on the Sabbath day. In his own person, he made God available to those who desperately needed God.

Let us face the fact that missionaries, no matter where they come from, cannot make God available to people if they come armed with doctrinal orthodoxy, value judgements, cultural immunity or moral standards. These they must leave behind them, ready to gaze into the abysmal depth of humanity crying out to God. You must be ready to accept their standards as your standards, their values as your values, their sins as your sins. You must assume their totality as human beings. Only in so far as you are able to do this, can you make God somewhat available to them. We have to come to terms with the fact that you cannot conduct Christian mission from a mission compound. The walls of the church, which look more like a citadel than a *Koinonia* of those who have come under the love of God, must be broken down before you can reach people God wants you to reach. In the last analysis, Christian mission does not consist in what you do for the people in a foreign country. It consists in what you are in relation to the people you seek to serve. Perceptions borne out of Christian presence with people will enable you to become involved in the problems of humanity in different cultural contexts. It is at this point that Christian mission really begins.

To change our metaphor, to make ourselves available for others is the same thing as putting ourselves at the disposal of or at the service of others. This metaphor makes us immediately aware that here we are dealing with one of the central teachings

of Jesus Christ, namely, denial of the self for the sake of others.
In reality this is what the mission of enfleshment is about. In the
person of Jesus Christ, we have the demonstration of God's denial
of His own self to the point of death on the cross. Because of
this self-denial of God, a new humanity comes into being in Jesus
Christ. The new man Jesus Christ is, therefore, both divine and
human. He is neither divine pure and simple nor human without further ado. As the result of God's self-denying act, room is
created for God to take humanity into Himself. He becomes
less God in order to make room for man in Himself. God's
mission of enfleshment thus results in the creation of the God-
man Jesus Christ. Jesus aptly explains this mystery of new life
when he says: 'If any one wishes to be a follower of mine, he
must leave self behind; he must take up his cross and come with
me. Whoever cares for his own safety is lost; but if a man will
let himself be lost for my sake, he will find his true self'.[21]

What all this implies for Christian mission is more than obvious. Those who engage themselves in Christian mission must lose
their own identity in order that a new identity in the context of
others may emerge. Harold DeWolf has expressed it this way:

> What we really crave and need is a love transcending not only
> self but also all individual isolation. Neither the 'I' nor
> the 'Thou' should be the exclusive object of concern. Rather
> both should be 'lost' in an inclusive 'We' in which both
> are 'found', that is fulfilled.[22]

Jesus Christ is the proto-type of this inclusive 'We'. Is it not
true to say that very few Western missionaries have found this
new identity in this inclusive 'We'? Christian mission, in so far
as it takes part in God's mission of enfleshment, must involve
missionaries as well as those to whom the Gospel is to be communicated in search of this inclusive 'We'. It is very humiliating
to realize that much of what has been done in the name of Christian mission has only a faint echo of God's mission of enfleshment.
But this should challenge us to a new commitment to follow Jesus
Christ in order to find ourselves and others in a new humanity.

2. Christ-centered Mission

Christian theology should begin with the creation, climaxing
in the incarnation and ending with the consummation of all things.

Through all these acts of God, Christ is the center of all things at every stage of the unfolding of God's will. This is in fact our argument in the foregoing pages. As has been stressed earlier, Jesus Christ is not to be considered as a historical point in the stream of time. Mathematical terminology such as 'point' is not only inadequate but incorrect to describe the event of Jesus Christ. If we continue in mathematical language here, we shall have to use dimension instead of point. Jesus Christ is at the intersection of the divine dimension and the human dimension at every stage of history from creation to incarnation. Can we, therefore, not say that in Jesus Christ God saturates the whole history of man and the world? In oriental thought, philosophy and art, the Asian, and particularly the Chinese, try to give expression to the saturation of God in nature. Without the discipline of Christo-centric thinking, these oriental expressions run the risk of falling into pantheism. That which is divine is saturated and sucked into nature. Christian theology must see to it that this should not happen. And Christo-centric theology in the sense we tried to understand above should be able to prevent this from happening. In this way, Christian faith can be said to contribute to the renewal of oriental culture.

What has been said so far seems to be a digression from our main concern in this chapter. Actually it is not a digression from our theme. For since Christian theology should be of the nature described above, Christian mission which is Christian theology to action should share this essential nature of Christian theology also. In other words, Christian mission should be the Christ-centered mission. Perhaps some will contend that this is nothing new, for it has always been the basic understanding among Christian theologians that Christian mission, by definition, is derived from Christ's mission. But this is not the whole picture, for is it not true that Christian mission, though derived from Christ's mission, is further qualified as the mission of the church? That is to say, is it not stressed that Christian mission begins with the church and ends with the church? The church is the context in which Christian mission is planned and carried out. In fact, Christian mission as we know and practise it is the church-centered mission.

There has been some rigorous re-evaluation of the validity of the church-centered mission. One of the authoritative voices in this regard comes from Hoekendijk, Professor of Mission at Union

Theological Seminary, New York. In his view, missiology and ecclesiology do not necessarily make compatible bed-fellows. He pointedly observes:

> To say that 'the Church is the starting point and the goal of the Mission' is after all only making a phenomenological statement. It may well be that we are so wrapped up in our church-centrism that we hardly realize any longer how much our ideas are open to controversy. Would it not be a good thing to start all over again in trying to understand what it really means when we repeat again and again our favourite missionary text, 'the Gospel of the Kingdom will be proclaimed throughout the *oikumene*—and attempt to re-think our ecclesiology within this framework of King-dom—Gospel—apostolate—world?[23]

Here Hoekendijk rightly advocates the reversal of our under-standing of the relationship between the church and the world. Instead of saying that we should view the *oikumene*—the world—through the stained glass windows of the church, he stresses that we should attempt to define the nature and function of the church which is mission in the context of the *oikumene*—the world. Such a radical shift of emphasis is based on his conviction that 'the church-centric missionary thinking is bound to go astray, because it revolves around an illegitimate center'.[24] This brings up the question of the relationship between Christ, the church and the world.

Let us stress once again that the legitimate center of Christian mission, to use Hoekendijk's words, is Christ in the context of the world. Where, then, does the church come in? Is there any place for the church in Christian mission? This is no place to elaborate on the doctrine of the church. What has to be stressed at this point is that the doctrine of the church badly needs redefini-tion from the standpoint of Christian mission. The lamentable fact is that in the course of the history of the church, ecclesiology tends to get separated from missiology. Especially when the church develops into the direction of a liturgical church, mission tends to be given only a nominal place. It has been emphasized again and again that the church is not only in mission, but the church is mission. However, owing to the fact that mission is left largely for the so-called mission boards to be responsible for in most branches of Christianity in the West, the church and mission are still regarded and treated as separate entities. A liturgical church divorced from mission is essentially a static church without the dynamics to demonstrate what God is doing in the world. The church can be mission only in so far as she is a mobile, dynamic and outgoing fellowship (*koinonia*) of the followers of Jesus Christ. The church can be mission only in so far as in whatever she does through worship, study, structure or actions she is responding to God's mission of enfleshment. Therefore, strictly speaking, we cannot say the church is mission. We can only say the church *becomes* mission.

Christ-centered mission defines the nature and function of the church. Accordingly, the church is an event rather than an organization, fellowship rather than church order. According to Hoekendijk, this is precisely what the church should be. He says:

> Where in this context does the church stand? Certainly not at the starting point, not at the end. The church has no fixed place at all in this context, it *happens* in so far as it actually proclaims the Kingdom of the world. The church has no other existence than *in actu Christi*, that is, *in actu Apostoli*. Consequently, it cannot be firmly established but will always remain the *paroika*, a temporary settlement which can never become a permanent home.[25]

The church as a social phenomenon cannot be identified immediately with the event of the *Koinonia* brought into existence in and through the act of Christ. That is why the church as we know and experience her must always live in tension. When the tension is broken, the church gets settled into her peaceful existence, losing her characteristic as mission.[26]

One of the mistakes committed by Western foreign missions in the past century consists in replacing Christ-centered mission with church-centered mission. Consequently, the relation between mission and the church is reversed. Since mission becomes an enterprise of a particular church and is conducted almost within the framework of the church, mission becomes the extension or expansion of the church concerned in form and in substance. That is why denominationalism is such a dominant factor in Western Christian mission. In the name of Christ, denominationalism is exported and sold to Christian converts. Western Christian mission enslaved Christian converts in the Third World with their denominationalism. It has not been possible for converts to let the church 'happen' in their contexts. Christ is preached and proclaimed, yes! but almost exclusively in subservience to a particular church or a particular denomination. From this standpoint alone, Christ-centered mission must take the place of the church-centered mission.

Christ-centered mission is a contextual mission, if we may borrow Paul Lehmann's terminology. Mission loses its contextual character when it is carried out under the rubrics of faith and codes of morality prescribed by the church represented by the missionaries. The often debated subject of polygamy in African society is a case in point. Faced with a problem such as this, Western missionaries tend all too quickly to forget the contexts in which their mission is carried out. The dynamic of God's act in that particular society is crystallized into the rules and standards of faith and morals in the missionary's own society and the practice of polygamy in African society is branded as being entirely out of keeping with the demands of the Christian church. It is highly instructive, therefore, to listen to an educated African Christian woman speak on this subject. During the All-Africa Lutheran Conference held at Maranga in 1955, the Hon. Mrs E. M.Mare-alle, wife of the paramount chief of the Chagga tribe, put the issue in these words:

> There was an advantage in this system of taking many wives and that was that the girls who reached the right age could always be assured of a husband. These days we think the system of marrying many wives is a bad thing but the towns are now full of young women who have no education with which to help themselves by way of work and not enough young men who are prepared to marry them. Many of our older people are often asking us if we think this is a good thing; we cannot reply easily because it is a choice between many wives or many prostitutes.[27]

If the choice is truly that between many wives and many prostitutes, Christ-centered mission certainly will not say many prostitutes be chosen in deference to the monogamous stance of the church in the West. In a situation such as this, the question is not what the church to which I owe allegiance would have me do, *but* what Christ would have me do. Christian mission becomes very exciting and redeeming when we always listen to Christ first in our particular contexts.

Someone may object and say, how can we listen to Christ apart from the church? After all, the message of Christ is interpreted by and handed down to us through the community of faith. True, but as we mentioned earlier, the church in this context has to be understood in terms of event or happening and not in terms of the institutionalized church as such. When Christian mission listens intently to Christ in a particular social context, a new event called church, namely, fellowship of beliefs or community of faith, comes into existence with new ways of responding to the demands of the love and justice of God. This is Christ-centered mission. This must not be regarded as merely a matter of inter-cultural understanding. It is unfortunate that nowadays many Western mission leaders think that obstacles of communicating the Good News of the Kingdom of God and the goodwill of the church in the West will be removed if Western missionaries spend more effort on understanding non-Western cultures. This, by itself, is a difficult task, and I have no intention of minimizing the importance of the efforts directed to this task. But obviously this is not enough. A far more important thing is for missionaries, especially those from the West, to divest themselves of practically all their cherished presuppositions and assumptions of their own historical churches. As we reflect a little more deeply upon the course which Western Christian mission has taken, we cannot help wishing that mission had been carried out in Asia and elsewhere less burdened with creeds, rules of faith, standards of morality, etc., historically and socially formulated in the Western contexts.

This brings us to speaking of the *nakedness* of Christian mission. In order for Christian mission to become contextually possible, it has to become naked. Is nakedness not another way of speaking about God's mission of enfleshment? For is the incarnation not the nakedness of God? The word nakedness may be too descriptive and mundane to apply to God. But is there any word too descriptive and mundane to be used of God? After all, what could be a more mundane act than the act of God enfleshing Himself in Jesus Christ? Because God becomes completely naked, He is able to assume the human flesh completely. The nakedness of God thus becomes the salvation of mankind.

Should we therefore not speak of the rich nakedness of God? The phrase rich nakedness seems a contradiction in terms, but this is precisely what God is in relation to man. God's nakedness has enriching power. He takes into Himself even that which is against Him and redeems it from corruption and destruction. What we witness here is the power of re-creation and not the power of self-propagation. Christian mission which refuses to become naked and chooses to operate from the richness of human resources and demands of religious establishments tends towards self-propagation. Mission becomes an expansion, enlargement of a church already in existence. But Christian mission which becomes naked will be given the ability and power to penetrate into the depth of humanity and become a leaven in the process of re-creating that humanity. In this way, Christian mission does not consist primarily in bringing people into the sphere of the Christian church but in taking part in God's mission to renew and to recreate humanity in different religious, social and cultural contexts. From this, it is not difficult to realize that Christian mission we are advocating here goes far beyond the traditional concept of mission and overlaps with the whole scope of the theological task of the church. That is to say, Christian mission is not something separable from Christian theology but forms an integral part of it. As has been mentioned before, Christian mission is Christian theology in action with the whole scope of the latter's concerns.

Christ-centered mission, furthermore, gives expression to the fact that Christ is the Lord of the church and not the other way around. Is this not the basic assumption of the faith of the church? Is Christ not always honoured as the Lord of the church? Does Christ not occupy the central place in Christian preaching? No matter how we may answer these questions, one thing is most sure, that is, we do not make Christ the Lord of the church. That Christ is the Lord of the church is an ontological reality. Or we can also say it is a divine reality. This means that as the Lord of the church Christ dictates what the church should be and do. By the same token, mission is Christ-centered only when the church lets Christ dictate what mission should be and do. One may wonder why this should be a problem. Surely it cannot be the question of the church 'letting' Christ dictate mission. But is it not true that Christian mission has become church-centered because the church with her theology, denominationalism, historical creeds and confessions has been preventing the Christian mission from being fully involved in social issues, quests for truth in other religions and in activities related to the liberation of people from bondage to the colonial past? With Christ as its center, the task of Christian mission *internally* is to urge and reform the church to take the Lordship of Christ seriously. It is Christ who forms and reforms the church. Thus Christian mission has the responsibility to wake the church out of her organizational security, doctrinal orthodoxy and structured immobility. To be more specific, Christian mission in the non-Western lands has internally an urgent task of breaking the Western pattern of the established churches. A thorough de-Westernization of Christianity has to be an essential part of Christian mission. Christian mission has to stress and demonstrate theologically and practically that alternative forms of Christian faith are possible under different social systems, such as communism and socialism. It has to spearhead the formulation of the contents of Christian faith *vis-à-vis* other religious faiths as non-Western thought forms. In this sense, Christian mission truly serves the cause of *ecclesia semper reformanda*.

Externally, Christ-centered mission proclaims through words and deeds that Christ is the center of history. The centrality of Christ in relation to history consists in Christ playing a decisive role in formation of historical events for individual persons, for nations, and for the world at large. This amounts to the messianic interpretation of 'histories'. Here is a basic assumption that messianic expectation is not limited to Israel, to the early church or to the history of the Christian church as a whole. The whole history of man and the world shares in messianic expectations in varied forms and in diversified ways. Messianism is no monopoly of the Biblical religion. This applies to non-religious as well as religious realms. It has been the experience of the modern world that secular messiahs are as powerful as, if not more powerful than, religious messiahs in commanding the allegiance of the masses of people and in blindly leading them to terrible destruction. The mission of the church externally has to address itself to history which is involved with messianism of one form or another. Christian mission is, therefore, an interpreter of history in the sense that it brings the decisiveness of Christ to bear on history. It has been well said by Bonhoeffer:

> . . . this Messiah Christ is at the same time both the destruction and the fulfilment of all the messianic expectations of history. He is their destruction in so far as the visible Messiah does not appear, but the fulfilment takes place in secret. He is their fulfilment in so far as God has really entered history and the expected one is now really there. The meaning of history is swallowed up by an event which takes place in the depth and secrecy of a man who is crucified. The meaning of history becomes evident only in the humiliated Christ.[28]

This concept of fulfilment taking place in secret has important bearing on our re-thinking of the nature and task of Christian mission.

For one thing, Christian mission would be actually frustrating the fulfilment in secret when it effects conversion in such a way that a person completely denies his past and leaves entirely his social and existential contexts to join the church—church understood in terms of organization and membership. Conversion means, of course, turning away from false messiahs to embrace the true Messiah. But the acceptance of the true Messiah implies that through that particular convert it now becomes possible to read the meaning of history in the light of the true Messiah *within* particular religious, social or cultural contexts. In other words, the fulfilment in secret begins to be displayed in the open. Christian mission consists in enabling the transition of fulfilment from secrecy to openness to take place. Through Christian mission what has been hidden has now become revealed. Revelation cannot be complete, of course. There are always elements of ambiguity in the very event of revelation. Nonetheless, in the midst of ambiguity what God wills for man in his historical contexts gets illuminated.

Perhaps one of the salient points which will serve to illustrate our discussion is the tragic reality which faces each and every one regardless of his background. When one is confronted with a tragic happening which disturbs the order of life and casts a dark shadow over one's being, one is bound to raise questions about the meaning of life and history. The tragedy that brings about loss of life and destruction of nature seems so non-sensical that it cannot possibly be willed by God who is good. It is true to say that this awareness and experience of the tragic reality of life has driven many a deeply spiritual man to seek solution in the life of meditation and asceticism. The Buddha, the founder of Buddhism, can be cited as an example. Although born to a royal family destined to inherit his father's kingdom, he was utterly overwhelmed by the tragic sense of life when he saw illness, old age and death threaten man's life with meaninglessness. He consequently left his palace and set out on a long tortuous road in search of enlightment on the mystery of life. He came to believe that the source of all evil and suffering was to be found in the self. A rather negative solution was proposed, namely, extinction of the self. This becomes the basic teaching of Buddhism. Buddhism, says D. T. Suzuki, the great Japanese Zen teacher:

> finds the source of evils and sufferings in the vulgar material conception of the ego-soul, and concentrates its entire ethical force upon the destruction of the ego-centric notions and desires. The Buddha seems, since the beginning of his wandering life, to have conceived the idea that the way of salvation must lie somehow in the removal of this egoistic prejudice. . . .[29]

From the standpoint of Christ-centered mission, what is important here is not the specific way whereby man is taught to become free from the sufferings of this world. In fact, we have to stress that the annihilation of the self would make salvation superfluous; for salvation in the Christian sense of the word is salvation from nothingness. If the self is to be relegated to nothingness, there would be no more salvation to speak of. Despite this being the case, is the Buddhist awareness of the tragic reality of life totally unrelated to Christian faith? Isn't there something here to which the crucifixion of Jesus Christ may address itself? In the crucifixion of Jesus Christ we have the suffering of the first magnitude. It is the most intense symbol of suffering which leads to salvation. This most intensive symbol of suffering, the crucifixion, gets broken into fragmentary symbols of pain and suffering in the whole world throughout history. Thus, these scattered symbols of pain and suffering become witnesses to the crucifixion of Jesus Christ which took place at a particular critical juncture in history.

Kitamori Kazo, the Japanese theologian whom we have already quoted, also stresses the inter-relatedness of man's pain and God's pain in his theological effort to grasp the nature and work of God through the concept of pain. This is what he says:

> We must always witness to the pain of God. Man's pain as a symbol must always be on hand. We must never allow pain to leave us, even when everybody else forgets his pain. Our very person must be in pain; pain must be our function.[30]

The symbolic character of pain is not limited to Christianity. Can we therefore not say that the universality of man's pain is witness to the universal fulfilment of God's love, although in a secret and hidden way? Is this not the reason why Bishop Bigandet found it possible to describe the Great Enlightenment of the Buddha in a strikingly Christian manner? When this great wonder of the Enlightenment took place, Bishop Bigandet writes:

> ten thousand worlds were shaken . . . all the trees of ten thousand worlds shot out branches, loaded with fruits and flowers. The lilies bloomed . . . the whole universe appeared like an immense garden covered with flowers. a vivid light illuminated the dark places . . . rivers suspended their courses; the blind received their sight, the deaf could hear, the lame could walk. The captives were freed from their chains and restored to liberty.[31]

Isn't here an adumbration of the inception of a Messianic age conceived in the Biblical faith?

Christ-centered mission thus has almost limitless frontiers. What it has to reckon with is the breadth, height and depth of the mystery of God's creation and salvation in the world. It is an operation that brings both agony and joy—agony because God's mystery is buried under the weight of man's pride and sin, but also joy because the same mystery of God gets broken out of the hiddenness every now and again to give fresh insight and new meaning to the humanity in both its grandure and humiliation. In this way, Christian mission, as Christ-centered mission, acquires

cosmic nature. It is the participation in God's work through Jesus
Christ to renew humanity and nature for the day when the new
heaven and new earth will appear.

3. Mission of Self-emptying

On the basis of what has been discussed, the following observation follows: Any act that reflects God's mission of enfleshment
is Christian mission, even though it may not take place within
the immediate sphere of the Christian church. Conversely, any
act that does not reflect God's mission of enfleshment cannot be
regarded as Christian mission, although it may occur in the Christian church. God's mission of enfleshment blurs the boundary
between what is Christian and what is not. How important it
is to bear this in mind when we speak of Christian mission is
illustrated by an observation such as follows:

> One Anglican compound I visited in Haifa remains in my
> memory as a symbol. The church, the pastor's house, and
> the group of institutional buildings were ringed with a high
> wall topped by a barbed wire fence, and the fence sloped
> inward, as if its purpose were not so much to exclude
> intruders as to keep the inmates in. Somehow in Iran, in
> the Arab world, and in Israel, the church must leap over
> the wall or perish.[32]

The security of the Christian compound is a false security. It is
built on the false premise that the Christian church or the missionary compound can be identifiable with the Kingdom of God and
thus the realm where the truth prevails. Such a view has been
shown to be erroneous, especially in view of the fact that radical
reinterpretation of Christian faith and re-definition of the nature
and function of the church in the non-Western cultural contexts
are urgently called for. We can no longer take for granted, for
instance, Calvin's view of the church. According to Martin Marty's
interpretation, Calvin

> built into the doctrines of the church that influenced Reformed-
> Presbyterian circles the suggestion that a test of the church
> was the solidarity of the brothers, the need for mutual
> assistance. And he sealed his version of ecclesiology by
> reference to the fact that those in the church were the elect,
> placed there by God.[33]

This kind of ecclesiology built on what we may call inner politics of election does not quite do justice to God's mission of self-emptying expressed so beautifully in a Christological hymn of the earliest Christian community used by Paul in his letter to the Philippians. I am referring to the famous passage in Philippians 2:5-11, and especially verse 7 which says:

> . . . but (Christ) emptied Himself, taking the form of a servant, being born in the likeness of man.[34]

In this section, it is our purpose to probe further into the nature of Christian mission in relation to the concept of self-emptying.

God's mission of enfleshment in Jesus Christ is the mission of self-emptying. This is the way in which Paul and his fellow Christians tried to understand the nature of the incarnation from the side of God. This can only be an afterthought, of course. It must be an inference from their experience of the fullness of God in Jesus Christ. And it is a realization of the costly nature of what God has to do in order to carry out His mission of salvation. The mission costs God nothing less than God Himself. Can God still be God when He so completely divests Himself of Himself? What happens to God during the earthly life of Jesus Christ? Paul and the early Christians did not pose the question in this way. These are the metaphysical questions which never entered their minds. The reality of God in Jesus Christ was for them an existential experience and not a philosophical speculation.

The New English Bible translates *heauton ekenowsen* as: '(Christ) made himself nothing'. This is a forceful rendering. Emptiness is nothing, literally nothing at all. It means one is stripped entirely bare. One has nothing to cover one's own body. But it goes beyond the physical emptiness of nothingness. When one empties oneself and makes oneself nothing, one gives up one's being entirely. The last citadel is gone. The final defence line is broken. One faces other human beings without pre-condition, reservation, claim, not to mention self-assertion. This is an act of total self-denial. This sounds negative. To state it positively, by this act of self-emptying and self-denial, a condition has been established, a room has been created, within me to receive my fellow creatures. Thus, self-emptying is not for the sake of self-extinction, but for the sake of accepting others and fulfilling the love of God.

Let us develop our train of thought here by the use of a different metaphor. By emptying himself and making himself nothing, Christ renounced all that he is as God. This is a suicidal act. Renunciation of one's being is nothing other than suicide. The cross comes close to the suicide of God. It is a terrible thing to say this. It may amount to blasphemy. But how else can we convey the meaning of Christ's mission of self-emptying with its pain and agony? The cry of dereliction on the cross is the cry of one whose being is about to be snatched away and done away with. 'My God, my God, why hast thou forsaken me?'[35] The agony of forsakenness—is this not what drives a man to suicide?

But God's mission of self-emptying in Christ is not a suicidal act. His is not the mission of a suicide squad. The act of self-emptying marks the beginning of a new form of being and a new set of relationships. After putting away all that separates him from all human beings, Christ assumes a new form of being, the form of a servant, literally a slave. By emptying himself, Christ has enslaved himself in God's service, thus becoming the most willing servant of God's mission of saving the world. To use Barth's words, this mission of self-emptying is 'the possibility of divine self-giving to the being and fate of man'.[36] In this divine act of humiliation and enslavement is the hope and salvation of man.

Christ's mission of service to mankind thus begins with a point of weakness rather than strength, of poverty rather than richness, of debasement rather than exaltation. Completely unarmed and willingly submitting Himself to humiliation, Christ sets the world on a totally new footing and in new relationships. This is a very crucial element which must be recaptured by Christian mission today. The temptation with Christian mission is that it always wants to begin from the point of strength rather than weakness. This is a very genuine human temptation. Even Christ, after having emptied himself of his divine glory, was tempted to assume the power, wealth and glory that the world could confer on him.[37] The temptation thus takes on a sinister look. What a tragedy and irony it would have been if Christ had yielded to the temptation of exchanging earthly glories for heavenly glories! No, he had to be a baby born in a manger; he had to sweat and toil for his daily living; he had to have no place where He could lay his head; and he had to be stripped almost naked, suffering pain and death on the cross. How different the world would have been today if only the historical Christian Church had been able to overcome the temptation to power, glory, prestige and respectability!

And there is a great temptation for security. Always being in the minority, Christians in Asia and elsewhere have come to claim security almost as their birthright. It is no exaggeration to say that in their method and approach Western missionaries have deliberately cultivated claims to security among Christian converts. Missionaries with their mission boards behind them came to be looked upon as dispensers of security. It goes without saying that this is a false security, but a sort of security nonetheless. The following observation made by D. T. Niles is very to the point:

> There is something to be said for a minority, and particularly a scattered minority, having not only churches to worship in but also having their own schools in which to educate their children, their own hospitals to which they go when they are ill, their own orphanages and old-age homes to meet such special need, and their own control of employment opportunities to find employment for their youth. But precisely at this point in the temptation, social security can and does become a preoccupation of a minority, but the temptation has to be faced.[38]

In other words, it pays to be a Christian. There are 'Christian dividends' that only membership in a church can promise. That is why a Christian church tends to grow inward instead of outward, preoccupied with her own members instead of those outside her domain.[39]

Be that as it may, it is true to say that many Christian communities in the non-Western world still do not enjoy great prestige in their society. Financially, they are weak. Politically, they still need to learn how to make their influence felt. Theologically, they cannot be said to be very productive. But let us not bemoan what they do not have. In fact, they have to learn to empty themselves of a great deal of what they already have. This act of self-emptying must precede the emergence of Christian communities which can embody God's purpose for their own culture and history. The church in the West too has much to divest of. In reality, the force of secularization has done, much more than anything else, much of the divesting and emptying for the church in the West. At last she is learning to do away with the medieval pompousness which made a mockery of God's mission of enfleshment. She at least begins to face the question of why she is losing more and more ground with modern secular man.

Particularly, this is a heart-searching moment for Western Christian mission. Why is the voice calling missionaries to go home growing louder and louder? Why is there increasing tendency to interpret the history of Western Christian mission more and more in relation to Western colonialism? Why is it that the liberation movement has also overtaken Christian mission so that those in the Third World are doing what they can to be liberated from missionary influences? It looks as if the weakness and nakedness of Western Christian mission has been exposed all of a sudden to the embarrassment of some and to the despair of others. But to the thoughtful Christians both in the West and in the East, Christian mission is at last enabled to become empty and make itself nothing in order for a new day of mission to be born. Let us remember, Christian mission must begin with an act of self-emptying, thus becoming ready to receive and communicate afresh the message of love and reconciliation in the midst of this terribly disturbed humanity. How can a Christian community regain the ability and confidence to engage itself in this mission of self-emptying? What should it do in order that it can become a part of Christ's mission? In a brief outline of a book he prepared in his prison cell, Bonhoeffer has made some practical but very radical proposals. This is what he says:

> The church is her true self only when she exists for humanity. As a fresh start she should give away all her endowments to the poor and needy. The clergy should live solely on the free-will offerings of their congregations, or possibly engage in some secular calling. She must take her part in the social life of the world, not lording it over men, but helping and serving them. She must tell men, whatever their calling, what it means to live in Christ, to exist for others.[40]

This poses a great challenge which I am afraid very few churches are prepared to meet. But there is little hope for a new era of Christian mission to dawn unless the challenge is seriously taken up. For as long as the church is preoccupied with her own endowments, welfare and security, she only pays lip-service to Christ's mission of self-emptying. And according to Bonhoeffer, for the church to exist for others, she must first divest herself of what she already has.

It has to be emphasized that the act of self-emptying creates the possibility of readiness for others. As has been pointed out earlier, self-emptying is a form of self-denial. In Buddhism, self-denial is carried to the extreme of extinction of the self, for the self is considered to be the primary source of all evil and illusion. There is profound existential truth and psychological insight in identifying the self as the source of evil and illusion, but the way to rid evil and illusion should not consist in ridding the self. Otherwise, it would be like throwing the baby away with the bathwater. What needs to be done is to restore authenticity to the self; and authenticity of the self consists, from the Christian view-point, in the self existing for others. What the Biblical faith is after is the fulfilment of the meaning of the self in the service of others.

This reminds us of one of the most important sayings of Jesus Christ which puts this whole matter in a nutshell:

> For even the Son of Man did not come to be served but to serve and to give up his life as a ransom for many.[41]

This saying in Mark's Gospel is cast in the context of dispute on greatness among Jesus' disciples. James and John, the sons of Zebedee, approached Jesus requesting him to assign them positions of honour and power, thus completely misunderstanding the nature of the reign of God. They had to be told again that the followers of Jesus Christ were expected to live and die for the salvation of others. Significantly, Luke arranges this dispute on greatness to belong at the Last Supper.[42] Here Jesus in the symbolic acts of breaking bread and drinking wine was acting out the drama of the cross. Soon he was to have his own body broken and his own blood shed. Such an act has little in common with the secular concept of greatness still held by his disciples. In the Gospel according to John, the writer goes even further. Not only is the exhortation on readiness to serve others as servants given in the context of the Last Supper but it is reinforced as an acted parable.   Jesus, rising from the Supper,

> laid aside his garments, and taking a towel, tied it around Him.   Then He poured water into a basin, and began to wash His disciples' feet and to wipe them with the towel.[43]

It was only after the resurrection that the disciples were to understand the meaning of this acted parable.   Here is the symbolic act of the Son of Man pouring out his being for the world as a ransom, as price-money, for man's salvation.   Readiness of the servant is the readiness to give up his own being in the service of others.

This, in essence, is Christ's mission.   Christ is mission.   His own very being is the personification of what God intends to do for man.   Christian mission should have no lower ideal and less lofty goal than this mission of Christ's.   Christian mission certainly is no exercise in charity.   It has nothing to do with an act of benevolence undertaken by the haves for the have-nots.   Nor is Christian mission an extra-curricular activity on the part of a well-ordered, richly-endowed and beautifully-decorated church.   The church, as the community and fellowship of believers, is mission. She does not take part in mission, regarding mission as something she does in inspired moments.   The church, if she is to be true to the reason for her existence, should be the witness of God's giving up of Himself in Jesus Christ for the world.   Thus, Christian mission is not to be motivated by the desire to become great in God's Kingdom, not to be used as a means to gain an assurance of a place in some blessed eternity.   Christian mission is not a means to an end.   If you give money for mission, you pour out your being to go out with your money.   If you offer yourself for missionary service, you go out to serve and not to be served and offer nothing less than your own self for those to whom you want to bring the love of God.

Lest there be misunderstanding, let me add this.   Of course, the money you have given serves the cause of Christian mission. And, of course, you may serve others as a medical doctor, teacher, technician or evangelist.   But if you fail to pour out your being for others along with what you do, you always remain stranger. Your relation with your fellow creatures is and remains tangential. No communion of humanity in God's love will take place in such a situation. You may be in mission, but you are *not* mission. Christian mission today and tomorrow must come out of such tangentiality and seek the dimension of embracement. It is instructive to refer again to the story of Jesus' washing His disciples' feet. You do not wash a stranger's feet. But the moment you wash a stranger's feet, he ceases to be a stranger. He becomes your friend, a member of your company, even a member of your household. For by performing the most intimate act of washing his feet, you have accepted him, embraced him and allowed him to enter your life. By thus opening the door to him to enter your life, you too enter into his life. That is why, when Peter hesitated, Jesus said to him: 'If I do not wash you, you are not in fellowship with me.'[44]

By saying this, Jesus drives home to his disciples the fact that foot-washing is no mere parable or ceremonial act. It is a reality through which you become a son of God in Jesus Christ. Christian mission, therefore, is an event, a happening in which people meet at their deepest spiritual level. It is not a call to those outside the Christian church to conform to the standards of social behaviour and morality set up by the church. Nor is it just a matter of asking people to subscribe to the creeds and confessions of the church. It is the communion of self with other selves, the communion inspired and made possible by the working of the Holy Spirit in the hearts of men. We may call this an ultimate communion because those involved in the communion, both Christians and others, are exposed to the truth of God which judges and redeems.

Yes, the integrity of Christian mission demands that Christians, among them missionaries, must be included in the judgement and redemption of God in the communion with others who do not bear the name Christian. In my own thinking, this is a very critical point not always recognized and admitted by those engaged in Christian mission, nationals or missionaries. The question is: How deeply does the central message of God's mission of enflesh-ment, which results in Christ being judged with us and on behalf of us, how does this basic tenet of the incarnation dictate the theory and practice of Christian mission? This Christological question must be asked again and again. As has been indicated, the age of secularization in which we all live has impacted the Christian

church in such a way that Christians must admit humbly that
they have no monopoly of the truth of God, and that what they
hold to be true may be wrong on the basis of new light shed on
the same truth of God contained in the Bible in different and
ideological contexts. There is no reason to believe that the
Western forms of Christianity are the only possible vehicles of
truth. In fact, it is true to say that the rise of secular ideologies
such as communism, the momentum in which the world heads
toward more and more secularization, empty churches, critical
appraisals of Western Christian mission as racist and colonialistic,
all these and many other factors are forcing Christian thinkers to
re-interpret the contents of the Christian faith.

One of such outspoken critical theologians is Hans Küng,
professor in the Catholic theology faculty of the University of
Tübingen. Writing in response to the announcement of holding
an Ecumenical Council by Pope John XXIII, he makes no secret
of his criticism of the church that in her narrowness and procras-
tination she perpetuates historical mistakes and resists *aggionamento*, bringing-up-to-the-present-day, when he writes:

> But we must ask ourselves here, is there not also a *refusal* to
> adapt which is just as much a sheer betrayal—a betrayal
> of Christ's missionary charge to the Apostles and of
> St Paul's call to be 'all things to all men,' a cowardly with-
> drawal from the present age into a spurious, self-righteous
> 'splendid isolation'? It would not be honest to deny that
> it has happened often enough; we in the church have
> failed to go half-way to meet men in situations where they
> had a right to expect it; we have bristled up defensively
> when we could have given cheerful approval; we have
> defended the good with evil weapons; we have defended
> the indefensible. We have invoked the authority of the
> Gospel in cases where nothing more was in fact involved
> than an established philosophy, mentality, culture or
> system, which we might have invoked or perhaps better
> not have invoked at all. We have condemned things that
> had later—when it was too late—to be admitted, and
> finally blessed and claimed as our own.[45]

This penetrating critique of the Roman Catholic Church equally
applies to the Protestant communions. Not only the Roman

Church needed an *aggionamento*, the Protestant churches, too, with their theology, ecclesiology and particularly their mission theology, badly need an *aggionamento*.

But Christian mission must go beyond an *aggionamento*. What we are faced with is not just a matter of bringing Christian mission up to date. This would keep us too much occupied with the past and the present. What the Third World is looking for is a future which is radically different from the past and the present, a future liberated from values predetermined by colonialism and neo-colonialism. Christian mission, if it is to be of service to God through serving human society, has the responsibility to be involved in this struggle and movement toward the future. It should provide the spiritual force that comes from God the Creator for the endeavours toward liberation from the past into the future. In the following chapters we will engage ourselves in further exploration of the implications of Christian mission for the future of mankind.

REFERENCES

1. John 1:14.

2. John Macquarrie, *Principles of Christian Theology*, p. 247.

3. Genesis 1:3.

4. Kazo Kitamori, *Theology of the Pain of God*, Richmond, Virginia: John Knox Press, 1965, p. 35. This is an English translation of *Kami No Itami No Shingaku*, published by Shinkyo Suppansha, Tokyo, Japan, 1958 (5th Revised Edition).

5. Romans 12:15.

6. John 11:35.

7. Luke 15:3-7.

8. Luke 15:8-10.

9. Luke 15:11-32.

10. Joachim Jeremias, translated by S. H. Hooke, New York: Charles Scribner's Sons, 1955, p. 103.

11. Luke 15:2.

12. Richard Bush, *Religion in Communist China*, Nashville and New York: Abingdon Press, 1970, p. 171.

13. I Corinthians 1:23.

14. Matthew 6:5.

15. Matthew 6:16.

16. Arend Th. van Leeuwen, *Christianity in World History*, translated by H. H. Hoskins, Edinburgh House Press, 1964, p. 419.

17. John 14:9.

18. D. T. Niles, *Upon the Earth*, p. 50.

19. Karl Barth, *The Humanity of God*, Richmond: John Knox Press, 1960. Barth stresses the concreteness with which God deals with the world in and through Jesus Christ. God does this by taking humanity fully into His divinity. He writes: 'Who God is and what He is in His deity proves and reveals not in a vacuum as a divine being for Himself, but precisely and authentically in the fact that He exists, speaks and acts as the *partner* of man, though of course as the absolutely superior partner. He who does *that* is the living God. And the freedom in which He does *that* is His deity. It is the deity which as such also has the character of humanity. In this and only in this form was—and still is—our view of the deity of God to be set in opposition to that earlier theology. It is precisely God's deity which, rightly understood, includes his humanity' (Op. cit., p. 45).

20. Matthew 23:13-15.

21. Matthew 16:24-25.

22. L. Harold DeWolf, 'The Gospel, the Church, and the Mission,' in *Christian Mission in Theological Perspective*, edited by Gerald H. Anderson, New York: Abingdon Press, 1967, p. 47.

23. Hoekendijk, 'The Church in Missionary Thinking,' *International Review of Missions*, Vol. XLI, 1952, pp. 332-333.

24. Ibid., p. 332.

25. Ibid., p. 334.

26. Paul Lehman's 'Contextual ethics' is also based on the dynamics of the church as an event, a fellowship (Koinonia). He calls contextual ethics as *Koinonia* ethics. He states the relationship between the church and *Koinonia* ethics in this way: The *Koinonia* is, however, neither *identical* with the *visible* church nor separable from the visible church. *Ecclesiola in ecclesia*, the little church within the church, the leaven in the lump, the remnant in the midst of the covenant people, the *Koinonia* in the world—this is the reality which is the starting point for the living of the Christian life and for our thinking about Christian ethics (*Ethics in a Christian Context*, p. 70).

27. The C.M.S. Newsletter of February, 1961. Quoted by D. T. Niles in *Upon the Earth*, p. 203.

28. Bonhoeffer, *Christ the Center*, introduced by Edwin H. Robertson and translated by John Bowden, New York: Harper and Row, 1966, p. 64.

29. D. T. Suzuki, *Outlines of Mahayana Buddhism*, New York: Schocken Books, 1963, p. 146.

30. Kazo Kitamori, *Theology of the Pain of God*, p. 64.

31. Bishop Bigandet, *The Life or Legend of Gaudama: The Buddha of the Burmese*, first printed and published in Rangoon, Burma in 1858; third edition published in London, 1879, p. 97. Quoted by H. D. Lewis and Robert Lawson Slater in *The Study of Religions*, Penguin Books, 1966, p. 66.

32. This is the observation of John Taylor, the General Secretary of the Church Missionary Society. D. T. Niles quotes it in his *The Message and its Messengers*, New York: Abingdon Press, 1966, p. 74.

33. Martin E. Marty, *Protestantism*, New York: Holt, Rinehart and Winston, 1972, p. 135.

34. The Revised Standard Version.

35. Matthew 27:46.

36. Karl Barth, *Church Dogmatics* IV/1, p. 180.

37. Cf. the story of the temptation recorded in Matthew 4:1-11 and Luke 4:1-13.

38. D. T. Niles, *The Message and its Messengers*, New York: Abingdon Press, 1966, pp. 75f.

39. The phrase 'rice Christians' used in China in the past is indicative of the situation described here. As a minority group, Asian Christians need to wrestle seriously with the tension between security in Christ and the security they seek in society. The test of Christian discipleship comes when they are forced to choose one or the other.

40. Bonhoeffer, *Letters and Papers from Prison*, edited by Eberhard Bethge, translated by Reginald H. Fuller, Macmillan paperbacks Edition, 1962, p. 239.

41. Mark 10:45.

42. Luke 22:14-27.

43. John 13:4-5.

44. John 13:8.

45. Hans Küng, *The Council, Reform and Reunion*, translated by Cecily Hastings, New York: Sheed and Ward, 1961, p. 20.

CHAPTER FOUR

The Sacramental Nature of Christian Mission

> Well then, about eating consecrated food: Of course,
> as you say, 'a false god has no existence in the real
> world. There is no god but one.' For indeed, if there
> be so-called gods, whether in heaven or on earth
> —as indeed there are many 'gods' and many 'lords'
> —yet for us there is one God, the Father, from whom
> all being comes, towards whom we move; and
> there is one Lord, Jesus Christ, through whom all
> things came to be, and we through Him.
>
> —*I Corinthians 8:4-6.*

1. Christian Mission as Enactment of the Last Supper

THE Last Supper Jesus had with His disciples on the eve of His crucifixion is a drama that sums up the whole event of the incarnation. In the words of Paul the Apostle, Jesus 'took bread and, after giving thanks to God, broke it and said: "This is my body, which is for you; do this as a memorial of me." In the same way, he took the cup after supper and said: "This cup is the new covenant sealed by my blood. Whenever you drink it, do this as a memorial of me." '[1] For Jesus, the Last Supper is not only the culmination of his ministry but a new point of departure for the future ministry to be carried on by his disciples. Filson is, therefore, correct in saying that the purpose of Jesus 'was not to give the later church a sacrament to observe, but to interpret his impending death to his disciples.'[2] In other words, the Last Supper can be meaningful only in the contexts of God's ministry of saving the world in and through Jesus Christ. The Last Supper, to use the theme of our discussion in the previous chapter, is the consummation of the mission of enfleshment.

It follows that the sacrament of the Lord's Supper must be set free from the liturgical bondage of the church, whether Catholic or Protestant, and be put back into the contexts of Christ's mission where it belongs. In fact, the language which has been developed by the church around the sacrament of the Lord's Supper is indi-

cative of the gross misunderstanding of the intention of Jesus
Christ as he sat at the supper table for the last time with his
disciples. The sacrament came to be *observed*, *celebrated*. Different denominations and churches competed with each other in
developing elaborate liturgical formulae to adorn the sacrament.
Abstruse theories were advanced to explain the 'real' presence of
Christ in the elements of the sacrament using terms such as tran-
substantiation and con-substantiation. There were also those who
laid stress on the spiritual and symbolic meaning of the Lord's
Supper. All in all, the Last Supper, which must have been a sober,
simple meal pregnant with forebodings and expectations, came
to be shrouded more and more in the maze of ecclesiastical and
theological argumentation. It also became loaded with liturgical
language remote from the reality of the life-situation in which
Jesus had his final meal with his men. This is not to say that
it has been entirely meaningless for the mind of the church to
wrestle with the mystery of the sacrament of the Lord's Supper.
What I am contending is that in such struggles and efforts the
central meaning and intention of the Last Supper tends to get
pushed out to the periphery.

The result has, needless to say, been disastrous for the church
as the body of Christ. The sacrament of the Lord's Supper, instead
of being what it is intended to be, namely, the visible expression
of God's saving love for the world, became an instrument in
deepening the dividedness of the Christian church. The celebration of the Lord's Supper could not but turn out to be a scandal,
for it became a mark of a particular religious persuasion effectively
barring the approach of those who happened to belong to different ecclesiastical traditions. If this has been most painful for the
church in the West, it has been no less calamitous to the newly
established Christian communities in the Third World. 'Many
nationals of the younger churches of Africa and the East,' so goes
the Report of the Theological Commission on Intercommunion,
the World Council of Churches, in 1952:

> also feel keenly the scandal of Christian disunity. They see
> the divisions of Christendom as mainly of Western origin
> imposed upon them by foreign missionaries, and they
> regard the imported restrictions upon intercommunion as
> shackles needing to be cast off in order that the indigenous

churches may find their true fellowship one with another. Here is a ferment of life which faces the whole ecumenical movement with crucial decisions.[3]

This was in 1952. Much change has, of course, been brought about by the ecumenical efforts to unite Christians for the healing of division in this divided church and the divided world. A great deal of liberalizing of restrictions has taken place in relation to the sacrament of the Lord's Supper when performed on ecumenical occasions. But have the shackles referred to above been completely cast off? Probably not. Is it not tragic that where the love of God should become most evident the divisive nature of man's sin also becomes most manifest? Is it not ironical that where freedom of man should become a reality the church gets trapped in self-made bondage?

It is our contention that most of the sacramental issues are raised and fought primarily because the sacrament of the Lord's Supper becomes divorced from Christ's mission of enfleshment. It ceases to occupy the central place in missionary thinking and mission activities. Thus, sacramental issues are not fought on the proper ground, namely, the mission of Christ. They become ecclesiastical, confessional and liturgical issues, whereas they should really be mission-oriented issues. The sacrament of the Lord's Supper seems to have lost its primary identity. There is, therefore, an urgent need to look at the sacrament of the Lord's Supper in its proper context, namely, mission. If this is done, the church is bound to gain new understanding of the nature of Christian mission. The church will also be able to find in her mission outreach the fulfilment of the meaning of the church in the contemporary world. It is to this situation that we will be addressing ourselves in this chapter.

Earlier we said that the Last Supper is the consummation of Christ's mission of enfleshment. This amounts to saying that Christian mission is the enactment of the Last Supper. The actual holding of the Last Supper was preceded by the ministry of Christ. It also ushered in a new day when the power of the crucified and risen Christ would be recognized. Thus, the Last Supper stretched backward to cover at least the three years of Christ's mission; it also stretches forward to the future in anticipation of the resurrection. This is to say that taken out of the whole ministry of Christ from birth to resurrection, the Last Supper becomes an isolated event without much historical and thus soteriological significance. It would become merely something which might appeal to our emotional, aesthetic or even religious sensitivity. In the observance or celebration of the Lord's Supper, is this not what happens? The Lord's Supper ought to be something much more profound than this. In emphasizing the centrality of the incarnation both for Baptism and the Lord's Supper, T. F. Torrance states that the sacrament is 'the sacrament of the *Word made flesh*, of the *Christ-event*, which includes the life, teaching, death and resurrection of Jesus Christ.'[4] The whole life and work of Jesus Christ is thus the sacrament in the primary sense of the word. Through his life and work, Jesus Christ enacted the sacrament for the sake of the salvation of the world.

This is the chief reason why we speak of Christian mission as the enactment of the Last Supper. It is what the Last Supper is, means and stands for that has to be enacted in Christian mission. To put it differently, Christian mission derives its meaning and task from the Last Supper. It follows that mission activities of the church ought to be sacramental. Each act of mission undertaken to make visible the saving love of God is a sacramental act. The profound intensity of the Last Supper is in this way transferred to and becomes embedded in Christian mission. In so far as Christian mission becomes related to the Last Supper and obtains such sacramental nature, it becomes living witness to what God has done in Jesus Christ for the sake of the world.

On the basis of what has been said above, I would like to assert that the proper place to hold the Lord's Supper is where the acts of mission take place. To be more accurate, the Lord's supper does not need to be held, observed or celebrated. The Lord's Supper happens. When asked by the disciples of John the Baptist whether he was the Messiah, Jesus replied: 'Go and tell John what you hear and see: the blind recover their sight, the lame walk, the lepers are made clean, the deaf hear, the dead are raised to life, the poor are hearing the good news. . .'[5] The healing of bodily disorder, restoration of broken relationships, elimination of social injustice, working for peace among men, in a word, becoming the witness to the reality of God in the world, are all literally the sacrament of the Lord's Supper. The Lord's Supper, therefore, is an action and not a ceremony. It is an event that happens here and now and not just a memory of what happened in the past. Furthermore, it takes place outside as well as inside the church. We can go so far as to say that the vitality of the Christian community depends on how often it becomes a part of the event of the Lord's Supper outside its own domain.

So, by the sacramental nature of Christian mission we mean Christian mission as the reliving of the experience of the life and work of Jesus Christ in the present day world. The sacrament is, therefore, interpreted in a broad sense of enacting the mission of enfleshment. In this way the sacrament of the Lord's Supper and Christian mission get related again in the arena of mission activities. When this happens, the Christian community will become a missionary-sacramental community. And only in this missionary-sacramental context the sacrament of the Lord's Supper becomes a celebration—celebration of what God is doing in the world through the Christian community.

The position I try to establish here in exploring the relation between Christian mission and the Lord's Supper has little to do with sacramentalism. This, I believe, is quite clear from the discussion above. Sacramentalism refers to 'the doctrine that in the sacraments themselves there is an inherent saving power.'[6] Needless to say, a doctrine such as this is a distortion of the meaning of salvation in Jesus Christ. Actually, it would make the event of the Word made flesh unessential to salvation because the sacraments are believed to have inherent saving power. According to such a view, the sacraments take the place of Jesus Christ. This is putting the cart before the horse, as it were. Theologically, sacramentalism is an untenable position. And the whole ecclesiastical and sacerdotal systems developed around sacramentalism are unfortunate misrepresentations of Christian faith. This explains all the more clearly the need for the sacrament of the Lord's Supper to become related back to Christian mission, thus regaining its true nature and meaning as something preceded by Christ's mission.

2. Christian Mission as Redemptive Presence

In what sense is Christ present in the sacrament of the Lord's Supper? And in what way does he make His own presence real to us? Is his presence in the sacrament to be regarded literally, that is to say, physically or spiritually? Or is he present in the sacrament symbolically? These are some of the key questions that underlie historical formulations of the doctrine of the Lord's Supper. It is not our task here to try to evaluate various teachings regarding the Lord's Supper. For our discussion on the nature of Christian mission, let us stress once again that to look for Christ's presence either physically, spiritually or symbolically, in the elements of the sacrament themselves is a futile exercise, as it has little bearing on Christ's mission. For those of us in Asia not brought up in and nourished by scholastic and metaphysical systems of the West, such ecclesiastical and theological exercises produce only confusion and bewilderment. As has already been hinted earlier, I really doubt whether it was Jesus' intention to be sought after in this way. The Last Supper, which the church attempts to experience and relive through the institution of the sacrament of the Lord's Supper, has more to do with the dynamic drama of God's saving act than with the question of Christ's presence with his disciples. In fact, the real presence which the institution of the sacrament tries to recapture is no problem at all in the immediate context of the Last Supper. Jesus Christ was there with his disciples. This was an existential reality beyond any question and search. What was at stake was the fulfilment or frustration of God's saving love for the world. This made the atmosphere of the room in which the Last Supper took place extremely sober, at least for Jesus Christ. The critical moment for the divine-human drama of salvation was soon to arrive. This was the dynamics behind those last moments Jesus had with his disciples. Therefore, Western theological traditions have gone too far, if not astray, in making the real presence of Jesus Christ in the sacrament a matter of metaphysical concern.

Furthermore, the real presence of Jesus Christ should be closely related to the act which heightens the intensity of the atmosphere surrounding the table of the Last Supper almost to an unbearable degree. This is the act of Jesus Christ breaking bread. He broke bread and said: 'This is my body'. Again it must be stressed that the verb 'is' in 'this is my body' is not so much a link between Jesus' body and the bread he was breaking as an allusion to the event in which Jesus' body was to be broken. In other words, the act of breaking bread was an anticipation of the actual breaking of Jesus' own body. Just as bread is broken in the presence of the twelve disciples representing new Israel, so Christ's body is to be broken on the cross before the eyes of the whole world. Salvation of the world consists in this act of breaking and not in the sacrament itself. Thus, 'breaking' constitutes the pivot around which the divine-human drama of salvation is played out for the whole world.

How important the act of breaking is in relation to Christ's presence is graphically illustrated by the story told by Luke about the incident on Emmaus road after the crucifixion.[7] According to the story, two of the followers of Jesus Christ were on their way to Emmaus utterly distressed, discouraged and saddened by Jesus' crucifixion in Jerusalem. They were joined by someone who tried in vain to enlighten them on the meaning of the death of the Messiah with scriptural and historical evidence. It was not until they sat down at the table and the stranger 'broke' the bread that 'their eyes were opened, and they recognized' Jesus. The whole story picked up momentum at this great turning point. These two people got up from the table at once, hurried back to Jerusalem and told Jesus' followers there 'how he (Jesus) had been recognized by them at the breaking of bread.'[8] Here the act of breaking bread is no longer an anticipation of what is going to happen to Jesus Christ on the cross. It becomes an event witnessing to the reality that God is present with us in Jesus Christ here and now.

The act of breaking bread is, therefore, an event filled with mission significance. What is Christian mission if not the task of the Christian community to make the presence of Jesus Christ real to the unbelievers as well as the believers? It is the encounter with Jesus Christ that Christian mission is expected to demonstrate. But how can there be such an encounter if the presence of Jesus Christ is somehow not quite real? If there is something special about Christian faith which is distinct from other faiths, it is no other than the reality of Christ's presence. Christian mission serves this real presence of Jesus Christ. In the last analysis, it is inconsequential whether Christian mission takes the form of evangelism, church growth or social action. The real danger lies in the tendency for some jealous Christians to uphold one form of Christian mission to the exclusion of other forms. When this happens, the presence of Jesus Christ is distorted.

As has been mentioned in the second chapter, polarization of Christian mission has taken place precisely because of such distortion of the Christian mission due to such exclusivism. Here is a good illustration of a very inadequate and biased assessment of action-oriented mission.

> Leaders who *as their paramount* duty are promoting social reconstruction or engaging in dialogue with other religions would wreck any such campaign (evangelistic) and preventing the church doubling in twelve months.[9]

Now a statement such as this is fraught with the misunderstanding of the nature and task of Christian mission. To the author of the statement church statistics are more important than the real presence of Jesus Christ. Doubling the number of churches gets priority consideration in his mission undertakings. We can sharpen up the issue here by asking the following question: In Vietnam after a decade of killing, bloodshed and destruction of social and human relationships, what is the crucial task of the Christian church there? What is most imperative for Christian mission to do in that war-torn country? And the church in the United States —which bears the collective guilt of the nation sadistically engaged in the laying waste of that backward agricultural society with mighty weapons of the most industrially advanced nation in the world, what forms should the Christian conscience of this church take if she is to be involved in the work of the church in Vietnam? Doubling the church in twelve months or social reconstruction which leads to the reconstruction and reconciliation of human relationships? The answer is obvious.

In addressing himself directly to what he calls 'the apparent opposition between the Gospel of personal conversion and the Gospel of social responsibility.' John V. Taylor pleads forcefully as follows:

> If we persist in maintaining this 'either/or,' the things we say on both sides will be naive and will sound more and more phony. We must face the issue and think it through to a synthesis, not a compromise. Whenever we are tempted once again to fall apart on one side or the other of these alternatives, Christ is surely saying to us, 'This ought ye to have done and not to have left the other undone.' We must enlist the passion for mankind in the service of all

men for whom He was content to die. We must enlist
the passion for mankind in the service of the Son of Man
whose face is 'like all men's faces.' This is the true synthesis
of the great Pauline affirmation: 'We preach not ourselves'
—not ourselves as the church, nor ourselves as the human
race—'but Christ Jesus as Lord and ourselves as your
servants for Jesus' sake.'[10]

There is so much preaching about ourselves in Christian mission
when particular life-situations are disregarded. Christian mission
is thus reduced to the soliloquy of Christians who now want to
have the last word on the salvation of man. To refuse to enter
into sharing of inexhaustible experiences related to matters of life
and eternity with men of other faiths is a sheer blindness to the
profoundity of the truth of God. To assume that the particular
way by which you believe you have grasped the truth of God is the
only possible way is spiritual imperialism. Is this not the human
hubris which prompted Adam and Eve to fall from the grace of
God? Soliloquy related to matters of the spirit is a dangerous
thing. Eve started this and involuntarily shut off God from her.
Religious soliloquy can thus prove to be fatal. Christian mission
must be set free from such a dangerous soliloquy. This can be
done only when Jesus Christ occupies the center of Christian
mission. It is Jesus Christ who makes Himself the supreme sacrament that must be the alpha and omega of Christian mission.
The test of Christian mission consists essentially in its truthfulness
and faithfulness to its sacramental nature. In comparison with
this, all other factors, including various forms of Christian mission,
become secondary.

What then is the most outstanding feature of Christ's presence in the world? What makes his presence real to us? The
answer is redemption. Christ's presence is redemptive presence.
That is why his presence in the world through the incarnation
is the Gospel. That is why he, himself, is the Good News. In
the Synoptic Gospels we cannot but be profoundly impressed by
His deep compassion for souls in trouble, His penetrating insight
into the weakness of human nature, his tender love for those in
tears, his anguish for injustice done to certain people, and his
readiness to forgive and save. In Jesus Christ we encounter the
love of God in action. In and through him is the gigantic mission

of God to bring redemption to individual men and women and to the whole of the creation.

If this is the mission of Jesus Christ, it should also be the mission of the Christian church. To put it differently, Christian mission becomes part of the mission of Jesus Christ in so far as it becomes instrumental in making the redemptive presence of Christ real to the world. Thus, the authenticity of Christian mission and consequently that of the church must be derived from the redemptive presence of Christ. Christian mission is authenticated when it serves nothing but the redemptive presence of Christ. In other words, the authentication of Christian mission as the mission of Jesus Christ does not come from the subjective conditions but from the objective reality which is the redemptive presence of Jesus Christ. When Christian mission seeks to authenticate itself through factors such as the structure and organization of the church, ecclesiastical traditions and historical-cultural privileges, it inevitably becomes distorted. Unless the church in Asia faces honestly this distortion of Christian mission, she will not be able to derive new meanings of the Gospel of salvation and find new applications of the Good News to her own life-situations.

At this point, the meaning of the breaking of Christ's body must be sharpened in order for us to see its implications for Christian mission. Let me quote in this connection an excellent statement from 'The Working Papers on the New Quest for Missionary Communities,' which resulted from the study authorized at the Third Assembly of the World Council of Churches in New Delhi in 1961 under the leadership of the Department of Studies in Evangelism. It says:

> . . . we know that Christians are called to be present with Christ in the life of the world and, corporately, to be a vanguard of the new humanity within history. This means at least making ourselves vulnerable to the full onslaught of the struggles which so engage our times. It means that any sort of hiding, either in ecclesiology or doctrine, to protect us from the anguish of decisions in particular problems which affect the lives of our fellowmen is not worthy of Christ.[11]

Christian mission can only be carried out with a great cost to those who are engaged in it just as Christ's mission is accomplished at the cost of the cross. Here the meaning of the breaking of Christ's body becomes central for Christian mission.

When Christ had his body broken on the cross, he laid his own being bare before the world and for the world. He denied to himself any help and protection that might come from man and God. The tradition and structure of the religious systems into which he was born proved not to be his protection but the very tool which was to bring about His death. At the last moment of his agony on the cross his disciples all left him, leaving a few helpless women weeping at the foot of the cross. And then from him came the final and most shattering words: 'My God, My God, why hast thou forsaken me?' Forsaken by both man and God, Jesus Christ carried out his mission to the very end.

If this is the mission of Jesus Christ, what implications does it have for Christian mission? In the first place, Christian mission, if it is to be true to the mission of Jesus Christ, must break out of the defence mechanism of the church. Christian mission has been, and still is, too much of a spokesman for the church. It defends what the church stands for in matters relative to faith and morals. It concentrates its effort on drawing a line between the church and the world. This strategy of Christian mission has made Christianity very visible as a religion but ineffective as the power which penetrates into the social structure of Asia. The church becomes a citadel from which the campaigns against the so-called non-Christian world are planned and launched. It is also a refuge where Christians find it possible to forget what is happening in the world. This is particularly true with the Chinese-speaking churches throughout Asia.

If the church in Asia is to be true to the mission of Jesus Christ, all such defences should be dismantled. Especially, she has to learn to do without the security which the Western church has provided for too long a period of time. The slogan of mission on six continents must not be used as a pretext for Western missionary forces to return through the back door. The umbilical cord which provided life-sustenance to the church in Asia must be cut. This must be done with resolution and integrity. We must confess that there is lack of integrity on the part of the church in Asia and signs of cynicism on the part of the church in the West when it comes to the matter of cutting the umbilical cord. The church leaders in Asia are not quite true to the mission of Jesus Christ when they demand in one breath freedom and autonomy of their own churches and the continued financial and personnel help from the church in the West. On the other side of the fence there are Western church leaders who, at the outburst of open accusation against the church in the West by the Third World Christian elite, ruefully and cynically murmur to themselves that these same people venting vindictives on the Western church will soon come to them with begging bowls. This seems to be one of the sentiments observed by some participants at the conference on 'Salvation Today' held in Bangkok, Thailand, December 29, 1972 - January 8, 1973, under sponsorship of the Commission on World Mission and Evangelism, World Council of Churches.[12] If the situation described here is true, there is still much soul-searching to do by both the Western church leaders and their counterparts in the Third World. Christian mission cannot be planned and conducted when church leaders are beset with false pretensions and mischievous cynicism. This almost amounts to making a mockery of the mission of Jesus Christ.

There is also much breaking to do for the church in Asia with regard to some of her basic assumptions of faith. This is essential if she is to enter into meaningful exchange of spiritual experiences with men and women of other faiths. There is very little new insight to be gained if Christians in Asia continue to operate on the doctrinal assumption that the Christian church has an exclusive claim to the truth of God and to the mystery of salvation. Such a claim fostered and upheld in the heyday of the Western dominance of the Third World is detrimental to the Gospel. On one hand, it tends to belittle the profound spirituality exhibited by cultures and religions in Asia; and on the other, it prevents Christians from experiencing the richness of God's revelation in the creation. Such an exclusive claim may have provided Christian mission with powerful incentive, but it cannot be said to be an accurate representation of the love of God in creation and redemption. Therefore, we cannot agree with Prudencio Damboniera, a Roman Catholic missiologist and former missionary in Asia, when he considers the crisis of mission to consist in compromise on the claim of exclusiveness. Here is his statement which is eloquent but questionable:

The missionary malaise is, to a great extent at least, a reflection of a deeper illness affecting the whole body of the church. I cannot avoid feeling that certain theologians have taken positions and issued principles which, carried to their logical end, would simply mean death for the mission of the church. One of those principles concerns the exclusiveness of Christianity in regard to all other religions, and consequently the need for Christian faith and conversion to attain salvation. If these truths are doubted or virtually denied, the missionary work of the church loses its meaning. For twenty centuries they have been the foundation of Christian missions. To shake them is inevitably to cause the whole edifice of mission to crumble.[13]

I am afraid it is precisely this kind of argument that immobilizes the church in Asia in an unproductive alliance with her historical inheritance. To amass and fortify this kind of argument by invoking the traditions of the past twenty centuries will only perpetuate such an immobilization. This must not be regarded simply as disrespect for history and tradition. We believe in history and tradition in so far as they are conducive to our understanding of God's act in our contemporary existential situations. And it is our conviction that the claim to exclusiveness by Christianity on the grounds of ecclesiastical and doctrinal traditions is not only nonscriptural but untruthful.

Thus, the crumbling of the edifice of Western Christian mission, to use Damboniera's expression, may not be lamented after all. The process of the crumbling which has already begun has forced open the eyes of the church both in the West and in the East to the old and new historical, cultural and spiritual realities that demand fresh recognition and interpretation. From the standpoint of Christian mission this should pose an exciting challenge. The horizon of Christian mission has definitely been widened. Personal conversion, which constituted the sole concern of the certainly powerful evangelistic outreach, must now be set and seen in the contexts of the transformation, justice and reconciliation of a society in Asia. No one can refute the fact that this is the Biblical vision related to the restoration of humanity and the whole of the creation. At the heart of this restoration is the justice of God which will be translated into actual realities of cosmic life

as well as the life of individual persons. This is the prophetic
vision of the day of the Lord. On that day the Lord of hosts:

> shall judge the poor with justice
> and defend the humble in the land with equity;
> his mouth shall be a rod to strike down the ruthless,
> and with a word he shall slay the wicked.
> Round his waist he shall wear the belt of justice,
> and good faith shall be the girdle round his body.[14]

Immediately after this eulogy to the divine justice which demands
right human and social relationships, the prophet goes on to describe the restoration of the cosmic order. He does this by referring
to the harmony restored between man and animals. At last, right
relationships prevail within God's creation. This is the ultimate
meaning of the Biblical concept of justice.[15] To be part of this
dynamics of justice is to be part of salvation.

The report submitted by Section II on 'Salvation and Social
Justice' at the Bangkok Conference on 'Salvation Today,' to which
a reference was made earlier, stresses this wholeness of the meaning of salvation. From the beginning the report makes it clear
that

> Our concentration upon the social, economic and political
> implications of the Gospel does not in any way deny the
> personal and eternal dimensions of salvation. Rather, we
> would emphasize that the personal, social, individual and
> corporate aspects of salvation are so inter-related that they
> are inseparable.[16]

It is doubtful whether the Conference succeeded in conciliating all
the deep-rooted differences of opinion with respect to personal
evangelism and social action. However, it endeavoured to show
that this is not a case of either/or but of both-and.

The question is: How can one maintain personal spiritual
health when there is no health in the society in which one lives?
And how can it fail to enhance personal spiritual health when an
unhealthy state of society is exposed and corrected? The answer
is so obvious that we cannot but wonder why Christian mission
has had to be vitiated with internal conflicts amounting to schizo-
phrenia. It is when Christian mission begins to witness to the
spirit in the body and also the body in the spirit that it will become

the sacramental presence of Jesus Christ for the disturbed humanity. The report to which we referred above, therefore, goes on to say how the concept of salvation is seen at work in society:

1. We experience the saving power of salvation in the struggle for economic justice against the exploitation of people by people.

2. Salvation works in the struggle for human dignity against political oppression of human beings by their fellow men.

3. Salvation works in the struggle for solidarity against alienation of person from person.

4. Salvation works in the struggle of hope against despair in personal life.[17]

One may question why salvation should be cast so much in the language of struggle, but salvation is a struggle. This modern interpretation of the concept of salvation vividly reflects the struggle of Jesus Christ during the last days of his mission of salvation, symbolized by the breaking of bread. By breaking his own body, he restores wholeness to man, to society, and to the entire creation. That is why the act of breaking becomes the event of his redemptive presence. Christian mission, in so far as it is derived from Christ's mission, becomes witness to the redemptive presence of Jesus Christ. This makes Christian mission sacramental.

3. Word in Action

Another way of looking at the wholeness of Christian mission is to regard it as word in action. Here the key to understand more deeply the nature of Christian mission is the unity of word and action. When this unity is impaired, the wholeness of Christian mission is jeopardized.

The separation of word from action or action from word is one of the greatest tragedies that has ever befallen man, for the health and truthfulness of his being depends essentially on the unity of word and action. Word, theologically speaking, is no mere sound produced by a man's vocal system. Word, to be heard, has to be transmitted through the vocal system as part of man's physiological structure. But it wells out from the deepest part of one's being with the purpose of reaching its destination, namely, comprehension by another human being. Strictly speaking, therefore, we cannot say 'mere' words, just as we cannot say 'mere' symbols. Paul Tillich stresses this point very strongly. There is an ontological relationship between a symbol and that which the symbol purports to symbolize. The symbol participates in the power of being of that which is symbolized. The same thing can be said of words. Primarily, words are of an ontological nature because they are the being of a person expressed vocally. Words are a being, in this case a human being, in utterance. That is why the same words may carry different weight depending on who utters them. Words spoken by those in higher echelons of a government or an organization certainly carry more weight and authority than words spoken by those in lower echelons of the same government and organization. The same is true in practically every phase of life and society.

The existential aspect of the word with its ontological nature is action. Words spoken must be heard and comprehended. And the best way for the spoken words to be heard and comprehended is through the corresponding actions and events. The spoken words will thus not become an abstract concept. Abstract concepts are for metaphysicians and not for those who have to live out their lives with direct confrontation with and involvement in the realities of this world. This is to say, spoken words need to be translated into events and actions in order to be seen and grasped. In this way a close correlation is formed between word and action. Words get translated into and become embodied in actions, while actions point back to the sources from which they came. The wholeness of a person consists, therefore, in the correspondence between word and action. The discrepancy between the two is the evidence that the discrepancy has invaded the being of a person. He is then no longer whole and healthy. An element of falsehood is introduced into his being. He *is* no longer what he *acts*. His action does not substantiate his words, and his words do not correspond to his actions. Here is the root of the problems that beset us human beings and our society. A wedge of distrust is driven into the mind of man, thus creating alienation not only within himself but also in the relating of one man to another. Unless human and social problems are dealt with at this ontological-existential level, we will continue to grope in the darkness of alienation and falsehood.

The Biblical faith shows us how God deals with this basic problem of man. According to the Biblical understanding, history is the Word of God in action. More specifically, in history the Word of God is uttered and takes forms in saving acts. History is, therefore, shaped by the Word-Action of God. It is from such perspective that the men and women of faith in the Biblical world try to read the meaning of events in history. For God there is a perfect correlation between His Word and His Act. Precisely for this reason we can know something of the ontological nature of God from events and acts in history. Exodus in the Old Testament comes immediately to our minds as the most illustrious example. From what they had to go through to get out of Egypt, the land of their bondage, the people of Israel inferred that Yahweh was the God who liberated them. Thus, they experienced Yahweh as having freedom as one of His chief characteristics.

The incarnation is, of course, the supreme expression of the unity of God's Word and His Act. Jesus Christ is the Word of God made flesh. That is to say the saving love of God becomes embodied in a particular person called Jesus Christ. Jesus Christ is thus the Word of God in action. To know Jesus Christ is to know God. To follow him is to follow God. That is why Jesus Christ says he is the way. Furthermore, since He is the perfect unity of God's Word and His Act, no falsehood is to be found in Him. For this reason he says he is the truth. The incarnation is the sacramental act of God. And through this divine sacramental act, salvation is brought to the world.

It is, therefore, most unfortunate that a doctrinal division has occurred within the church with regard to the sacrament of the Lord's Supper. On one hand, there are the churches of the Reformation tradition laying much emphasis on the Word of God over against the sacrament. The inherent meaning of the sacrament as the embodiment of the Word and the Act in unity is thus endangered. To quote John Macquarrie, 'Calvin set out with the intention of holding word and sacraments in proper balance, but in fact, he subordinated the sacraments to the word by making them *verbum visible*. So, in spite of his intention, in the Calvinist tradition (as in Protestantism generally)' preaching has quite overshadowed the sacraments. . .'[18]   The sacrament, in this view, is not a self-sustaining event.   It is not self-explanatory. The Word must be injected into it to make it meaningful. Perhaps the sacrament as an institution of the church needs the help of the Word to become witness to the sacramental act of God in the mission of Jesus Christ.

The divorce of the Word and the sacrament is further seen in Roman Catholicism. There the sacrament has acquired the importance and meaning of its own in separation from the Word. The theory of *ex opere operato* reinforces this separation. The absence of the Word 'makes the sacraments into automatically effective rites which are scarcely to be distinguished from magic.'[19]   This leads to the situation in which the event of Jesus Christ, though it should be central, does not constitute the primary importance. The sacrament becomes a substitute for Jesus Christ, supposedly making impacts on believers quite independently of him.

Neither the Protestant view nor that of Roman Catholicism is true to the nature of the sacrament in its original sense.   The mission of Jesus Christ is the sacrament *par excellence*. As has been said, Jesus Christ is the Word of God in action.   This divine mission of salvation culminates in the Last Supper during which Jesus Christ, by both words and acts, enacts in advance the drama of the cross.   Utterly awed and overwhelmed, the disciples did not comprehend the meaning of it all until after the resurrection. They did not quite grasp the dynamics of the Word of God communicating itself to men in the ministry of the suffering of Jesus Christ.

Christian mission becomes sacramental, that is, instrumental in communicating the saving love of God, when its words take form in action.   When the unity of the Word and action becomes manifested in Christian mission, the divine saving power is released to judge and save.   It is at this very point that Christian mission is tested as to its validity and authenticity. This reminds us of the judgment often passed on the church by modern man both inside and outside the church.   The church is pronounced to be irrelevant to the contemporary world largely because she has lost her validity and authenticity. Her validity as the one body of Christ is threatened by her own internal strife and divisions; while her authenticity as the witness to the saving love of God is questioned on account of her inability to substantiate her words with actions. The words thus spoken by the church become hollow words, words without substance. Once the words of the church become deprived of their very substance, the church becomes dispensable. She does not have to be taken seriously. Such a church becomes a church without promise. What is this church without promise? It is the church which lives on the past. Her present is at most the re-living of the past without much relevance for the present and challenge for the future. Such a church tends to avoid the realities and responsibilities of the present. She will have nothing to do with socio-political issues. She has no future to offer. That is why we have seen people, especially modern intellectuals and young people, turn away from her. The church with a double or triple standard with regard to her involvement in the world cannot command respect of the people who have to face daily struggle with the realities of life. The mission of the church, which has one foot in some euphoric future and the other foot in the present, can only become half-hearted. This very easily leads to the idea that whatever good you do in the present is counted towards the acceptance by God in some remote future. Some religions explicitly make this the sole aim and purpose of their teachings and practices. The worldly realities thus lose their intrinsic value and meaning. They exist only to serve as means to achieve other-worldly goals. Christian evangelism, narrowly conceived, has too often been carried out with such an other-worldly motivation.

Some theological implications for the church and Christian mission can be drawn from our discussion above. The first implication is this: the church becomes sacramental when Christian mission truly exhibits its sacramental nature, that is, when it reflects the Word of God in action. Contrary to common understanding, the church does not become sacramental on account of the altar or the communion table placed in her midst. The church, if she is to be Christ-centered church, must be mission-centered and not altar- or communion-table-centered. After all, the church, in the primary sense, is not an ecclesiastical or a religious institution endowed with some magical sacramental power. Strictly, the church has no structure of her own separated from her mission. But the fact is that Christian mission has too long been shaped by the church. That is why Christian mission has demonstrated too much of denominational idiosyncrasies. And traditionally the explicit purpose of mission is to plant the congregations patterned after the particular ecclesiastical backgrounds from which missionaries came.

In line with our argument here, it is Christian mission which should determine the shape of the Christian community brought into existence as the result of mission endeavours. The church, in its original sense, is the gathering of people who have come under the impact of the witness to the saving act of God. Thus, she does not have a pre-determined shape or structure. Her doctrinal contents may not have to be so rigid either. Although historical formulations of the contents of Christian faith will give us insight into the past, they often become a hindrance rather than a help, especially for the church in Asia, in finding her own way of confessing Christian faith. A particular congregation in a particular context should thus be confessional in character. Unless the church in Asia learns to be confessional in character, she will not be able to encounter Jesus Christ in the realities of this world.

The second implication is this: Christian mission as sacramental is needed where conflicts are. As has been pointed out, most human conflicts occur on account of the tragic disruption which has invaded the being of man—the disruption of word and act. God's act of salvation in Jesus Christ has its chief purpose in restoring the unity of word and act to man. It follows that Christian mission must identify areas of human conflicts. These areas can extend from personal and inter-personal to social-political arenas. That is to say, there should be no area marked off-limits to Christian mission. Just to single out one area to the exclusion of others will not do justice to the sacramental nature of Christian mission. Jesus Christ came to the world not just to save individual men and women, but to redeem the world. His body is broken for the alienation of the whole world from God as well as the alienation of man from God. The healing of individual men and women is called conversion. The healing of conflicts relative to society may be called restoration. The doing away with religious corruption may be termed reformation. Whether it is conversion, restoration or reformation, what is thus brought about through Christian mission is closely related to God's salvation. In this way the sacramental nature of Christian mission demands that no boundaries be drawn for Christian mission with regard to its involvement in the mission of Christ.

A corollary may be drawn from this. Christian mission should be directed as much to the Christian church as to the world outside the church. This may sound strange at first, but in reality it is not so. The history of the Christian church is full of internal conflicts as well as the service which the church renders to the world and mankind. For this reason, the church cannot be exempted from the thrusts of Christian mission. In the Old Testament days, the prophets directed their activities largely to Israel. Israel, the nation chosen for a particular divine purpose, was their mission field.

This is no less true with the church and the Western world which the church has helped to shape and build. The notion that nationalism or resurgent religions in the Third World constitute big obstacles to Christian mission cannot be accepted without further thought. The statement such as follows is as provocative as it is true:

> The greatest threat and obstacle to the mission of the church is not the world it faces but the church itself. In what we do we are to become like Him, to grow into His likeness. Jesus lived His life entirely for others. Have we learned to do this, so that our time is radically filled with God's glory?[20]

One cannot help questioning the integrity of Christian mission carried out by the church which has become an obstacle to her own principal task. In order for the church to regain her integrity as the body of Christ, the sacramental nature of the mission of Jesus Christ must be restored to her.

4. Christian Mission in a Sacramental Universe

Our effort has been to give Christian mission wider contexts in which to operate. Without a wider connotation, Christian mission would continue to produce rigid church structures and narrow definitions of the contents of the Christian faith. The concept that I find most useful in further assisting our effort here is the concept of the sacramental universe adopted by Donald Baillie in developing his theology of Christian sacraments.

According to Baillie, the concept of the sacramental universe can be explained as follows: The sacramental universe points to

the idea that the sacraments in the specific sense are but con-
centrations of something very much more widespread, so
that nothing could be in the special sense a sacrament unless everything were in a basic and general sense sacramental.[21]

We are reminded again of the importance of setting the essential
contents and practices of Christian faith such as sacraments in the
context of the creation. As has been argued previously, the
parochial characteristics shown by ecclesiastical and theological
traditions is the end result of virtually isolating salvation from the
creation. When the divine act of salvation loses its ground in the
divine creation, salvation becomes a monopoly to be handled solely
through the historical and sacerdotal structures of the church.
Christian mission has been the instrument of this church.

But the concept of a sacramental universe such as expounded
by Baillie brings the creation back to the center of Christian faith.
He is not a lonely voice in this effort. Paul Tillich, for example,
expresses a similar view when he observes that 'no part of
encountered reality is excluded beforehand from the possibility
that it might become sacramental material; anything can prove
adequate for it in certain constellations.'[22] It goes without saying
that the term sacramental is not to be interpreted in a narrow
liturgical sense. It points to the reality which becomes a focal
point of the divine-human interaction. It is the reality which
conveys the meaning of the divine in the midst of the human.
Such reality can be encountered both in the church and outside
the church. It is mistaken to regard such reality taking place
only within the precincts of the church. This largely accounts
for the one-way traffic in Christian mission, namely, to call people
into the precincts of the church. The idea of a sacramental
universe strongly speaks against this traditional approach of Christian mission. Instead, it implies that Christian mission can become sacramental in that it makes visible anywhere in the world
the dealings of God with man. Thus, the idea of a sacramental
universe affirms the universal nature of God's saving acts in the
whole of the creation. Christian mission, understood and conducted in the contexts of a sacramental universe, should be able
to give witness to the universal nature of God's salvation.

This brings up the question of universalism. Christian mission
and universalism have been posed as antithetical. If all men are

to be saved in the end—this is what universalism means after all—then why Christian mission? Further, is this not to obliterate distinction between the righteous and the wicked? Does it pay to be good and righteous if the wicked are to be saved eventually? These questions are often charged with emotion which stems from selfishness and narrow-mindedness. This is to see God's work of salvation not from the perspective of the entire creation and the eschatological hope but from the standpoint of personal likes and dislikes. We would rather agree with John Macquarrie when he says:

> If God is indeed absolute letting-be, and if this letting-be has power to overcome the risks of dissolution, then perhaps in the end (so we must speak) no individual existence that has been called out of nothing will utterly return to nothing, but will move nearer to the fulfilment of its potentialities, as the horizon of time and history continually expands and it is set in an ever wider reconciling context. In other words, we prefer a doctrine of 'universalism' to one of 'conditional immortality', and this seems more in line with the eschatological hope that all things will indeed find their fullness in God.[23]

What is Christian mission if not an active participation in the process of all things finding their fulfilment in God? In this new era when man's horizon is unprecedently expanded not only on the frontier of space but also on the frontiers of culture, Christian mission has to take up the task of working out the meaning of fulfilment in different cultural contexts. As long as the church in Asia is preoccupied with converting people, expanding the church and enlarging her membership, Christianity in Asia will assume more and more sectarian characteristics, failing to play an essential role in the spirituality of Asia. Fulfilment has its negative aspects, too, of course. There are things in Asian spirituality that must be negated, especially that part of spirituality which stops short of reaching the ultimate. This may be one of the reasons why worship of idols proliferates. There is also this inclination to look away from the abysmal depth of the meaning of life for fear of having to face questions and issues that may disrupt their pursuit of life. But this negative aspect of fulfilment should not continue to make us neglect, as has been in the past, our responsibility to discover the meaningful aspects contained in the Asian spirituality.

Thus, Christian mission understood in the light of sacrament is an event charged with universal significance. It is in the contexts of universal significance that we regard it true to say: 'the universal is always in the trust of the particular—particular persons, conditions, occasions and places'.[24] Christian mission is this particular entrusted with the universal. Christian mission bears the responsibility to awaken in other particulars under certain conditions and places the consciousness of being part of the universal. In this way, Christian mission should be the adventure filled with excitement and expectation. In the course of its endeavour, Christian mission will encounter the particulars that bear the mark of the universal. This should prove to be an occasion for joy and celebration. But those who are engaged in Christian mission have often been hesitant to affirm this for fear of syncretism. They turn away from the signs which point to the ultimate reality for which Christian faith stands simply because they are found outside the domain of the historical Christianity. It is only in recent years that Christian mission can no longer ignore the impacts that the non-Christian particulars are making on the spirituality of men and women in Asia. At last it should now become possible for Christian mission to look upon these non-Christian impacts not with hostility but with a profound sense of awe towards the mystery of God's creation and revelation. This amounts to an emancipation of Christian mission from self-imposed restrictions on the acts of God in the world.

In this connection, I would like to refer to what Karl Barth calls 'biblical universalism'. His consistent concentration on Christology has often given rise to the misunderstanding that his theological system is based on a very narrow understanding of God's revelation. However, when one wades laboriously through his thick volumes of *Church Dogmatics*, one cannot help being struck by the wide scope of his theological enterprize. What particularly interests us here is his universalistic application of God's action in Jesus Christ. He stresses that 'we have no option, therefore, but to understand realistically in this sense the very positive statements of the Bible concerning the general human situation. They describe this situation as it really is in virtue of the fact that it has been altered and determined by God's action in the history of Israel and of Jesus Christ enacted within it'.[25] If this is the case, what is the task of Christian mission? What is it that Christians are commissioned by Jesus Christ to witness? In a word, what is the nature and task of the mission of the church? Barth's answer to these questions is something as follows:

> Hence their witness (the positive statements of the Bible referred to in the above quotation)—and this is the root and meaning of biblical universalism—had also, and even primarily, to be a declaration concerning others, the world and all men, namely, the declaration that the action of God in His covenant with Israel and His unity with the one man Jesus Christ was and is His gracious judging, yet also justifying and sanctifying action for them and to them.[26]

What we can infer from this statement is this: Israel, and for that matter, the Christian church, must not be posed as antithetical to other nations or to those outside the church. What we see done to Israel and the Christian church is also to be done to other nations and to those outside the church. Israel and the church are thus the particulars symbolizing the relationship between all the particulars and the universal. Christian mission consists in making such a declaration.

But the relationship between the particular and the universal is far from being uniformal in its expressions. To assert that this relationship should be uniformal has been a major error on the part of Western Christian mission. The Christian church in the West represents one of the types that can be conceived of in the relationship between the particular and the universal. Even within this type there are minor and major variations such as denominational differences. And from the standpoint of orthodoxy, sectarianism is an aberration of the main type which orthodoxy represents. Since this is the case, there is no reason why this particular type of relationship should also be the type of relationship between the particular and the universal in the non-Western settings. The Biblical account of the creation affirms implicitly that the meaning of the particular, be that represented by Israel, the church or others, derives its meaning from the universal. We can, therefore, assume that a relationship is already in existence between the particular in a particular context and the universal. This basic biblical and theological principle must be asserted by those engaged in Christian mission.

This affirmation or assertion is accompanied by negation or judgment. What has to be judged and negated is the distortion of the relation between the particular and the universal. The most common form of such a distortion is to be seen in the replacement of the universal by something less than universal or by something devoid of the meaning pertaining to the universal. Here we are, of course, referring to idolatry. Idolatry distorts and confuses the relation between the particular and the universal. It seeks to replace the infinite by the finite, the universal by the particular. Since idolatry distorts the relationship between the universal and the particular, it cannot bear witness to the universal. On account of this, it must be judged and negated. No wonder the prophets in the Old Testament never cease to attack idolatry. Second Isaiah, for example, bluntly declares that idols are the creation of man's hand and thus cannot be the object of worship. He taunts idolatry saying:

> Those who make idols are less than nothing;
> All their cherished images profit nobody;
> Their worshippers are blind,
> Sheer ignorance makes fools of them.
> If a man makes a god or casts an image,
> His labour is wasted.
> Why! its votaries show their folly;
> the craftsmen too are but men.
> Let them all gather together and confront me,
> All will be afraid and look the fools they are.[27]

Religion is more often than not an expression of man's weakness. Unable to fathom the depth of the universal, he takes an easy way out by attempting to particularize the universal and localize it for easy access. But once the universal is particularized and localized in images and idols, the universal eludes his grasp and apprehension. What he worships is no other than the work of his own hands. Having this tendency towards idolatry, religion can be an illusion of man.

This criticism of religion with respect to its idolatrous aspect must not, however, blind us to the possibility that the universal may choose to manifest itself in the way we least expect it. In other words, we cannot pre-determine how and where the universal should make itself known. But Christian mission in Asia has not always shown openness to this freedom which is inherent in the very nature of the universal. It tends to reject other forms of religious expressions as having any vital relation with the universal. It has to be pointed out that the church in the West too has those who are inclined to think that Christian witness is well-nigh impossible in a society in which social system and political ideology are different from theirs. Charles West, for instance, observes and says:

> It is those who find themselves most comfortably at home in our Western society who find it hardest to believe that one can live a Christian life and bear a Christian witness in a communist-dominated land or even in a nationalist ex-colonial country. Fed by the descriptions of Orwell and Koestler, they picture Communism as a demon who leaves no power for God in the regions where he rules, so that the only Christian answer can be suffering, flight or a hopeless rebellion.[28]

Not only Christians in the West are obsessed with this dark picture of communist-dominated countries; America's foreign policy, too, until very recently has been largely influenced by it. This results, for example, in the strategy of containment the United States has adopted *vis-à-vis* Communist China. The vulnerability of the strategy became apparent when it had to be replaced by that of co-operation for the sake of the peace of the world with tacit acknowledgement of the viability of different social structure and political ideology.

We want to emphasize, therefore, that the primary question for a Christian or a Christian community in a communist-dominated land is not: How can a communist be converted to Christianity? but: What must the followers of Christ do to become sacramental so that God's love and reconciliation proves to be a reality in their society? The life of the Christian in such a society should be sacramental living. It is not by word of mouth but by deeds that the cross and the resurrection of Christ may begin to have impact on a particular society.

Let us be reminded again of the central meaning of a sacramental universe. It means in essence that anything is potentially sacramental simply because this world of ours is created by God and redeemed by Jesus Christ. Bread, wine and water represent the most ordinary and yet the most indispensable things in our daily lives. They are chosen for sacramental use to remind us that other things and events too can equally become sacramental in different situations. There is a telling example of this in the experience of Peter at Joppa. In a vision he was asked to kill and eat 'four-footed creatures of the earth, wild beasts and things that crawl or fly.'[29] Peter was absolutely horrified. How could he degrade himself by committing such a sacreligious act? How could he dare to tamper with the strict Jewish law by having to do with these 'unclean' animals? Thus, he refused to obey the order. But he was sternly told: 'It is not for you to call profane what God counts clean.' This experience had a traumatic effect on Peter. It proved to be a radical change in his concept of mission. For before long, we see him in Jerusalem taking the lead in successfully silencing the objections of his fellow Jewish Christians to the mission to the Gentiles.

This extraordinary experience Peter had at the inception of the mission to the Gentiles also clearly implies that there is no validity whatsoever in the artificial differentiation between the profane and the holy. The division which we too readily make especially in our religious conceptualization is more the projection of our own subjective likes and dislikes than the reality embedded in the objective world. The imposition of such a division on the world actually amounts to putting into question God's creation as essentially good not only in itself but in its relation to man. Thus, rigorous self-examination must go on at the very heart of religious beliefs and practices lest in the very act of worshipping God, we are in fact challenging His sovereignty.

Another interesting point to observe in Peter's vision is this. Peter was not asked to apply any religious rites to make these animals clean. They were presented to him as already clean. What Peter was asked to do was to recognize this as de facto and proceed to prepare them for eating. Applied to the mission to the Gentiles, can this not be interpreted to mean that the Gentiles are already accepted by God and that the mission of the church is to affirm and proclaim this fact of acceptance? We would like to stress that Christian mission should be carried out on the basis of this note of acceptance rather than rejection. It is, therefore, a very crucial part of Christian mission to be open and ready to respond to what God has already been doing among those men and women whom the church through her mission tries to reach.

The concept of a sacramental universe ought thus to be able to help us broaden the purview of Christian mission. It reminds us that there is no so-called religious realm well defined for carrying out Christian mission. Christian mission has to do with man's cultural and social concerns as well as his religious needs. Let us, therefore, emphasize what has already been said earlier: Christian mission should not be a by-product of a self-perpetuating religious community. Instead, it should be instrumental in bringing into existence communities openly and explicitly conscious of their relation with the universal through what God has done in Jesus Christ. On account of this, a theology of Christian mission needs to deal with areas and subjects related to man's diverse cultural activities.

REFERENCES

1. I Corinthians 11:23-25. Cf. also Mark 14:22-25; Matthew 26:26-29. Luke's version is somewhat different from these three reports. Both the Revised Standard Version and the New English Bible follow some early manuscripts which 'omit Luke 22:19b-20. In this shorter form of Luke, Jesus first took a cup, gave thanks, and gave it to the group; then he took bread, gave thanks, broke it and gave it to them saying, "this is my body"; but there is no word about a cup after the bread or about repeating the rite, although some think this shorter text is probably the original form' (Floyd V. Filson, *A New Testament History*, Philadelphia: The Westminster Press, 1964, p. 141). This is no place to discuss what Jesus actually said and did at the Last Supper. One thing is sure, that is, the early church soon came to celebrate the Lord's Supper with the bread and the cup with the wording reflected in Paul's version.

2. Floyd V. Filson, *ibid*.

3. *Inter-communion*, edited by D. M. Baillie and John Marsh, New York: Harper and Brothers Publishers, 1952, p. 23.

4. T. F. Torrance, 'Eschatology and the Eucharist,' *Inter-communion*, p. 305.

5. Matthew 11:4-6.

6. *A Dictionary of Religion and Ethics*, edited by Shailer Matthews and Gerald Birney Smith, New York: The Macmillan Company, 1921, p. 390.

7. Luke 24:13-35.

8. Luke 24:35.

9. Donald A. McGavran, *Understanding Church Growth*, Grand Rapids: William B. Eerdmanns Publishing Company, 1970, p. 27.

10. *The Uppsala Report 1968*. The World Council of Churches, Geneva, 1968, p. 28.

11. *Planning for Mission*, edited by Thomas Wieser, The U.S. Conference for the World Council of Churches, New York, 1966, p. 55.

12. At this writing, the official report of the conference is still in preparation and thus a comprehensive analysis has to await its appearance. It was said, however, that at the Conference the Third World voice dominated for the first time in ecumenical gatherings. Though there might have been both sadistic and masochistic tendencies in such East-West confrontation, I believe this is a stage in the process of mutually growing into maturity.

13. Prudencio Damboriena, S.J. 'Aspects of the Missionary Crisis in Roman Catholicism' in *The Future of the Christian World Mission*, Studies in Honor of R. Pierce Beaver, edited by William J. Darker and Wi Jo Kang, Grand Rapids, Michigan: William B. Eerdmanns Publishing Company, 1971. (pp. 73-88), p. 78.

14. Isaiah 11:4-5.

15. Justice or righteousness in the Old Testament according to *The Interpreter's Dictionary of the Bible* is 'the fulfilment of the demands of a relationship, whether that relationship be with men or with God. Each man is set within a multitude of relationships: King with people, judge with

complainants, priest with worshipers, common man with family, tribesman with community, community with resident, alien and poor, all with God. And each of these relationships brings its specific demands, the fulfilment of which constitutes righteousness.' (Vol. R-Z, p. 80).

16.   The quotation is contained in the introductory part of the Report.

17.   Section III of the Report.

18.   John Macquarrie, *Principles of Christian Theology*, New York: Charles Scribner's Sons, 1966, pp. 399-400.

19.   *Ibid.*

20.   John D. Godsey, 'History of Salvation and World History,' in *Christian Mission in World Perspective*, edited by Gerald H. Anderson, Nashville-New York: Abingdon Press, 1967, p. 75.

21.   Donald M. Baillie; *The Theology of the Sacraments*, New York: Charles Scribner's Sons, 1955, p. 42.

22.   Paul Tillich, *Systematic Theology*, Vol. IV. The University of Chicago Press, 1963, p. 123.

23.   John Macquarrie, *Principles of Christian Theology*, p. 322.

24.   Kenneth Cragg, *Christianity in World Perspective*, New York: Oxford University Press, 1968, p. 18.

25.   Karl Barth, *Church Dogmatics* IV, 3, Second Half, translated by G. W. Bromiley, Edinburgh: T and T Clark, 1962, p. 489.

26.   Karl Barth, *ibid*, p. 490.

27.   Isaiah 44:9-11.

28.   Charles West, *Outside the Camp*, New York: Doubleday and Company, 1959, p. 145.

29.   Acts 11: 5f.

CHAPTER FIVE

Mission of the Exodus

When Israel was in Egypt's land
  Let my people go!
Oppressed so hard they could not stand.
  Let my people go!
Go down, Moses, way down to Egypt's land,
  Tell old Pharaoh
  Let my people go!

—*Negro Spiritual*

1. Let My People Go !

Our discussion in the last chapter brings us to the conclusion that the divine mission of enfleshment is sacramental in nature. It culminates in the Last Supper which is the symbolic enactment of God's salvation in Jesus Christ on the cross. The task of Christian mission consists, therefore, in constantly opening up the frontiers of reality in Asia in such a way that what has been implicit with regard to the working of God may now become explicit.

Where do we then see God acting on behalf of man? How does His saving love become a reality in our experience? What are some of the concrete events which enable us to say God is with us in the world? Or to formulate our question differently: Are there happenings in the world demonstrative of sacramental nature? In other words, what are the happenings in us and around us which can be said to be of redemptive nature and quality? In the following two chapters we shall try to answer these questions in the light of the Bible and also in the light of the present situations in Asia.

One great theme which dominates the Bible, if not exclusively at least out of proportion, is the theme of the exodus. The Biblical writers of the Old Testament did not comprehend the love of God conceptually. They did not try to grasp the meaning of God's salvation in a rarified spiritual atmosphere often prevailing in worship services today. Instead, God's salvation for them was something that affected them to the very depth of their being. Naturally, the event of the exodus became the pivot of their faith in God. And for subsequent generations of the people of Israel the event of the exodus was to be relived and re-experienced over and over again in different contexts and situations.

We are dealing here with the exodus as a sacramental act embodying the reality of God's salvation. It is no wonder that the exodus becomes the central theme in the confession of faith. What we read in Deuteronomy 26:5-9 is a model form of such a confession of faith:

> My father was a homeless Aramaean who went down to Egypt with a small company and lived there until they became great, powerful and numerous nations. But the Egyptians ill-treated us, humiliated us and imposed cruel slavery upon us. Then we cried to the Lord of God of our fathers for help, and he listened to us and saw our humiliation, our hardship and distress; and so the Lord brought us out of Egypt with a strong hand and outstretched arm, with terrifying deeds and with signs and portents. He brought us to this place and gave us this land, a land flowing with milk and honey.

This historical experience of the exodus is woven into the structure of the religious life of the people of Israel throughout their history. It forms the basis of their relation with God. And it serves as the reminder that Yahweh their God is the God who interferes with the affairs of man and the world. It is through the experience of the exodus that their outlook on life and the world is formulated.

For this reason the faith of Israel is an historical faith. It is a faith that not only goes back to an historical root in the event of the exodus but also is defined in the ages to follow by that historical root. On account of this, the Old Testament, as the record of those people who responded to the acts of God in history, is built on the foundation of the exodus. Thus we are told:

> As the foundation stone of faith the exodus tradition came to be more and more the *pièce de résistance* of the description of the history of salvation in the history books. It became

one of the strongest pillars of Israel's religious life, too, but also of legal and moral thinking, the starting point of both the message of judgment of the prophets and their message of hope.[1]

It is, therefore, no exaggeration to say that the exodus is the key to understanding the message of the Old Testament. Without deep understanding of what the exodus is about, it will be difficult to really grasp the faith of the Bible.

At this point, we recall how the exodus is re-enacted in the person of Jesus Christ It was to Egypt that Joseph and Mary had to flee for the safety of the infant Jesus. Is this not another indication that the historical experience of the exodus is crucial to the extraordinary mission with which Jesus Christ is entrusted? 'Out of Egypt have I called my son'.[2] Through this re-enactment the historical link between the acts of God in the past and those in the future is established. The continuity is assured. But this is not all. Through Jesus Christ the event of the exodus gains messianic significance. From now on, the experience of the exodus is not to be confined only to Israel. It will become the experience of all men and women. The power inherent in the historical experience of the exodus in relation to Israel will now be released and become available to all mankind. Thus, in Jesus Christ the meaning and intent of the exodus is fulfilled. The mission of Jesus Christ is, therefore, the fulfilment of the mission of the exodus.

The question we must now ask is this: What makes the exodus stand out as the most outstanding experience in the history of Israel and in the life of the people of Israel? The answer is to be found in the powerful demand Moses made on behalf of his people before the Pharaoh to let his people go. In the account of the confrontation of Moses with the Pharaoh, Moses demanded no less than seven times: 'Let my people go!'[3] Here is a spiritual leader of Israel making a political demand. More concretely, 'the essential happening in the exodus was the going forth of the Israelites from bondage to freedom.'[4] The mission of Moses is, therefore, a political mission. It is for the purpose of setting his people free from the political bondage that Moses is called to be the leader. Consequently, we do not find him engaging his people in spiritualizing their predicament. He does not resort to counselling patience and submission. On the contrary, the life of bondage has become so intolerable and humiliating that Moses has to face the powers that be with an uncompromising demand: Let my people go!

This is the mission of great deliverance. The people of Israel first came to know their God in this existential context. It is not in some abstract spiritual atmosphere that they encountered their God. Their God is the God who acts in history. That is why the experience of the exodus becomes the backbone of the faith of Israel. As has been pointed out, it constitutes the core of their confession of faith. And very often the prophets had to confront the people of Israel with this event of great deliverance from Egypt in order to bring them back to right relationship with God. This is what Amos tried to do. Utterly frustrated in the midst of the unrepentant people of the Northern Kingdom of Israel, Amos burst out into these passionate words:

> Listen, Israelites, to these words that the Lord addresses to you, to the whole nation which he brought up from Egypt:
>
>> For you alone I have cared
>> among all the nations of the world;
>> therefore will I punish you
>> for all your iniquities.[5]

The mission of the exodus thus continues. The prophets rightly see in it the powerful means to awaken their people out of spiritual and social decadence. It is to the historical experience of deliverance from the house of bondage that the prophets turn for the renewal and revitalization of their nation. The mission of the exodus, begun with Moses, is carried forward down through the history of Israel. And, as has been mentioned, it gains much wider and deeper spiritual meaning when it is relived by Jesus Christ. The mission of the exodus is the messianic mission.

According to Luke, Jesus Christ announced the beginning of His ministry by the declaration of the theme of deliverance. In the synagogue in Nazareth he stood up and read those poignant words from the Deutero-Isaiah:

> The spirit of the Lord is upon me because he has anointed me;
> He has sent me to announce good news to the poor,

To proclaim release for prisoners and recovery of sight for
the blind;

To let the broken victims go free,
To proclaim the year of the Lord's favour.[6]

In quoting this passage from the Deutero-Isaiah, Jesus Christ makes
it clear that His mission consists in setting men and women free
from both physical and spiritual bondage. In other words, he is
going to fulfil the meaning of the exodus in his own person.
Resolutely He declares: 'Today in your very hearing this text has
come true.'[7]

For Jesus Christ his mission of the exodus is the mission of
deliverance from both internal and external bondages that make
men and women unfree. In him the internal and the external,
the spiritual and the physical, the eternal and the temporal, have
merged into one. This is a colossal mission, the mission that
constantly seeks to break out of human bondage in its various
cruel forms. True, the mission of the exodus under the leadership
of Moses is spiritualized, but it is not spiritualized to become a
nice religious ceremony to be performed in the quietness of a
sanctuary. It is spiritualized to take forms in vigorous, concrete
and actual situations in which individual men and women find
themselves. It is spiritualized to reinforce the power of con-
cretization in cultural events.

The mission of Jesus Christ as the mission of the exodus does
not speak to a spiritual vacuum. It addresses itself to the humanity
struggling against poverty, social injustice, political bondage and
physical pain. The Kingdom of God as preached by Jesus Christ
is never divorced from these. He brings good news to the poor,
proclaims release for prisoners and performs healing of the body.
When he condemns sin, it is not so much moral or religious sin
as the distortion and violation of justice that is meant. When he
deplores the hardness of heart on the part of his fellow man, it
is their insensitivity to human needs that arouses indignation in
him. Whatever form human bondage may take, it proves to be
an assault on God's creation and the belittlement of God's love
for man.

But one may ask: Is the mission of Jesus Christ not quite
different in substance from that of Moses? As far as we know,

there was no direct political involvement on the part of Jesus Christ. He did not confront the Roman authorities in Palestine with a demand to set his fellowmen free. Instead, he seemed to avoid any direct confrontation with the political powers of his day by speaking of the religion of the heart. He preached and practised forgiveness. And one of the last things he said on the cross was to ask God to forgive those who crucified him. In all this and in many other instances he was at pains to show a qualitative difference between the Kingdom of God and the Kingdom of this world. In the sermon on the mount we are given a picture of what a man as a follower of Christ should be and do. Thus, he tells us:

> Do not set yourself against the man who wrongs you. If some-one slaps you on the right cheek, turn and offer him your left. If a man wants to sue you for your shirt, let him have your coat as well. If a man in authority makes you go one mile, go with him two. Give when you are asked to give; and do not turn your back on a man who wants to borrow.[8]

The picture of a man depicted here simply does not fit the realities of the world with which we have to cope. Perhaps this is an ethic meant not for this world but for a different kind of world.[9] Surely this is a far cry from a direct and imperative demand which Moses laid before the Pharaoh.

Are we to conclude from this that the mission of Jesus Christ had little to do with the mission of the exodus especially in its social, economic and political dimensions? On more careful reflection, we must say that this cannot be our conclusion. What Jesus Christ did was to deal with the social, economic and political problems at the most basic level. He did not ostentatiously demand the Roman authorities to let his people go from the yoke of oppression. But all the time he was engaged in a most funda-mental task of paving the way to radical and genuine social, economic and political transformation not only for his own race but also for all mankind. A revolution of a most profound kind was being conceived here through his ministry. And he accom-plished his task by turning the mission of the exodus to the mission of the cross.

His mission of the cross at first threw his disciples and those around him into confusion and desperation. When he revealed his intention to face the final ordeal of his ministry in Jerusalem, Peter was completely taken aback. Peter 'took him (Jesus) by the arm and began to rebuke him: "Heaven forbid!" he said, "No, Lord, this shall never happen to you." '[10] Jesus must also have disappointed those who welcomed him with great enthusiasm at his triumphant entry into Jerusalem. There is something to be said for the view that Jesus Christ 'was convinced that it was his duty to announce the coming Kingdom in his country's capital and to try to force a decision there for or against its demands. Such a motive might account for the public nature of his entry into the city . . . and for his act in purging the Temple.'[11] But it was debatable whether Jesus really intended to force his contemporaries to accept the ethic of love which constitutes the cornerstone of the Kingdom.

Be that as it may, we want to stress that the mission of the cross proves to be the ultimate fulfilment of what the mission of the exodus stands for, namely, deliverance from social, economic and political bondage. The mission of the cross makes it possible for the coming into being of new men and women becoming instrumental in a reshaping of a social order based on the ethic of love envisioned for the Kingdom of God. A most spectacular example of this is to be found in the new type of community that emerged among the first converts to the Gospel. At least among this group of converts under the leadership of the Apostles, the traditional order of society and conventional structure of economy were temporarily suspended. According to the account in the Book of Acts, the earliest Christian community was started on a communal basis:

> All whose faith had drawn them together held everything in common: they would sell their property and possessions and make a general distribution as the need of each required.[12]

Presumably, this sort of communal life lasted only for a short period of time. Without completely committing oneself to the vision of the new man in the new Kingdom, it is not possible to put all of one's possession and energy for the service of other people. This is illustrated by the episode of a man by the name of Ananias and his wife who kept to themselves part of the proceeds from the sale of their property. They had to pay with death the penalty of violating the law of the communal life.[13] Despite such an unfortunate incident of which there must have been a few in the primitive church, there was no question about the fact that the mission of the cross was intended to be the most radical force through which man might be delivered from various forms of human bondage to the freedom of God's love. On account of this, the cross became the hope of a new world order.

Inherent in the cross, therefore, is the germ of revolution that begins with man himself and extends to the system, structure and environment which define human society. Inspired by this revolutionary spirit of the cross, which seeks freedom in personal and extra-personal relationships, countless men and women, both inside and outside the Christian church, have dedicated their lives to humanity. We thus do not entirely agree with the view which sees no validity in the 'claim that all modern revolutions are essentially Christian in origin, and this even when their professed faith is atheism.'[14] By disagreeing with such a view, we are not saying that all revolutions can be literally traced back to the Bible. But the revolution which stands for the freedom, equality and basic human rights of man is not possible without direct or indirect influence of the spirit of the cross. In a case such as communism which has now found, outside Eastern Europe and Russia, a new home in China with its distinctively Chinese flavour, we see a revolutionary force which brings into being a ruthlessly secular version of a new social order. In the words of van Leeuwen,

> Communism is a Christian 'heresy' which has achieved independence and stands, as it were, on its own authority. It is a counter-church; and its typically heretical character consists in its having fastened, with fanatical single-mindedness and in necessary and fully justified protest against a prevalent bourgeois version of Christianity, upon a *partial* truth which it exalts into the one complete exclusive and infallible dogma at the expense of all other aspects and points of view. This fixation stifles . . . the free play of the revolutionizing powers secreted in God's proclaimed word.[15]

To say that communism is a Christian heresy is nothing new. But the realization that it has a substantial relation, although in a negative way, to 'the revolutionary powers secreted in God's proclaimed Word' should urge us to examine carefully the life-style of the church in a capitalist society. Especially in Asia such a self-examination of the church will have very important implications for Christian mission.

It is accurate to say that the church in Asia brought into existence by Western Christian mission failed on the whole to come to grips with the meaning of the exodus. She exhibited a strong tendency to spiritualize and allegorize the mission of the exodus both in the Old Testament and the New. The result is that the social, economic and political implications were set aside. For Christians in Asia the exodus had to do with sin, moral and religious. The 'new' man that came into being as the result of the exodus from sin simultaneously made his exodus from the world. To them, the exodus became an allegory, having no real impact on the social contexts in which the 'new' man continues to live. In this way, the place of the new man in the construction of a new social order disappeared.

It goes without saying that the prophetic role of the church under such circumstances is seriously impaired. The church in Asia has definitely become a priestly church. Her major concern is how to cater to the spiritual needs of individual Christians. She completely fails to realize that Jesus Christ intended to bring about a radical change of social order through a radical change of individual men and women. Conversion, or a radical change, is never meant to be a merely private matter fulfilling the so-called spiritual needs. It is a radical change which happens to a man, but this change is to entail change in interpersonal and social relationships as well. Thus, conversion is not simply a personal affair. It should be a social event contributing to the emergence of a new social order. Here is a basic theological reason for Christians to become involved in the struggle for peace, freedom and equality. In the following section, we want to discuss how the black people in America have woven the exodus theme into their efforts to overcome oppression from the predominantly white community. This will be a case study enabling us to see the relevance of the exodus theme for the contemporary world.

2. The Black Experience of the Exodus

The experience of the exodus does become alive and real for the black people in the United States. In order to bring this experience to the level of articulate consciousness for the black people in general, black theologians have exploited the biblical theme of the exodus to the full. To many of them, the exodus is the greatest event in the whole message of the Bible which has closest and most relevant bearings on their situation today in America. They, therefore, not only attempt to interpret the Bible in the light of the theme of the exodus but also to weave it into the texture of black consciousness. For them, God is the God of the exodus from the house of bondage in Egypt in the historical sense. At the same time, God is the God who stands on their side in their struggle to be liberated from white oppression. Hence, they see a remarkable parallel between the people of Israel in ancient days and the black people in twentieth century America. It is very seldom that we see a biblical theme so closely linked with an existential situation as this one. For those who are interested in the problem of theological hermeneutics, black theology provides a case study. But this is not our principal concern here. Our chief interest here is to examine the meaning of the black experience of liberation on the basis of the mission of the exodus we discussed in the foregoing pages.

The black theologian most articulate in relating the biblical experience of the exodus to the experience of the black people in America is James Cone. For him, theology is 'that discipline which seeks to analyse the nature of the Christian faith in the light of the oppressed.'[16] Such a definition of theology is quite a departure from the traditional approach to the exposition of the contents of Christian faith. In traditional theology the condition of man to which Christian faith addresses itself is that of sin. It is the sinful nature of man that constitutes the main burden of the message of salvation. Consequently, the doctrine of sin occupies a central place in the Christian understanding of man. When such a theological understanding of the nature of man is translated into the practical aspect of religious life, asceticism, moralism or puritanism becomes a predominant feature in the practice of Christian faith. The history of the Christian church gives us ample examples of how one-sided emphasis on the sinful state of man may be carried to the extremes of legalism. Instead of enjoying new found freedom in the love of God, man becomes a captive to the self-imposed bondage of the law. Martin Luther's experience of justification by faith is a dramatic example of how man needs to be emancipated or liberated from the bondage of religion. In this aspect, Christianity shares much in common with other world religions.

Christian mission is thus considered and carried out almost solely as the mission effecting conversion from the darkness of sin. People are challenged to repent of their sins, sins conceived morally. The Christian community made up of such converts cannot but become a spiritually introverted community. When they venture into the outside world, it is for the purpose of snatching repentant sinners away from this sinful world to join the community of saints. Thus, Christian mission tends to become uprooted from its messianic foundation and to take root in moral teachings. The challenge of faith becomes a demand of moral codes. Needless to say, such a tendency completely obscures other equally important, or perhaps more important, dimensions of the message of the Bible.

By relating the particular experience of being black in white America to the biblical experience of the exodus, black theology does succeed in becoming liberated from morbid preoccupation with sin and thus opens up a new dimension for theology and mission. To quote Cone again:

> . . . God's call of this people (Israel) is related to their oppressed condition and to his own liberating activity already seen in the exodus. *You have seen what I did!* By delivering this people from Egyptian bondage and inaugurating the covenant on the basis of that historical event, God reveals that He is the God of the oppressed, involved in their history, liberating them from human bondage.[17]

As in the ancient days when God was on the side of the people under Moses, enabling them to leave the land of oppression, so black thinkers such as Cone believe that God stands beside the black minority over against the white majority in their struggle for liberation from white oppression.

Cone pursues relentlessly and singlemindedly the black interpretation of the Christian faith based on the theme of the exodus.
With his characteristic pungent language he declares:

> If God has made the world in which black people *must* suffer,
> and if he is a God who rules, guides and sanctifies the
> world, then he is a murderer. To be the God of black
> people, he must be against the oppression of white people.[18]

Here is an existential issue which, to black people, is a matter of
life and death. If we believe that faith is a response to God who
acts in concrete historical situations, we then have in black theology a very genuine expression of that faith. That is why black
theology is radically different, in style at least, in the form represented by people like James Cone. It is a missionary theology
because it takes its rise not in the quiet sanctuary of the church
but in real concrete situations which black people in America are
facing today.

But liberation from oppression does not constitute the whole
experience of the exodus. The people of Israel, after having won
liberation from the land of bondage, had to press towards the land
of promise through the agonizing journey in the desert. As
Gayraud Wilmore has put it: 'The Egyptian captivity of the Jews,
the miraculous deliverance from the hands of the Pharaohs, and
their eventual possession of the land promised by God to their
fathers—this was the inspiration to which the black religionist
so often turned in the dark night of his soul.'[19] In other words,
redemption is not complete. until the promised land is reached
and won. For this reason, theological language of black theologians
must be translated into practical actions which will make manifest
the freedom which black people in principle have won.

Thus, we have had to witness the fact that both blacks and
whites in the United States have no alternative but to face the
reality of power squarely. Sentimentalism, charity and favourit-
ism must be cast aside in order that the cause of justice for the
oppressed may not be compromised. The Civil Rights Movement
under the leadership of Martin Luther King engulfed this nation
with cries for freedom, justice and equality. It was a radical form
of Christian mission which the black church leaders undertook
toward white America. The black experience of the exodus becomes inevitably embodied in black revolution. The pain of

revolution experienced by both blacks and whites is in reality the pain of the cross. It is deeply religious and spiritual, and it has its aim in the redemption of both blacks and whites from the sin of racism—the sin of abusively treating a certain group of mankind by another group, thus desecrating the creation of God. How true it is to say:

> Reconciliation must pass through the revolution of the cross . . . Reconciliation in the race issue has simply been translated as integration. Whereas the church should have recognized that integration which bypasses 'Black Power' demands means a resurrection without a cross.[20]

The church in America must bear the cross of black power before she may emerge out of the darkness of death as the church triumphant.

One of the dramatic expressions of black revolution was the appearance of James Formann in a number of white churches, claiming retribution money. He was armed with the Black Manifesto issued by the National Black Economic Development Conference in Detroit, Michigan on April 26, 1969. The Manifesto in part says:

> . . . we have been forced to come together because racist white America has exploited our resources, our minds, our bodies, our labour. For centuries we have been forced to live as colonized people inside the United States, victimized by the most vicious, racist system in the world. We have helped to build the most industrialized country in the world. We are, therefore, demanding of the white Christian churches and Jewish synagogues that they begin to pay reparations to Black people in this country. We are demanding $500,000,000—This total comes to fifteen dollars per nigger.[21]

This sounds all very monetary, but the intention of the Manifesto was to formulate 'a comprehensive strategy for the development of pride, unity and self-determination as the first step toward the orderly and intelligent control of the Black Community, its institutions, resources and skills.'[22]

What was the reaction of the white churches to the demands of the Manifesto? Was it viewed as the cross to bear in order

to reach reconciliation and resurrection? Or was it regarded as
a disturbance disrupting the worship service? William Stringfellow, attorney and lay theologian, remarks as follows:

> There is dismay (in the White churches and synagogues)
> because the direct implication of the reparations Manifesto
> is a challenge to the integrity of White worship and an
> exposé of those who still attend such worship while count-
> enancing the inherited and continuing alienation of the
> races in this land and in most of its churches.[23]

How dreadful it is to realize that Christians can lie at the very
heart of the practice of their faith, namely, worship. Worship
should be the visible expression of the relation between God's
love and man's response to that love. It should be a witness to
the reconciliation that takes place between God and man and
between man and man. For this reason, Jesus wants us to be
reconciled to our brothers and sisters before coming to lay our
gifts at the foot of the altar.[24] A Christian worship which denies
anyone on the grounds of his race, religion or profession is no
longer Christian. It amounts to a slap in the face of God who
loved the world so much that He sent His only Son to redeem it.

This is, in fact, one of the chief burdens of the prophets in
the Old Testament. Their vehement contentions are often directed
at the worship in the temple because it has become the height of
hypocrisy and lies. The religious activities of Israel have actually
become a burden to Yahweh. Listen to these words of Isaiah:

> Your new moons and your appointed feasts
>   my soul hates;
> They have become a burden to me,
>   I am weary of bearing them.[25]

The piety that we show at worship services is no guarantee of
our acceptance by God. In good prophetic tradition, Jesus Christ
tried to demonstrate this again and again in his dealings with
the pharisees and scribes. If a worship service is held with all
sorts of false pretensions, it can become our own condemnation.
Indeed, the judgment of God begins with the Christian church.
God judges the Christian churches through racial crises in the
States, in South Africa and elsewhere. God judges the Christian
churches in the communist dominated countries, especially in

China, because of their other-worldly oriented religion. God also judges the Christian churches in Asia through the resurgence of old religions and the emergence of new religions. And when the churches in Asia tenaciously cling to the out-dated contents and forms of missionary Christianity representing a particular period in the history of the Western church, God judges them by the invasion of secularism. The church, the Christian mission, which loses its sacramental nature and is thus entrenched in the dichotomy between word and act, is a dead church, a dead mission. It becomes the church and mission which perpetuates human interests alone and thus bears the name of Christ in vain.

It will not be incorrect to say that blacks in the States not only challenge the integrity of the white church but actually become the latter's conscience. Furthermore, this black revolution has a third world connotation, for it also challenges the integrity of the mission carried out overseas by the white church in the States. All in all, it is a challenge to the church and mission which shows more interest in updating statistics, conducting body counts, indoctrinating converts with dogmatical formulae than in really coming to grips with human problems. It is against this kind of church and mission that Bonhoeffer spoke in 1936:

> Because the church is concerned with God, the Holy Spirit and His Word, it is, therefore, not specially concerned with religion, but with obedience to the Word, with the work of the Father, i.e., with the completion of the new creation in the Spirit. It is not religious question or religious concern of any form which constitutes the church—from a human point of view—but obedience to the Word of the new creation of grace. In other words, the church is constituted not by religious formulae, by dogma, but by the practical doing of what is commanded.[26]

The plea of this martyred theologian is that the church must not allow herself to be undermined by the divorce of word and act. As soon as the divorce of word and act takes place in the church, the world ceases to take her seriously. The reason is simple. The church, whose words are not accompanied by deeds, becomes innocuous. Her mission becomes words without substance. It is a *religious* undertaking without existential meaning. Bonhoeffer wants the church to go beyond a mere religious institution.

It is true to say that Black Power in the United States has exposed the weakest point of the church which is primarily oriented to the needs and aspirations of white Christians. And together with this, there is the most vulnerable aspect of Western Christian mission. Thus, the Black Manifesto pointedly relates black oppression to colonization with military power. 'We are not threatening the churches', says the Manifesto:

> We are saying that we know the churches came with the military might of the colonizers and have been sustained by the military might of the colonizers. Hence, if the churches in colonial territories were established by military might, we know how deep within our hearts that we must be prepared to use force to get our demands. We are not saying that this is the road we want to take. It is not, but let us be very clear that we are not opposed to force and we are not opposed to violence. We were captured in Africa by violence. We were kept in bondage and political servitude and forced to work as slaves by the military machinery and the Christian church working hand in hand.[27]

This is a forceful and candid statement. Violence, which is negative use of power, is not glorified but acknowledged as a means of achieving liberation after other means have proved ineffectual and unfruitful. Here is a tragedy which repeats itself again and again in the history of mankind. There is, therefore, no use in just condemning violence. The church has to inquire why blacks are driven to violence and proceed to eliminate one by one those conditions which generate violence. In fact, violence is a desperate expression of those who feel that no ordinary means will bring back to them the integrity of being human.

Thus, the oppressed groups have to take fate into their own hands in order to be their own masters. This is a deeply spiritual problem involving life and death for those who find themselves in the midst of struggle for liberation. Very often the Christian church does not fully understand what is going on in such struggles. She fails to discern the spiritual forces at work to give birth to liberated men and women. The spiritual dimension of revolution often eludes her. Because of this, she tends to find excuses to continue her alliance with the *status quo*, to hold on to the security she has built up over the years and centuries, and to be the tacit collaborator of the powers that be. This is too easy a way out in a most difficult and demanding situation. Not only has the church in America often tended to take such an easy way out in her dealings with blacks, but her mission overseas has more often than not had recourse to it. Just to give an example, we may quote Paul A. Cohen who, in the cause of tracing the causes of Chinese anti-foreignism way back in 1860-1870, observes:

> . . . the missionary made his power felt on the local scene by abusing his treaty rights or by using them with a minimum of discretion. Catholic and Protestant missionaries accepted, at times with considerable delight, the application of force to obtain redress.[28]

It may not, therefore, be totally unjustifiable to say that the seed of Chinese anti-foreignism with its culmination in the period of the communist takeover was partly sown by missionaries themselves. It has to be stressed that the integrity of Christian mission, and that of the church for that matter, cannot be maintained if Christian mission forms alliance with the powers that be. Once again, we must remind ourselves of the prophetic spirit in the Old Testament which never loses its critical function in relation to the political and social establishments. When Christian mission departs from this prophetic spirit, it becomes less Christian. Although there is a danger of it becoming a cliche, it is still true to say that the communist rise to power in China is the judgment of God on Western Christian mission. Can we not also say that black power is the judgment of God on the white church in America?

3. Stride Toward Self-determination

The exodus, both that of Israel and of blacks in America, is a gigantic stride toward self-determination. It is a resolute rejection of an outward authority imposing its will on those without power and incarcerating them in bondage and servitude. It is a declaration of No to the power that exercises control over them and determines their fate. The courage to say No to those who hold power over one's life and death is the courage to assert one's humanity. By saying No, one comes to realize one's individuality over against others. As long as one shrinks back from saying No, one is still not a full person. And in so far as one is conscious of being a person, one is able to become a responsible member of society.

The exodus of Israel from Egypt is such a No to the Pharaoh and the Egyptian taskmasters. Under the leadership of Moses, the Israelites took the first step towards growing into full humanity. The exodus itself, namely, the departure from Egypt in defiance of the Pharaoh's objections, was a mere beginning. Although the subsequent long treks in the wilderness were to prove that the stride toward self-determination was far more difficult than anticipated by both Moses and those who followed him, nonetheless it was the course they had to take in order to become responsible members of humanity. Faced with heat, thirst, hunger and enemies, their courage to say No faded and their determination to march toward the land of promise wavered. They challenged Moses and said: 'If only we had died at the Lord's hand in Egypt, where we sat round the fleshpots and had plenty of bread to eat! But you have brought us out into this wilderness to let this whole assembly starve to death.'[29] But they had already reached the point of no return to the fleshpots of Egypt. They had no choice but to continue their long journey toward self-determination. It was in the course of this long tortuous journey that they grew into a coherent group of men and women with a vision of a common future. The foundation for the birth of a new nation was thus laid.

Furthermore, self-determination leads to self-fulfilment. We may put it differently and say, self-determination is a prerequisite of self-fulfilment. As long as a man is deprived of the right to determine his own destiny, there will be no self-fulfilment for him. He fulfils himself as he decides what to do and what not to do. He can speak of self-fulfilment only in so far as he can choose what to be and what not to be. Of course, this choice or this determination may not come easily. If has to be won, often with great difficulty and much struggle. A price has to be paid for the right of self-determination. The Israelites had to pay the price to win self-determination. They had to leave behind them the security of fleshpots, the security of a slave, nonetheless a security. They had to put up with extreme hardships in the wilderness. The threat of death was never far from them. But without paying these prices, there was no way for them to reach their destination, enabling them to enjoy self-fulfilment.

For the Israelites who took part in the exciting drama of the exodus, this self-determination/self-fulfilment component is expressed in their desire to worship God away from Egypt, the house of bondage. In his demands to the Pharaoh, Moses repeatedly said: 'Let my people go in order to worship the Lord.' For them self-determination/self-fulfilment is a religious act. It is a profoundly spiritual event which culminates in the act of worship. Worshipping God in the land of freedom is the integral part of the political and social struggle for liberation.

Self-fulfilment means, in part, the bringing out the best in a man in order to put it to the best possible use for which it is originally intended by God. Described in this way, self-fulfilment becomes extremely difficult, if not impossible, if a person lives in the state of bondage or oppression. His sense of justice has to be suppressed. His sensitivity towards basic human needs and aspirations is expected to go blunt. His love for his fellowmen is not allowed a free expression. In a word, he is expected to behave as less than a full person. That is why the oppression in a totalitarian state tends to bring out the worst in man. It thrives on the dark side of human nature. It is the self-fulfilment in an absolutely reverse sense.

We may side-track a little, but it has to be mentioned that here we seem to touch upon a very essential element in Christian worship. We would like to affirm that worship service should be the occasion to celebrate the self-fulfilment of believers in the love and grace of God. In the worship service the fact that we are children of God, that we are His own creatures, is affirmed and confessed. This is the basic element in human self-fulfilment. We can fulfil the meaning of our being precisely because we are created by God. We can see hope and future in our lives only because God has given it to us through Jesus Christ. There should be confession of our sins, repenting our failures in responding to the love of God. But the worship service cannot stop short at confession of sins and repentance of our failures. Worship service can become oppressive if it does not go beyond this. Indulgence in sins is bad, of course; but indulgence in exploiting sins, which is often done from the pulpit, is even worse. The church tends to turn inward toward herself when worship service is conducted in this way. She becomes an introverted church, busy fending off sins, both real and imaginary, coming from the outside world.

Evangelism, especially in its narrow sense of converting people into the fold of the fellowship of the repentant, often proves to be the opposite of the self-fulfilment just described. The way in which the evangelist pounces upon the audience by giving gruesome pictures of sin and hell becomes almost a threat to the integrity of man as God's creature. His assault on the sin of the world leaves little room for goodness, truth and beauty in God's creation. To make the matter worse, the sin that he attacks so vehemently is invariably related to the moral aspect. There is little attack on social injustice, the abuse of power by those in political power and the exploitation of the powerless, and so on. Thus, the picture or image of an evangelist in Asia, and perhaps in other parts of the world as well, is that of a moralist and not of a prophet in the Old Testament sense of the word. It goes without saying that this kind of evangelistic approach is the seed-bed of narrow sectarianism. It not only thwarts ecumenical co-operation among Christians of differing backgrounds, but also obstructs any meaningful contacts with men and women of other faiths. It also adopts a defensive attitude towards secularization. It responds negatively to the social changes brought about by the process of technological developments. It is no wonder that those who have close association with sectarian Christianity do not show much interest in the struggle for self-determination in which their fellowman is involved.

For the church and the Christian mission to break out of this self-imposed sectarian restriction, what is needed is an articulate theological expression with regard to the subject of self-determination and self-fulfilment as an essential part of God's design for man. In the contemporary scene, this kind of theological articulation is provided most unequivocally by black theology. This we have already shown in the previous pages as we dealt with the black experience of the exodus. Let us bring to a sharper focus at this point the attempt of black theology to probe into the basic problem of human destiny.

For some black theologians the very first step in coming to grips with self-determination and self-fulfilment is the acceptance of what one is as a black person. This is a very legitimate and logical step. If one denies the very self which constitutes one's own being, it will be contradictory to speak of the determination of this self or the fulfilment of this self. As the center of consciousness and being, the self must be the starting point. Deotis Roberts, another black theologian, is thus right when he says:

> Blackness is a fact of life for the Negro. It is a given. It must be accepted—it cannot be ignored, escaped or overcome. Acceptance of blackness is the only healthy stance for the black man. In Tillichian language, 'he must have the courage to be black.'[30]

Basically this statement has its grounds in the theological understanding of the relation between God and man in and through Jesus Christ. God's dealing with man in Christ begins with the acceptance of man by God; and in accepting man, God wants him to accept himself. Jesus Christ is the most radical expression of what takes place between God and man. Jesus Christ, though representing God, though being of the divine nature, becomes and is one of us, literally one of us. Without his acceptance of man, there will be no salvation, no restoration of relationship between God and man, and between man and man.

But acceptance can mean for some people resignation, the rationale being that since this is the fact of life, you have to accept it. There is not much that you can do about it. But this is not the theological meaning of the word acceptance. Nor does Roberts advise his fellowman to accept blackness as a fact of life and resign himself to it. That is why he goes on to say:

> One of the most wholesome and positive aspects of the black revolution is the assertion that 'black is beautiful' and that we should seek 'black pride'.[31]

This is the acceptance of life with meaning for the present and hope for the future. The quality of beauty and pride here is not to be simply understood aesthetically or ethically. It is a quality that gives black men and women confidence of being equal partners with others in the human community. Lacking this confidence, it will probably be difficult for them even to accept the love of God. There would always be nagging questions in their minds: Does God truly love me as He does others such as the white man? What kind of place do I have in the providence of God? But perhaps the most depressing question will be this: Why has God made me so?

Herein consists the essence of black Christian mission, if we may coin a term in line with terms such as black theology or black power. The primary task of black Christian mission is to be actively engaged in the effort to make beauty and pride an integral part of black consciousness. It would be irrelevant and harmful even for evangelists addressing themselves to a black audience to dwell on the subject of sin as the one single important issue. The morbid fear of sin especially in its moral aspect only serves to make one retreat farther into the secret corner of one's heart where anxiety and uncertainty are harboured. This does not mean that the word sin should be dropped from the vocabulary of Christian theologians. It does mean, however, that the concept of sin must be redefined in the light of the Bible and of the existential situations in which the concept is to be understood and communicated.[32]

Having taken the first step in accepting oneself as one really is, black theologians go farther in asserting the fulfilment of one's being as the goal of their endeavours. Thus, we are told:

. . . freedom is not doing what I will but becoming what I should. A man is free when he sees clearly the fulfilment of his being and is thus capable of making the envisioned self a reality.[33]

For black theologians such as Cone, the self thus envisioned is not an abstract concept without reality. Nor is it a utopian picture of a man of perfect virtues. There is no actual counterpart of such a man in the real world. What black theologians are after is a black man who is fully conscious of humanity and who demands the white man to recognize his full humanity. Therefore, Cone continues to tell us that:

As long as man is a slave to another power, he is not free to serve God with mature responsibility. He is not free to become what he is—human.[34]

In other words, the givenness called blackness provides the framework of meaning for black people to be human. It is through his blackness that a black person may come to grips with his own humanity and come into touch with humanity as a whole. Consequently, to accept blackness as the givenness in God's creation and to be human amounts to one and the same thing for him. If he refuses to accept his blackness and escapes it, he will be in fact refusing his own humanity and escaping it.

It is on these grounds that the mission carried out among the black people must be criticized and appraised. For instance, it is said of missions in the inner city: '. . . when one looks into the work which was performed, one sees, until the very recent past, no concern for or appreciation of the religious background of the people of the inner city and no development of relationships with the black churches of the ghetto. Black religion was to be upgraded; that is, made to conform to mainstream white Christianity and the models had more of a relationship to Greenwich Village than Harlem or Georgia.'[35] This is exactly what happened also in Asia and elsewhere in the Third World. The uniformity thus created was to give rise to the problem of identity for Christians surrounded by non-white culture. It has also made it necessary for the church in the Third World to be dependent on the Western church for her well being. It is of interest to realize that the black church in the States had to agonize over the same problem besetting the church in Asia.

In view of this situation, the mission of the black church must be quite different from that of the Western church. It consists of

> the task of making black life more human, of getting black people to accept their acceptance, and of helping to bring into existence mature, authentic black persons.[36]

We cannot agree more with this statement. It will be utterly wrong to criticize it as being humanistic and therefore contradicting the main thrust of Christian mission. Such a criticism is entirely beside the point. For one thing, the concept of Christian mission under which Western missions operated, especially that of conservative trends, has no normative claim over the form and content of Christian mission in the contexts of the Third World, including the black church in the United States. In fact, conscious effort is now being made to come up with a different concept and practice of Christian mission which will depart essentially from the traditional one. In the light of this, the concept of the task of the church implied in the statement just quoted is a viable one in the life and historical contexts of the black people.

The statement is not only existentially viable. It can also be defended theologically. Humanity is the basis on which the relation between God and man becomes possible. This seems to be one of the implications of the biblical insight which sees man as created in the image of God. It is a well-known fact that Karl Barth speaks of the humanity of God in his later theology. Although he insists that this is by no means a diversion from his Christocentric theology, it does indicate that he has come a long way from his earlier theological career in which the qualitative difference between God and man was his major theological emphasis. Applied to our discussion here, the humanity of God seems no other than the image according to which God created man. Man, therefore, differs from other animals in that he is endowed with this humanity. And it is by means of this humanity that he is able to communicate with God. The communion between God and man becomes possible on the basis of this humanity.

Does it not follow that the most essential task of Christian mission consists in helping people to regain their humanity and to become human? Does this not mean that for Christian mission to become actively involved in redressing the conditions which deny full humanity to certain people because of their race, colour, or social status is part and parcel of the ministry of the church? Is it not obvious that as long as oppression exists, there are people who are deprived of the basis on which they can be in communion with God?

In addition, humanity is the bridge which relates not only man to God but also man to man. Interpersonal relationship is not possible without this humanity. The political power and social system which uses coercion and oppression to control people poses a serious threat to the humanity of man. That is why interpersonal relationships are most easily disrupted in a dictatorial country. Under such circumstances, suspicion takes the place of trust, faithfulness is replaced by treachery and truth is confused with falsehood. This reinforces our belief that the Christian mission must begin by removing obstacles to humanity such as this.

This analysis has shown beyond the possibility of doubt that the traditional concept of Christian mission is no longer relevant.

Perhaps we may go so far as to say that it has misrepresented the basic understanding of the task of the church. Thus, there is every justification for saying that

> Christianity cannot rob the black man of his blackness unless it desires him to be something less than a man. The black church and black theology thus seeks to permit the black man to be both black and Christian.[37]

It is self-evident that this blackness of the black man, namely, his humanity, does not merely mean the colour of his skin. In blackness is embodied the whole past history of the slavery a black man went through individually and corporately. It stands for the whole of culture built on the basis of that history. Furthermore, blackness represents the future hope of the black man and his community. Christianity must speak to this blackness. Any form of the work of the church which belittles this blackness becomes irrelevant. It betrays the soul of the black man.

The same quest for identity has been going on in Asia and in other parts of the Third World for quite some time already. Only it has not come out in forceful and blunt statements such as the ones we have been quoting from black theologians. The basic issue is the same, although historical circumstances and existential situations differ greatly. It amounts to this: Christian mission must seek to permit the Asian to be both Asian and Christian. This requires the church in Asia to give up all her heritages, precious though they may be, that hinder her search for identity. She must seriously question the validity of her relationships with the Western churches maintained through Western personnel and financial assistance. These relationships are becoming more fragile than before. This is all to the good both for the church in Asia and the church in the West. They must make every possible resistance to strengthening these relationships on the old basis. In fact, in order for new relationships to come into existence, the old relationships must be broken. This is precisely what black Christians try to do through their theological effort. Theirs is a resolute No to the Christian heritage thrust upon them by the white church. They rightly insist that they cannot build the new structure of faith and life on the basis of the old. The new wine needs new wineskins.

However, this critical approach to the Christian heritages is only one aspect of the task in the quest for identity. Another important, and perhaps more important, aspect of the question is that of culture to which one is born. Thus, the black Christian's search for identity plunges him into black culture. The black Christian's identity can be genuine only if it comes out of ·his deep experience of what it means to be black in the white society. Not only this, it can be found only when he permits himself to be involved in struggles that may usher in a new day for his own people. Black theology, therefore, cannot but take on a revolutionary tone. It will be a mistake to think that the revolutionary and militant tone of black theology is the result of the black theologian's frustration with the black man's situation in America. Let us quote Moltmann just to show that such judgment on black theology is not true. He says:

> . . . the missionary proclamation of the cross of the Resurrected One is not an opium of the people which intoxicates and incapacitates, but the ferment of new freedom. It leads to the awakening of that revolt which in the 'power of the resurrection' . . . follows the categorical imperative to overthrow all conditions in which man is a being who labours and is heavily laden.[38]

We cannot lightly speak of 'overthrowing all conditions in which man is a being who labours and is heavily laden,' for this is a highly revolutionary statement. We just cannot empty it of all social and political implications and fill it with a harmless spiritual interpretation. Let us face it. The cross is a revolutionary event. It literally seeks to overthrow those conditions which enslave man. How can the theology which seeks to interpret the meaning of the cross be anything but revolutionary?

The quest for identity has, needless to say, its fertile field in arts also. Consequently, black theologians endeavor to read theological meaning in cultural expressions of black consciousness. What Preston Williams says about the phenomenon of 'soul'[39] is very revealing:

> Soul is the constant feeling of one's two-ness, of being a part yet not being a part. It is a warring of two thoughts, two ideals, two unreconciled strings within one dark body. Soul is the expression of both the black man's freedom and

his bondage. It is a spontaneous and free response to life. Yet also the stolid-stoical response to a fate one can barely endure and from which one can never fully escape. Soul catches up both the heroism and the pathos of black life, its frenzies of joy and its sullen dark sorrow.

Soul is elusive and vague, it is contradictory and confusing: it is the heart and marrow of black existence. When then the black church/black theology phenomenon gave expression to soul it was affirming the black man's right to be himself.[40]

Does this interest of black theology in soul not indicate that any cultural expression can be the subject of theological reflection? Can we not draw a conclusion here that the richer one's cultural creation is, the fuller the content of theology would be? Therefore, theology done outside a particular cultural context is a poor theology. It is an abstraction separated from the dramas of the real life. For the church in Asia, as well as for the black church in America, we need to bring into existence the kind of theology firmly rooted in a particular culture. Christian mission not predicated on theological reflection on culture often becomes anticultural. The divorce of Christian faith from culture has been the result of such Christian mission. In this event, faith has little implication beyond individual men and women. They are peremptorily torn away from their living contexts and placed in a domain which has no vital relation to the reality of this world. The strength of black theology consists in its effort to reflect on the meaning of Christian faith in the living contexts of black people. If black theologians persevere in this effort, they will be able to come up with creative alternatives not only in doing theology but also in applying Christian faith to their social and cultural situations.

REFERENCES

1. Th. C. Vriezen, *An Outline of the Old Testament Theology*, second edition, revised and enlarged. Oxford: Basil Blackwell, 1970, p. 193. Gerhard von Rad expresses the same view when he writes: 'Whenever it occurs, the phrase "Jahweh delivered his people from Egypt" is confessional in character. Indeed, so frequent is it in the Old Testament, meeting us not only in every page (down to Dan. 9:15), but also in the most varied contexts, that it has in fact been designated as Israel's original confession' (*The Old Testament Theology*, Vol. I, The 'Theology of Israel's Historical Traditions', translated by D. M. Stalker, New York: Harper and Brothers, 1962, pp. 125-126).

2. Matthew 2:15.

3. Exodus 5:1; 7:16; 8:1; 8:20; 9:1; 9:13; 10:3.

4. Jack Finegan, *Let My People Go*, 'A Journey Through Exodus', New York: Harper and Row, Publishers, 1963, p. 59.

5. Amos 3:1-2.

6. Luke 4:18-19.

7. Luke 4:21.

8. Matthew 5:39-42.

9. According to W. D. Davis, this is the ethic of a new order. In his words: 'A new order has come—an order when God's grace is revealed and fully given. This new order is, in one sense, a return to the primordial will of God in creation, to his pure will uncorrupted by the necessities of history, by the disobedience of man. And this will of God imposes a demand for grace. To receive the Kingdom is to know also the demand of the Kingdom. To be forgiven is to know the demand to forgive. This is the real absolution of the moral teaching of Jesus—it is a call to those who have received grace to show grace (*Invitation to the New Testament*. New York: Doubleday and Company, 1966, p. 195).

10. Matthew 16:22-23.

11. John Knox: *The Death of Christ*, New York: Abingdon Press, 1958, p. 119.

12. Acts 2:44-45.

13. Acts 5:1-6.

14. Hannah Arendt, *On Revolution*, New York: The Viking Press, 1963, p. 18.

15. Arend Th. van Leeuwen, *Christianity in World History*, p. 344.

16. James H. Cone, *A Black Theology of Liberation*, Philadelphia and New York: J. B. Lippincott Company, 1970, p. 18.

17. *Ibid.*, pp. 18-19.

18. James Cone, *Black Theology and Black Power*, New York: The Seabury Press, 1969, pp. 124-125.

19. Gayraud S. Wilmore, *Black Religions and Black Radicalism*, New York: Doubleday and Company, 1972, p. 52.

20. J. Christian Beker, 'Biblical Theology Today,' in *New Theology*, No. 6, edited by Martin E. Marty and Dean G. Peerman, London: The Macmillan Company, 1969, p. 31.

21. *Black Manifesto*, edited by Robert S. Leeky and H. Elliot Wright, New York: Sheed and Ward, 1969, p. 119.

22. Gayraud S. Wilmore, *op. cit.*, p. 280.

23. William Stringfellow, 'Reparations: Repentance as a Necessity to Reconciliation,' in *Black Manifesto*, p. 52.

24. Matthew 5:23–24.

25. Isaiah 1:14.

26. Dietrich Bonhoeffer, *The Way to Freedom*, letters, lectures and notes 1935-1939, translated by Edwin H. Robertson and John Bowden, New York: Harper and Row, 1966, p. 48.

27. *Black Manifesto*, pp. 125f.

28. Paul A. Cohen, *China and Christianity*, the Missionary Movement and the Growth of Chinese Anti-foreignism 1860-1870, Harvard University Press, 1963, p. 128.

29. Exodus 16:23.

30. J. Deotis Roberts, 'Black Consciousness in Theological Perspective,' in *Quest for a Black Theology*, edited by James J. Gardiner and J. Deotis Roberts, Philadelphia: A Pilgrim Press Book, 1971, p. 64.

31. *Ibid.*

32. James Cone has attempted a redefinition as follows: 'If we are to understand sin and what it means to black people, it is necessary to be black and also a participant in the black liberation struggle. Because sin represents the condition of estrangement from the source of one's being, for black people this means a desire to be white and not black. It is the refusal to be what we are. Sin then for black people is the loss of identity' (*A Black Theology of Liberation*, p. 190).

33. James Cone, *Black Theology and Black Power*, New York: The Seabury Press, 1969, p. 39.

34. *Ibid.*

35. Preston N. Williams, 'The Ethics of Black Power,' in *Quest for a Black Theology*, p. 86.

36. *Ibid.*, p. 87.

37. *Ibid.*, p. 88.

38. Jürgen Moltmann, 'Toward a Political Hermeneutics of the Gospel,' *Union Seminary Quarterly Review*, Vol. XXIII, No. 4 (Summer, 1968) pp. 313-314. Quoted by James Cone in *Black Theology and Black Power*, p. 37.

39. 'Soul, as expressed in Afro-American music is hardly definable in any clear, literal sense. To be sure the complexity of this concept is as complex as the Afro-American life-experience itself. Soul music is reflective of that complex experience. And as evasive as it may be, it is easily identified in all the musical forms which blacks have generated. It resides in so-called jazz, gospel, rhythm and blues, rock and roll. Soul is by its nature, a reality manifested in visceral experience and continues to defy rational containment'—M. William Howard, Executive Director, Black Council, Reformed Church in America.

40. Preston N. Williams, *op. cit.*, p. 84.

CHAPTER SIX

From Bondage to Freedom

> It is well to repeat constantly that man is a being who is full of contradictions and that he is in a state of conflict with himself. Man seeks freedom. There is within him an immense drive towards freedom and yet not only does he easily fall into slavery, but he even loves slavery. Man is a king and a slave.[1]
>
> —*Nikolai Berdyaev*

1. Great Movements Toward Liberation

THE Christian mission is the mission of the exodus. It is the mission which leads men and women from bondage to freedom. This is the main theme of our discussion in the previous chapter. We also attempted to show how black theologians in the United States contemporized the biblical event of the exodus and read its meaning in the light of their historical and existential situations.

For us, therefore, the exodus is more than a metaphor. It is an event that can happen to us too. And in so far as it happens to me in the course of my life, it is historical. It is historical not only because it happened to the Israelites in the Egyptian bondage but because it can be a reality which transforms my being in relation to God and other people. We cannot, therefore, let the exodus have no more than a metaphorical meaning.

The exodus in our present day is expressed in various forms of liberation. In liberation we encounter the exodus in a global dimension. The exodus is no longer an experience limited to a certain group of people or a certain nation. It is a global phenomenon involving most of the nations in the world. Furthermore, the exodus is seen not only in a strictly political arena in which people struggle to be liberated from tyranny and servitude, but also in various sectors of human life in which oppression of one kind or another is practised. We can, therefore, rightly speak of the secular meaning of the exodus. Unless Christian mission in Asia comes to grips with this secular meaning of the exodus, it will not be able to become creatively and redemptively involved in the destiny of Asian peoples.

Liberation is thus the great spiritual movement of our day. Whatever forms it may take, it represents the assertion of the human spirit over against any form of coercion, oppression and dehumanization. This is the glory of man endowed with the spirit. Physically and physiologically man shares much in common with other animals. It is the spirit that makes him stand up and stand out in the animal world. The authors of the more primitive version of the creation of man in the second chapter of Genesis are at pains to stress this distinctive quality of man. It is said that God 'breathed into his nostrils the breath of life' so that man became a living being. It is through the spirit of God that man gains his identity in God's creation.[2]

The word spirit both in Hebrew (*ruach*) and in Greek (*pneuma*) etymologically means wind. It is closely associated with the concept of power. It is this *ruach* of God that 'swept over the face of the abyss'[3] to turn the chaos into the ordered universe. Those who have experienced the terror which typhoons can inflict on nature and man know well the power of the mighty wind. The wind that rages in fury through space when a typhoon strikes is the power that will not permit anything in its way to stand intact. The Spirit of God is, of course, not such a destructive power. It is the power that constructs and builds up. Even if it may have to destroy and tear down, it does this for a reconstruction of man and his world. In receiving a call to be a prophet on the eve of the fall of Judah, Jeremiah heard God address him saying: 'I put my words into your mouth. This day I give you authority over nations and over kingdoms, to pull down and to uproot, to destroy and to demolish, to build and to plant.'[1]

It is this Spirit of God in man that makes man God's coworker in the creation. He is ordered to tend his inhabited world. He is to see that order is maintained. Moreover, his spirit becomes embodied in the work of his hands. In arts, science and technology, the creative spirit of man has its dynamic expression. It is true to say that the history of culture is the history of how man's creative spirit tries to bring into concrete forms the mystery of God's creation.

But the spirit of man is not an unlimited power. This can be a source of frustration and a man may misuse his limited power as if it were unrestricted and uninhibited. Consequently, the spirit in man agitates to burst open the frame of man with its limitations in space and time. The story of the Fall in Genesis 3 can thus be viewed as the conflict of man against himself in an effort to break out of the frame of space and time to which he is ordained. In doing so, he realizes that the ordering of the creation under which he has to live is the ordering of none other than God. This realization makes him rebel against God. He begins to question the legitimacy of God's injunction with regard to the fruits of the tree planted in the midst of the garden. Eventually, he decides to defy that injunction. He takes the fateful step by stretching out his hand to pluck the forbidden fruit. He wants to become like God. The limitations ordained for his benefit become unbearable to him. He finally reaches the point where he must take his fate into his own hands.[5]

This is the tragedy of man as a being endowed with the Spirit of God. The height of the glory of man as a spiritual being proves to be at the same time the height of the tragedy of man fallen victim to his own spirituality. That is why great tragedies in both Eastern and Western literary history cannot but touch us to the core. They are the product of the deeply troubled human spirit—the spirit that defies in vain the limitations of space and time as part of his being. Due credit must be given to the biblical writers for bringing out into the open this basic ambiguity in the nature of man. In man his glory as the creature of God and his tragedy as the victim to his own spirituality reside unreconciled. We are reminded of what Sarte, the French existentialist, has said: 'Man is free . . . is condemned to be free.'[6] Undoubtedly, this stresses the fact that freedom is part and parcel of man's being. Without freedom man ceases to be fully man. But at the same time, the fact that freedom is not there readily available, that it has to be fought for and won, indicates the limited and ambiguous nature of the freedom man possesses.

Another important insight into the nature of man's freedom can be gained from the Genesis story of the fall. It is this: man too often gains his freedom at the cost of those related to him. Man gains freedom from God by putting God into question, challenging His sovereignty and thus jeopardizing the relationship with Him. The new-found freedom, instead of bringing man closer to God, makes him estranged from God. It is to this estranged situation that God comes in Jesus Christ. Man's pretension to freedom costs God His only Son. In the cross, we see what a price God has to pay for the freedom man has striven to gain for himself. And in this act of redemption, God overcomes man's estrangement and bestows on man a new freedom.

At the horizontal level of human relationships, one man's freedom can be another man's enslavement. That is why tragic elements can never be absent in human society, even in the exalted moments of human accomplishments. Man actually lives on the border line between freedom and slavery. Why does freedom become such a self-contradictory reality in the life of man? What makes freedom turn into a form of slavery? There is much truth in what Berdyaev says about this paradoxical nature of man's existence. 'The fall of man', he writes, 'finds expression most of all in the fact that he is a tyrant. He is a tyrant, if not on a great scale, then on a small, if not in the state, if not in the pages of world history, then in his family, in his shop, in his office, in the bureaucratic establishment in which he occupies the very smallest position. Man has an unconquerable inclination to play a part and in that to assign a special importance to himself, to play the tyrant over those around him. Man is a tyrant not only in hatred but also in love. A man in love becomes a dreadful tyrant. Jealousy is a manifestation of tyranny in a passive form. A jealous person is an enslaver who lives in a world of fiction and hallucination.'[7] This is an observation which has much deep insight into human nature. Freedom is thus not a simple concept which can be easily transformed into a reality.

Despite the fact that the concept of freedom is itself not free from such an ambiguous and paradoxical nature, we must acknowledge that it constitutes the basic yearning of the spirit of man. A man without this yearning is a castrated man who is deprived of the ability to live a full life. He becomes a spiritless man and condescends himself to the sub-human level. It is, therefore, with real excitement that we have witnessed the phenomenon of liberation movements which have come to enjoy great fruition after World War II. These movements are mainly political in nature.

Both domestically and internationally they express the assertion and claim of political power made by the oppressed groups over against the oppressing groups. In these political movements, the indomitable spirit of man not to submit itself to oppression comes to assert itself. Therefore, liberation movements must not be viewed and evaluated only in terms of success or failure in relation to the struggle for political power. Their full significance has not been appreciatively and properly assessed until they are seen in the light of change that has come over to the people involved in the movements. And together with the change in man, we will do well to probe deeply into the fundamental changes that have taken place in social structures and social behaviour. In other words, liberation movements give rise to new understanding of man and new forms of society. In this case, China provides a most fascinating example. By way of illustrating our analysis here, we can quote John Saar, *Life* journalist, who, after his visit to China with the American Table Tennis Team, makes the following remark: 'Here was an Asian nation that owed nothing to anybody, and in consequence one looked them in the eye and they looked you right back. They seemed very content within themselves, content with their lot and sure of themselves, knowing where they are going.'[8] Here is a most outstanding example of the effect which liberation from feudalism and colonialism had on people and their society and their country. Any Christian mission which does not take full recognition of this fact is likely to make a horrible kind of blunder when it contemplates and plans mission work among the Chinese of this transformed nation.

In thus stressing the spiritual dimension of liberation movements, we have set the concepts such as liberation and freedom in theological contexts. The theological answer to liberation and freedom is neither an unconditional Yes nor a categorical No. This is based on theological understanding of the relative nature of the phenomenon of man and society. That is why the liberation movement is an on-going process. It is a forward movement which negates the old and brings the new into existence. It does not only negate others who pose as a corrupting and oppressing power structure. It also directs its negation to itself in an effort not to let what has been achieved become eroded from within by its own corruption. For this reason, Christians, though personally involved in liberation movements, must retain a transcendence that comes from the awareness that ultimately they do not serve liberation movements, but God, who through liberation movements, wants to bring into fulfilment the freedom He has in store for man. We have, therefore, the following statement from the Asian Ecumenical Conference for Development:

> Power is best used when it serves justice in the forward move-ment to the full liberation of man. All men have the need and the obligation to participate not only in the struggle for the liberation of man from all forms of oppression, exploitation and ignorance, but also in the positive effort to master all wisdom and power in love so that all may attain to the fullness of the liberty of the children of God.[9]

The key phrase in this statement is 'the fullness of the liberty of the children of God.' When Christians participate in liberation movements motivated, guided and directed by this phrase as the expression of their ultimate goal, their actions take on a confes-sional character. In other words, it is their confession of faith that is being expressed through social and political involvements. For them, the line between what pertains to their faith and what does not is removed. Undertaken with this theological under-standing of liberation movements, their social and political actions are as much evangelistic as evangelical rallies are. It is, therefore, imperative for the church in Asia to relinquish once and for all hesitancy and reluctance to become involved in 'world affairs', fearing that in so doing they may be compromising the Christian faith. Actually, the opposite should be the case. Their non-involvement can only make their confession of faith a lip-service, for how could people agree that God is the Lord of history when Christians would have little to do with historical events?

We have said that liberation movements, at their best, repre-sent the spiritual dimension of man's being in the world, as well as social economic and political dimensions. This is so because freedom for which man is to be liberated is the integral part of man's spirituality. Through liberation movements, man strives to throw away whatever yokes of oppression are placed on him and to be man in the fullest sense. Here Christians cannot help perceiving the impact of the power which transcends man's being on the process of world history. The divine spirit is at work in the depth of humanity. Rubem Alves has well said:

Only when freedom becomes historical through power, through an activity that changes concretely the subjective and objective conditions of history, is the history of bondage brought to a stop, thereby giving birth to the possibility of liberation. Through this activity, transcendence comes to the midst of life. And only as such, as a reality in the midst of life, is transcendence an element of the language of the community of faith, so it is determined by the historical experience of liberation.[10]

It is, therefore, obvious that Christian mission in the Third World cannot go on preaching the Gospel of freedom as if it has nothing to do with liberation movements. Dynamism of the biblical faith comes from the awareness that the world is the arena of God's activity, that the community of faith is the instrument through which God's will for love, justice and freedom is to be expressed. Without such dynamism, Christian mission becomes no more than practice in pious talks which, though having some effects on troubled souls, exerts no impact on the realities of life in the world.

Jesus Christ himself is the personification of this dynamism of the biblical faith. In the synagogue in Nazareth, he announces the beginning of his ministry by quoting from Second Isaiah:

> The spirit of the Lord is upon me because he has
> anointed me;
>
> he has sent me to announce good news to the poor,
> to proclaim release for prisoners and recovery of
> sight for the blind;
>
> to let the broken victims go free,
> to proclaim the year of the Lord's favour.[11]

It is by no accident that Jesus chose this passage to announce the inception of a totally new era. His own people lived under the colonial rule of the Roman Empire and were subject to political injustice and oppression. They needed to be liberated not only spiritually, healed physically, but also emancipated politically. Thus, justifiably he was looked upon by many as their liberator.

At the same time, nor is it by accident that Western Christian mission in the third world chose not to take seriously this manifesto of Jesus Christ. It did not help people to see the evil of oppression and injustice committed by colonialism on one hand and feudalism of national governments on the other. Very often it was under the protection and recognition of these latter that Western Christian mission went about conquering the souls of the so-called pagans. No wonder Jesus' message of liberation and freedom was not communicated, if not suppressed. The church in the West was to learn her mistake too late. As Moltmann has pointed out:

> . . . Christians are obligated to bring, with the Gospel and with their fellowship, the justice of God and freedom into the world of oppression. Men do not hunger for bread alone. In the most elementary way, they hunger for recognition and independence. Since the Church has limited itself to the forgiveness of moral and spiritual sins, the hope for justice wandered out of the Church and entered into revolutions for freedom. Many of the revolutions which today go through Africa, Asia and the Americas are declarations of independence.[12]

The church in the West was too slow and too reluctant to grasp the full meaning of this assertion of independence. But there is no excuse whatsoever for the church in the Third World, and especially in Asia, not to be part of struggles for independence and freedom. For this purpose, the church must be equipped with theological sensitivity to the conditions of political bondage and human oppression. She must teach impatience instead of patience in the face of powers that dehumanize people. Christians must be told that patience is not a Christian virtue when injustice is committed against those without power. In Asia today, Christians are very much in need of the courage to stand on the side of the oppressed, the powerless and the poor. In other words, she must find her place and role in the midst of revolution.

2. Christian Involvement in Liberation

Our argument that the church should be involved in liberation movements does not mean that we accept all that is done in the name of liberation and freedom. We cannot ignore the fact that liberation movements, just as any other human enterprise, contain in themselves seeds of corruption and danger, especially when they lose sight of lofty ideals with which the movements are launched.

Furthermore, like any other human activity there is nothing absolute and eternal about these movements. Without being fully aware of their limitations living and working in a finite spatio-temporal framework, those engaged in liberation movements may begin to absolutize what they believe and do. Thus, they will create contradictions which defeat the purposes they have set out to accomplish. We may cite the concept of absolute freedom as an example. My freedom presupposes the freedom of others. If my freedom is attained at the cost of the freedom of others, it is no longer freedom in the true sense. It becomes, in reality, despotism, the exact opposite of freedom. From this consideration alone there can be no blind involvement in liberation movements on the part of Christians. At the same time, this raises a question with regard to the role Christians should play in liberation movements on the part of Christians. In this section our purpose is to discuss some essential theological presuppositions in relation to efforts towards the achievement of liberation and freedom.

First of all, the biblical faith views God's intervention as essential for man's act of liberation to obtain soteriological character. This is the way the people of Israel look back upon the exodus and the subsequent events in their history. God's intervention is thus the fulfilment of man's desire for liberation. This is salvation in the historical sense. Salvation in the Old Testament is primarily related to deliverance from enemies. Salvation in the sense of deliverance from physical pain, moral failures and sins is secondary. This magnificent message of God's deliverance leading man to salvation is accentuated in many events highlighting Israel's contacts with other nations.

This points to the central emphasis of the biblical faith with regard to the role God plays in man's liberation from oppression and injustice. It is to be noted that the verb 'to deliver' in the Bible almost always has God as its subject. One prays to God to deliver one from one's enemy (Psalm 143:9). God assures Jeremiah that He will be with him to deliver him from danger (Jeremiah 1:8). Therefore, God is 'my rock, my fortress and my deliverer' (2 Samuel 22:2). It is this same God who has 'delivered us from the dominion of darkness and transferred us to the Kingdom of His beloved Son' (Colossians 1:13).[13] Theologically, we must, therefore, stress that man's effort towards liberation should be conceived in the context of the divine deliverance. Liberation which accepts God's intervention becomes God's act of deliverance, leading to real freedom. On the contrary, liberation which refuses to make room for God's intervention may become a deadly weapon in the hands of those who possess power and thus may easily turn it into an instrument of brutality and oppression.

To illustrate biblically what has been said above, let us return again to the story of the exodus. Moses, as the story of the exodus begins to unfold, first sought to take the liberation of his oppressed fellowmen into his own hands. It might be that he thought he was launching the first signal of the liberation movement when he killed the Egyptian beating a Hebrew. It was, however, not long before when he discovered that his self-styled leadership was not going to be accepted by his fellowmen without question. In fact, his leadership was challenged by his own people. 'Who set you up as an officer and judge over us?'[14] Without proper credentials he would not be accepted by his own people. But the time he spent in the wilderness taught him to recognize the hand of God in delivering his people from bondage to freedom. The repetition of the divine 'I' in Exodus 3:7-8 shows how this conviction grew firm in Moses:

> The Lord said, 'I have indeed seen the misery of my people in Egypt. I have heard their outcry against their slave-masters. I have taken heed of their sufferings, and have come down to rescue them from the power of Egypt, and to bring them up out of that country to a fine, broad land; it is a land flowing with milk and honey. . . '

In this way, the personal involvement of God in the history of a particular people is affirmed right from the beginning in Moses' expedition to lead his people out of the land of slavery to the land of freedom. In fact, the subsequent events of the exodus show that when the divine 'I' is lost sight of, or set aside, their stride toward freedom becomes infected with vested interests, vitiated with suspicion of leadership and hampered by an ugly power struggle.

Liberation without God is, therefore, blind. It confuses the means with the end. It loses sight of the dimension that brings meaning to one's struggle. It can become a form of idolatry, demanding blind obedience. It begins to dictate to people, allowing for no difference of opinion. To the leaders of liberation this means self-exaltation. Their power is enhanced. But to the masses of people this leads to self-debasement. Instead of leading to humanization, what is achieved is just the opposite, namely, dehumanization.

It appears that here we have a clue to the Christian understanding of revolution. Revolution becomes human necessity when it first of all becomes the divine necessity. Revolution becomes the divine necessity when certain basic things in relation to God's creation are seriously threatened. It is when man is dehumanized, when he is treated less than as the creature of God, that revolution becomes inevitable. To put it differently, when a social system dehumanizes man, it has to be challenged. When a particular ideology demands exclusive and absolute loyalty from man, it must be opposed. When economic factors are treated as solely determinative in relation to man's dignity and worth, they should be rejected. When a religious belief or practice leads to the unleashing of demonic forces in man, as in the case of inquisition, it ought to be negated. In all this, revolution, from the standpoint of Christian theology, must ultimately deal with man himself. Poverty, injustice, oppression and so on are symptoms of a corrupt social and world order. These have to be dealt with politically, economically and socially. Some radical measures may have to be employed to bring about the change. But unless the change also leads to the revolution of man himself, it will soon give way to corruption. And man can never get out of the vicious circle of constant revolutions.

It is, therefore, true to say that the ultimate goal of revolution should be the revolution of man himself, namely, a radical change in man in such a way that the structures of society will also be radically affected. As Jacques Ellul has well observed:

> Revolution is man himself. I believe that man comes into being through his revolutionary acts. By radically challenging the totality of his environment down to its structures and values, he enters upon a new existence and changes in the process of changing his environment.[15]

In the language of faith, this change in man is called conversion. Jesus Christ demands a radical change from his followers. It is a total demand because the whole person has to be involved in the change. Without a change of a radical nature in man, it will not be possible to see a new social order emerge out of the old. Thus, it should be stressed that Jesus Christ is no social reformer. He is the reformer of man, enabling men and women to leave behind them old values. A fundamental change in social structures can come into existence only when such a radical re-orientation in man has taken place.

The Christian role in revolution and liberation movements is to humanize the power held in the hands of revolutionaries and liberators. This means that the power must be commanded and used by those who have been made conscious of being under the sovereign power of God. It is only in this way that power can be kept from being abused and thus becoming a tool of tyranny. There can be nothing more dangerous than to put power in the hands of those who have chosen to ignore God. Theirs will be a blind power bringing about misery and destruction.

To humanize that power also means to regulate it for the purpose which God has ordained, namely, for the betterment and enjoyment of life within the ordering of God. Power in the hands of man must serve the purpose of God for mankind. When it becomes corrupted and begins to serve itself or serve the interests of those who hold power, it will deny God and dehumanize man. Moses' constant turning to God thus proves to be the redeeming factor for the army of liberation under his command. Man's liberation is in constant need of God who delivers him from his chief enemy, that is, man himself, from his pretensions, from his evil motivations, from the satanic power latent in each and every one of us attempting to be self-destructive and at the same time destructive to other people.

How it is then possible to humanize revolution? How can the power of liberation be used to humanize the structures of society? And how is it possible to bring about a radical change, a conversion, to a man in the middle of struggle for freedom and justice? Nestor Paz, a seminarian studying for priesthood and one of the seventy-five young men who organized a guerrilla force in the Bolivian jungle only to suffer death, had these words in his journal:

> . . . I want my capacity to love to increase with my ability as a guerrilla . . . that is the only way of qualitatively and quantitatively improving the revolutionary impulse.[16]

For an activist such as Nestor Paz engaged in revolution and guerrilla to the extent of suffering death, love would have been a most remote concept. And yet he sees in the love manifested in Christ the only way to give meaning to revolution. It is true to say that with the power of love Christ revolutionalized human relationships. And with the same power of love he revolutionalized the world order in which the justice of God would prevail. What we earlier called God's mission of enfleshment in Jesus Christ is the mission of love. There are demands and agonies in such love. But there is also joy because through it restoration of humanity as created by God becomes possible. And it is at this point that we seem to begin to understand and fathom the depth of Christ's injunction: 'Love your enemy!'

Christ's command to love one's enemy comes from the heart of God's deliverance. In fact, we are greatly conscious here of the limitation of human language. In the truly Christian sense of the word, love knows no enemy. It does not set boundaries around itself in the forms of religion, culture, nationality or ideology. Love with a boundary is not love, at least not the love with which Christ commands us to love our enemy. Christ is true to his own injunction right to the last moment of his earthly life. For those who nailed him on the cross, his prayer was the prayer of forgiveness. The cross is the external expression of God's internal anguish for man. God's love is His anguish and pain in saving action. Love and pain are integrally related. This love-pain constitutes the chief element of the Christian faith. Christian involvement in rèvolutionary activities should reflect this divine love-pain for the world. It is in the exercise of such love-pain that Christians can be free from partisan strifes and hatred.

The Christian revolutionary is the one who demands justice with love. One dominating concept in the contemporary world of revolutions is, of course, the concept of justice. People want justice in all levels of their lives. They cannot tolerate injustice, and rightly so. Poverty is economic injustice imposed on the poor by the rich. The loss of freedom is the political injustice committed by those in power against the powerless. Racism is cultural injustice perpetuated by those obsessed with the sense of racial superiority. And we see various form of social injustice existing in our world today by virtue of one's birth, profession and circumstances. The intent to commit injustice seems to be ingrained in human nature. It is the desire to take advantage of other people's weakness for one's own profit. Thus, injustice reflects the sinister aspect of man's nature. It has to be confronted, defeated or at least subdued. The society in which injustice gains the upper hand is not only hell for those who live in it but also an affront to God's creation. God is the God of justice. He cannot allow injustice to dominate the life of man and the course of history. That is why we have observed earlier that human revolutions often, though not always, reflect the divine necessity of revolution. The exodus was God's response to the injustice which the people of Israel were suffering at the hands of the Egyptians. Amos' calling was his answer to God's will to put to an end injustices committed in the northern Kingdom of Israel. It is the divine compulsion which forced Amos out of his life of seclusion and peace:

> The lion has roared; who will not fear?
> The Lord God has spoken; who can but prophesy?[17]

Then came these mighty words like a torrent from the mouth of the prophet:

> But let justice roll down like waters,
> And righteousness like an ever-flowing stream.[18]

There will be no peace in the world until the justice of God is done. Granted that the justice we achieve is relative justice, but the world is sustained by relative justice which has its root in the divine justice.

But the justice Christians are after must be the justice with love. As Reinhold Niebuhr has said, justice

> cannot exist without love and remain justice. For without the 'grace' of love, justice always degenerates into something less than justice.[19]

God Himself has demonstrated justice with love in the person and work of Jesus Christ. The justice of God demands that man be punished for his sin of disobedience against God. This would mean an end to man's existence. In the Old Testament the story of Sodom and Gomorrah and the account of the flood give us a picture of what it would be like if God's justice were to be carried out. But the message of the Bible is that the saving love always accompanies the execution of divine justice. Consequently, Jesus Christ is both God's justice and His love. In Jesus Christ, man is at once punished for his sin and saved by God's love. In this way, justice ceases to be merely a legal concept. Through the presence of love, justice is enriched and fulfilled. Thus, from the Christian point of view, love of justice must be expressed through the justice of love.

We can, therefore, begin to understand why people like Gandhi and Martin Luther King firmly advocated and practised non-violence. For the Indians to be freed from the long colonial rule, bloodshed seemed inevitable. But it was Gandhi who refused to resort to the use of force that eventually brought independence to India. It cost him his life, but in his life and death is reflected the mission of enfleshment culminated on the cross. It was the same with Martin Luther King. His struggle for freedom and justice on behalf of black people in America never deprived him of the capacity to love his white brothers and sisters. In his exhortation to his fellow black brothers and sisters, he had this to say:

> There will be no permanent solution to the race problem until oppressed men develop the capacity to love their enemies. The darkness of racial injustice will be dispelled only by the light of forgiving love. For more than centuries American negroes have been battered by the iron rod of oppression, frustrated by day and bewildered by night by unbearable injustice, and burdened with the ugly weight of discrimination. Forced to live with these shameful conditions, we are tempted to become bitter and to retaliate with a corresponding hate. But if this happens, the new order we seek will be little more than a duplicate of the old order. We must in strength and humility meet hate with love.[20]

These are not the words of an idealist. On the contrary, they come from a man who knew what it meant to be a black person in White America, a person who experienced the agony of social and spiritual injustices committed against him and his fellowman for no other reason than the colour of their skin being black, from a man who tasted the bitterness of jail for a crime he had not committed, and finally from a person who constantly faced death because of his conviction that all men and women, regardless of the colour of their skin, are created equal.[21] Love is the powerful force that transforms individuals and social conditions. It not only prevents a new-found justice from lapsing into injustice, but enriches it and makes it more durable. It humanizes justice in such a way that justice is serving people and people are not mere instruments to the system of justice. For Martin Luther King, therefore, non-violence is the only way to meet the injustice and hate that has enslaved him and his fellowman. Non-violence in this case is not a passive attitude towards injustice, oppression and enslavement. It is a positive spirituality filled with the power of love to bring about changes in man and in society. It is a categorical No to injustice, an imperative Yes to a new order of being in which justice prevails, and an indefatigable hope for the future of mankind in the Kingdom of God.

It is to be expected that for years to come the nations in Asia and those in the rest of the third world will press for more freedom and greater justice both nationally and internationally. In the midst of all this, there will be a greater concentration of power on a few politically and economically powerful people. This concentration of power will be done in the name of national security and stability.[22] Unlike in the past, people will no longer be fooled by this. There will continue to be unrest among the people who are deprived of their basic human rights. Inevitably, there will be more agitation for liberation. There will be a resort to arms, violence and destruction, for when people are driven to rebel, this seems to be the natural course of action for them to take.

What should the church do in such situations? What is her task as the community of faith committed to follow Jesus Christ? In a word, what is her mission? Of course, it is out of the question to side with the powers that be. She cannot be indifferent to the injustice that keeps the masses of people under the rule of terror. The church cannot escape the demand of her faith to stand with the masses in their struggle for justice, equality and freedom. But she cannot agree to the use of power that will bring bloodshed and instigate hatred. At the same time, she cannot be a silent witness to the tragedy which would destroy the very structure of justice which the people desperately seek to build.

The mission of the church should thus consist in providing the foundation of love on which, and on which alone, the meaningful and relatively durable structure of justice can be erected. The church, through her members, must be able to meet hate with love, to overcome suspicion with trust, to dispel despair with hope, and to bring life into the midst of the threat of death. The mission of the church in Asia is first to become herself. Such power of love then seeks ways to let this power of love become incarnate in the realities of day-to-day struggle towards justice, freedom and equality.

In the event of political and social turmoil, it is easy for the church to adopt one or the other of the following approaches: Either she goes all the way with the movements of liberation, even in extreme forms, losing all sense of critical judgment and redemptive function; or she shrinks back in trepidation, finding an excuse for her non-involvement in what professes to be her primary concern for saving the soul. The former attitude is that of Christian radicals, while the latter is that of Christian conservatives. Needless to say, neither option is tenable. The church should *be* the power of love, with her whole-hearted support for the quest and struggle for justice. At the same time, with her power of love, she should play a redemptive function among people, between the ruler and the ruled, the oppressor and the oppressed. The reality of evil in man, no matter whether he is the oppressing party or the oppressed party, dictates that this redemptive function through the power of love is indispensable in the emergence of a relatively sane, just and free society and world order. And who else is it but the Christian church endowed with the redemptive power of love by God through Jesus Christ which can make redemption a reality in this complex world in which conflicting interests militate against each other?

3. Freedom—God's Gift to Man

A theological analysis of revolution will not be complete until the concept of freedom is discussed from the Christian perspective. Man is born with an innate desire to be free. Freedom is an essential part of man. Thus, to be deprived of freedom is to be deprived of part of his nature. Liberation from bondage to freedom becomes, therefore, imperative, if man is to be truly man. But what is this freedom? Does the fact that he is born to be free mean that he has a capacity for freedom? Or does he receive freedom as a gift from someone?

The following statement tells us that freedom is not a gift. Man has the right to freedom. When he loses it, he has to fight to get it back.

> Freedom is not something you get as a present. . . You can live in a dictatorship and be free . . . on one condition: that you fight the dictatorship. The man who thinks with his own mind and keeps it uncorrupted is free. The man who fights for what he thinks is right is free. . . You cannot beg your freedom from someone. You have to seize it . . . everyone as much as he can.[23]

Freedom is often associated with such a militant note. It is perfectly understandable that it has to be this way. In a world in which freedom always goes with power, freedom is not attainable to those who do not possess power. The loss of freedom is the loss of power. To put it differently, you lose your freedom because you do not have enough power to keep it. Of course, the loss of physical freedom does not necessarily mean that your spiritual freedom is lost too. But in that case you still need to possess enough spiritual power to keep yourself free spiritually. Conversely, the fact that you have physical freedom does not automatically mean that you are in possession of spiritual freedom. Under a totalitarian society the citizens are all too often forced to forfeit their spiritual freedom in order to maintain their physical freedom. In a situation such as this, we often witness the crucifixion of truth, goodness and beauty.

Furthermore, since freedom is bound with power, you cannot receive it as a gift. If freedom is received as a gift, it is no longer freedom. For in a very subtle way, a gift of freedom disqualifies you from being yourself fully. It binds you to the giver of the gift in such a way that you are no longer free in relation to him. You capitulate yourself to him and to his power. Freedom thus has to be earned to be freedom. Revolution has its immediate aim in forcing the dictator to surrender his power so that people may have free access to freedom.

Does what has been said above apply to God as well? Does it mean that man cannot even receive freedom as a gift from God?

The answer has to be in the negative. From the Christian point of view, we must confess and say that freedom is God's gift to man. God makes it possible for man to be truly free. By giving freedom to man as a gift, God does not make him surrender to His power. How is this possible? How does God make freedom a reality to those who receive freedom from Him as a gift? God does this by becoming weak Himself. In Jesus Christ, God makes Himself so weak that by receiving freedom as a gift from Him man is not enslaved to His power. In His weakness God offers freedom to man. In this paradox of the incarnation, man becomes free from sin and coercion. He can now maintain his spiritual freedom, even if he may lose his physical freedom. He finds himself so close to the source of life that even death loses mastery over him.

This consideration of freedom as a gift from God in the light of the incarnation cannot but make us wonder whether we should continue to speak of God as an almighty and absolute being. In the modern history of Christian thought, it is neo-orthodoxy which puts exclusive emphasis on God as being absolute, incomprehensible and beyond the reach of man. In such a theological system, the doctrine of the incarnation almost becomes a necessity. It would appear to be a device of theologians to make the inaccessible God somewhat accessible to man. Thus, there is much insight in what Berdyaev has said:

> God is not the Absolute. God is relative to creation, to the world and to man, and with Him takes place the drama of freedom and love. . . When men have attempted to know God Himself as Absolute . . . then a monarchical understanding of God has been accepted, which is a source of theological seduction and slavery. Christianity is not the revelation of God as an absolute monarch. The Christian revelation of the Son of God who sacrificed Himself, suffered and was crucified, saves us from that. God is not an absolute monarch. God is a God who suffers with the world and with man. He is crucified love; He is the Liberator. The Liberator appears not as a power but as crucifixion.[24]

Indeed the church has, for the past two thousand years, taught that God is an absolute monarch. Although this contradicts the revelation of the divine love on the cross, it may have served the purpose of communicating the human understanding of God in a feudalistic and monarchical society. However, since the contemporary world has definitely ceased to be feudalistic, the concept of God as an absolute monarch only serves to alienate man from God. The bankruptcy of the traditional church both in the West and in the East is partly due to the bankruptcy of the concept of God as an absolute monarch wielding absolute power and authority. To quote Berdyaev again:

> God reveals Himself as humanity. Humanity is indeed the chief property of God, not almightiness, not omniscience and the rest, but humanity, freedom and sacrifice. . . Humanity is the image of God in man.[25]

Jesus Christ is this humanity of God. In Him, God has given us freedom as a gift. Jesus Christ lived, acted and died in utter freedom. It is this kind of freedom that transforms his followers into men of responsibility towards God and their fellowman.

True, the crucifixion represents a kind of power. But it is not the kind of power that humiliates and dominates man. On the contrary, it is a power that accommodates itself to the weakness of man. It is a power that sets man truly free. It does not bind him to conditions that may render his new found freedom unreal. It empowers man to find his identity and place within the order of God's creation.

Once we realize that from a Christian point of view freedom is a gift from God, we must insist that no one may use whatever power he may have to take away this gift of freedom from other people. For someone to take away freedom from other people amounts in fact to usurping the right of God. He sets himself against God and pretends to have the power that does not belong to him. This is why a totalitarian system is atheistic in nature. It cannot allow intrusion of power, be it human or divine, into its system. It will have to do everything possible to consolidate all power under its authority alone. That is why a totalitarian system is at the same time demonic in the expression of its authority and power. It will employ every possible means to ensure that no one will dare to challenge its authority. Once freedom as God's gift is gone, what we see is the degradation of man. Man without the divine gift of freedom is not man. Indeed, a totalitarian system poses itself as a challenge to God's creation. It changes and re-shapes man at its will to suit its own purpose. Humanity, which is the image of God in man, to use Berdyaev's phrase, is abused and distorted.

This is sin far more serious and sinister than moral offences which evangelists have a special delight in exposing in the hope of winning their audience to the Christian faith. Political changes that have taken place in Asia in the recent past predict that the church must be prepared to face the challenge of totalitarianism in a more intensified way. Reference has already been made earlier to certain countries in Asia which have taken measures to restrict the freedom of the people and to enhance the power of the rulers.[26] Another obvious example is, of course, that of China. There is no question about the fact that for China to be able to emerge from total chaos only to become a unified nation with a maximum degree of order and a great deal of equality cannot be viewed as less than a miracle. It indeed is a twentieth century miracle. But the Western nations and churches, in their admiration for China, coupled with their sense of guilt for their past dealings with her, are in danger of being uncritical to the sin of totalitarianism from which the new China is certainly not exempted. To speak of Western Christian mission returning to China without being prepared to face the implications of this colossal sin of totalitarianism is simply preposterous. What would be likely to happen, should Christian mission find its way back to China, would be a repetition of the old evangelistic approach of trying to save individual souls while having no impact whatsoever on the system and structure of society. What China and countries in Asia need is not this kind of emasculated Christianity. What the church through her mission must present is a faith tough enough to uphold the freedom of God in man and the integrity of humanity expressed through free, constructive and responsible actions towards the community, the society and the nation. If the church believes in the God of the exodus, the God of the crucifixion and the resurrection, she cannot avoid this task. In being faithful to this task, the church will find the fulfilment of her meaning in the world, namely, fulfilling the meaning of humanity in man who is created by God for freedom.

4. Freedom for Others

Christians do not seek freedom with their bare fists. First and foremost they must acknowledge that freedom is a gift from God. This is the main theme of our discussion in the preceding section. Now we must carry our discussion farther by asking: Freedom for what?

Our answer to the above question is this: in accepting freedom as a gift from God, we gain freedom for the service of others. At first, this may appear to be a simple and stereotyped answer which can be dismissed as no more than pious talk. But if we consider it more carefully and deeply, it will not be difficult for us to realize that here we actually touch upon one of the most basic elements of Christian faith. In fact it has far reaching bearings on the nature and task of the church. It also ought to have enormous effects on the shapes of the Christian community in the world. The self-understanding of Christians too cannot remain unaffected.

Earlier, if we remember, we made the observation that the election of Abraham, and consequently the election of the people of Israel, was not only for the sake of Israel herself but for all the nations in the world. It was through Abraham and Israel that other nations and peoples might be blessed. This was a decisive religious insight which molded and shaped the history of Israel. This does not mean that Israel always remained faithful to its calling. More often than not, it misused the privilege of election, trying to turn it into their own advantage alone. The result is that the history of Israel was often marked by conflicts between nationalism and universalism.

Of course, there is a lot to be said for nationalism, especially in the case of Israel, a relative newcomer to Palestine. Understandably, the rulers of Israel directed their efforts to establishing Israel as a political entity among the tribes and nations. Their identity and freedom as a nation could not be maintained without political unity and military strength. But on the other hand, there was a strong prophetic voice issuing a warning to Israel not to become a self-contained and self-sufficient entity. When the loosely organized tribes of Israel were about to be formed into a kingdom under the necessity of circumstances, the conflict between the political consideration and the religious concern was brought out in the open through events surrounding two leading personalities, namely, Samuel and Saul.[27]   Of course, the conflict can be interpreted as the struggle for power between religious leaders and political leaders, which was to result in Saul, the political leader, being a loser.   This episode gives us a picture of the end of an era in the history of Israel in which religious leaders also acted as political and military heroes.   From now on there is going to be a division of labour, and religious leaders have to witness the popular support of the people going to political leaders who, by virtue of their courage and expertise in matters of war, can lead their people into victory over their enemies.

But the conflict between Samuel and Saul has a far-reaching meaning beyond the feud between two powerful personalities representing different interests.   Looking back from the perspective of the later history of Israel, we can perhaps point out that for Israel to become a politically consolidated nation might result in Israel becoming disqualified as a servant of God, carrying God's mission to the nations.   This becomes apparent as the history of the Davidic Kingdom unfolds itself.   Both internally and externally, Israel as a political entity is to be beset with problems which threaten her survival.   There is little room left for her to live up to the expectation that through her all nations will be blessed.   In retrospect, therefore, we can affirm that political and military defeats which Israel had to suffer, leading eventually to her disintegration as a nation, gain profound meaning in the history of salvation.   Israel must be freed from nationalism in order to be God's servant to all nations.   But the trend towards nationalism is hard to resist. And in the time of Jesus Christ it was Judaism which had come to embody the nationalistic aspirations of the Jewish people.   Jesus tried to break open the closed door of Judaism, hoping to restore freedom to his own people so that the latter could be once more freed to serve other nations and peoples.   Consequently, he himself, became the embodiment of such freedom.   By totally identifying himself with man to the extent of death, he made himself free for all mankind.

Out of his profound experience as a man freed for the service of others on account of the Gospel, Paul writes to his fellow Christians in Corinth saying:

I have become all things to all men, that I might by all means save some.[28]

Paul's freedom in Jesus Christ enables him to cross the boundaries of race, culture, religion, ideology and even politics. He becomes the first apostle to the Gentiles, bringing the Gospel of salvation out of the Jewish environment into the Roman world. Paul thus builds the church on the foundation of Jesus Christ who gave up himself completely in order that the world might be saved.

This Christian freedom for others is to accept others on their terms and not on your own terms. It is this kind of freedom that leads to the fulfilment of other people. It enables you to enter empathetically into the heart and mind of others. And in the fulfilment of others, you will come to experience your own fulfilment. Here is the secret of Christian freedom. This shows a relational character of freedom. Freedom can be genuine only in so far as it is sought in the context of 'freedom for someone or something' as well as 'freedom from someone or something'. If this dual relationship is lost in a quest for freedom, what you have attained through that quest is not freedom at all. If your freedom from someone or something is not followed by freedom for someone or something', you will become imprisoned in your self-centeredness which denies the freedom of others. This is the freedom of a despot, which is no more than a caricature of true freedom.

At this point, we have to seriously raise one question with the church in the so-called free world. Is the church capable of becoming free for others? Perhaps one would hesitate to answer the question affirmatively. The Christian church has, in the course of the centuries, become physically overloaded. Even the church in Asia is no exception. She is too loaded with traditions which have lost meaning for the modern world. Particularly she is too loaded with financial burdens. Her property too often becomes cumbersome to the Gospel. We are reminded of the rich young man who came to Jesus Christ in search of eternal life. He kept all the commandments. He was a model youth, so to speak. He had little to blame as far as social and religious standards of that day were concerned. It was, therefore, astonishing that he was not commended by Jesus. Instead, Jesus said to him: 'If you wish to go the whole way, go, sell your possessions, and give to the poor, and then you will have riches in heaven; and come, follow me'.[29] The young man could not face such a blunt challenge because of his great wealth. 'He went away with a heavy heart', so Matthew tells us.

This episode is followed by Jesus' dictum that it is easier for a camel to pass through the eye of a needle than for a rich man to enter the Kingdom of God. One may call this Jesus' prejudice against the rich because of his humble origin. Perhaps this is his bias prompted by his inferiority complex towards the rich people. However hard one may try in this way to make light of an episode such as this, there is no mistake about the fact that Jesus did have some very harsh words to say about the rich, the privileged and the powerful. Those who are rich and self-sufficient will have no use for the Gospel. For the rich, religion can be a matter of pastime. It is a luxury which he makes use of at his own convenience; whereas for the poor, faith is a life and death matter. It is either his all or nothing. For them faith is a serious matter.

So there is much truth in what Jesus said about God and mammon.[30] One cannot serve God and mammon, namely, money or property, at one and the same time. What has happened in China since 1949 may be a strong indication that the future of Christian mission in Asia depends very much on the choice which the church will have to make between God and mammon. If the life-style of the church developed in the West based on the economic power of a competitive capitalist society does not seem to be quite in conformity with the central teachings of Jesus Christ, surely it cannot be adopted by the churches in the Third World without critical scrutiny. It is no secret that in the so-called 'free' nations in the Third World, the political, economic and social exploitations of the masses by the politically and economically powerful class are simply scandalous. Unfortunately, these exploitations have largely been made possible by the intervention of Western powers. In view of this, the involvement of Western nations in the political and economic affairs of Third World countries in modern history is, in a real sense, tragic. A very important lesson of history must be learnt by the governments in the Third World at this point. Both in theory and in practice, it will not pay in the long run to rely on economic and military capitals from the West for the consolidation of one's political power, although some Third

World governments may seem to thrive on them for a time. Without meeting the human needs and human issues which beset the masses of the people living on the boundary between the human and the sub-human level, the powers that be in the Third World will not be able to gain genuine support of their people. And it is almost inevitable that sooner or later the murmurings of the people will turn into open protest, thus laying the ground for social revolution. When the chips are down, there is no question as to where the politically oppressed and economically exploited masses will move. Ominous signs in Indo-China strongly and tragically reflect this tendency of mass loyalty and mass movement.

What does all this say to the life and mission of the church in Asia? It says that the Christian Gospel preached with urgent ideological fervour will prove to be increasingly difficult to filter down in the mind of common men and women and win their hearts. After all, the words of Bonhoeffer quoted in the first chapter saying that the church should get rid of her investments and properties in order for her to be able to serve humanity cannot be brushed aside as nonsensical and impracticable. But the fact is that this is an extreme measure which in all probability none of the churches in Asia, not to say the churches in the West, is able or inclined to follow. Such advice will be most likely dismissed as unrealistic. This alone shows that the churches in Asia need a lot of repenting to do in order to be reshaped into a new spiritual force with which the people in Asia must reckon.

Someone may retort and say: Oh, yes, but surely no church in Asia is numerically and financially strong. She is a minority in the country of her adoption, and more often than not she has to fight for the right of existence. This is a weak apology if we consider the fact that the church started out in Jerusalem in the very beginning as a small insignificant group of people who had nothing but the vivid and irresistible memory of Jesus Christ. The mistaken assumption here is that the ministry of salvation depends on the numerical and financial strength of the church, that a church with organizational security will do a better job of leading people to the foot of the cross. Nothing could be farther from the truth than such an assumption. Is it not almost a platitude to say that Israel was chosen not on account of her strength but on account of the sheer grace of God's election? The truth of the matter is that when they became numerically and politically strong, they began to fail God and the cause to which God had called them.

It is the same with the church, the new Israel. As Israel needed the prophets to remind them of their particular relation with God and with other nations, so the church has had reformers who bring home to her the obedience of discipleship. The church cannot do without reformation. The medieval Roman Catholic church had to go through the traumatic experience of the Reformation and the Counter-Reformation to become part of modern history. The spirit of Protestantism is not content with the present *status quo.* The church cannot move forward unless she is prompted by the need to reform herself. Therefore, the church, in order to be faithful to her nature and task as the body of Christ, must be *ecclesia semper reformanda.* The church which has ceased to reform herself is no longer the body of Christ. She falls victim to her own dogmatic rigidity and internal strife.

The reformation of the church has to have a two-fold objective. On one hand, the church, through a reformation, must return to the root or origin of her faith. Therefore, the reformation must be first of all revitalization of the biblical faith. But this is not enough. The fresh insights gained in this revitalization must serve as the foundation of building up something new. A new Christian community relevant to the contemporary world that gives hope to the future must come into existence. For this reason, reformation is an exciting adventure. It is an adventure of faith. It enables the church to serve God by serving humanity.

The form and content of the church must be determined by her service to humanity. Since this service to humanity, from the Christian point of view, is no less than Christian mission, the form and content of the church must be predicated by Christian mission. We have argued before that it is Christian mission that should determine the form of the church. When Christian mission is understood as the service of the Christian community for humanity or as the freedom of Christians for others, this must be stressed again. Needless to say, this understanding of the relation between the church and her mission is derived from the incarnation. In order to carry out His mission of salvation, God in Jesus Christ leaves behind Him the glory of being God and becomes man. Since the church is founded on the foundation of such act of God, she will be betraying her nature if she allows things to stand between her and her mission with the result that she fails to reflect the central meaning of the incarnation.

What Bonhoeffer suggested is, after all, far from unrealistic. In fact, he points out the very basic task which the church should be doing in the world today, namely, to reform and reshape herself in order that she may be enabled to become free for the service of humanity. As far as the church in Asia is concerned, what will be required of her in the midst of change and challenge is a thorough reformation. To begin with, she must decide once and for all not to subsist on foreign aid. The structure that cannot be supported and maintained by local resources must go. The projects that cannot be operated without continuous financial assistance from outside should be discontinued. Furthermore, she should initiate the study and experiment of what the church should be and what role the church should play under a socialistic system of society. She must become long-sighted. Most nations in Asia, with the exception of China, are under the impact and pressure of the Western capitalist economy. And the over-hasty development towards industrialization has placed these nations even more at the mercy of Western economic and political manipulation. But such a situation cannot go on forever. There are signs that internal social upheavals will hasten the day when the social system that fosters the privileges of the few and turns a deaf ear to the needs and claims of the masses can no longer stand intact. How can the church play a significant role in the future, if she does not begin to reshape and reorganize herself towards the direction of socialization, if she does not begin to reinterpret the contents of her faith with this future socialistic context in view?

On the surface, the church would have too much to lose if she were to venture into this new direction. But how can the church gain new integrity as the body of Christ without losing what has to be disposed? Here the experience of East German Christians will give us help and encouragement. F. Skladny expresses his conviction that 'Our balance of now 27 years life in a socialist society shows losses *and* gains.' He then mentions some of the losses and gains:

> We—as organized Church—lost our *power*, *position* and our *traditional privileges*—And we are gaining a trustworthiness that this process of losing power and privileges just

does not push us into isolation, but—on the contrary liberated us from the isolation of a power, which is separated from the masses and directed against them. We lost our beloved belief in individualism and salvation of the individual and together with it the stronghold of our Church in the rural areas, which was based on the individual property of the so-called 'free' peasant; we lost individual 'freedom'. And we are gaining the real freedom of renouncing individual rights for the sake of the development of collective life and work and of a new responsibility for the community and the society as a whole.[31]

This is an eloquent witness to what Christian freedom means in a socialist country. In the case of East Germany, the change was forced upon the church. In Asia, do we have to wait until a similar change is to be imposed on the church? Should we not be instrumental in creating something new in advance for the life-style of the Christian community and for the interpretation of faith and culture more in keeping with what is intended in the Bible?

Thus, it is imperative that the church in Asia has to renew and relive the experience of the exodus at this juncture in the history of Asia. Asian Christians must be delivered from their past 'Christian' traditions and be given the freedom of becoming all things to all men, to use Paul's expression. It is when this missionary principle of Paul's becomes a reality to the church that she will find her identity as the body of Christ in the particular situations in which she is called to give witness to the love, justice and truth of God.

REFERENCES

1. Nikolai Berdyaev, *Slavery and Freedom*, New York: Charles Scribner's Sons, 1944, p. 59.

2. The 'breath' of life here is no other than the 'spirit' of life originated in God. Thus Lindsay Dewar observes: '. . . from the first *ruach* in the Old Testament signifies not only the wind or breath but also the "spirit" of God and "the spirit of life" in a living organism. Thus, for instance, we read in the early narrative in Genesis 7:22: "All in whose nostrils was the breath of the *ruach* of life died." This, of course, includes human beings. And it is quite clear from the early account of the creation of man in Genesis 2:7, in which we read that God "breathed into his (man's) nostrils the breath of life," that *ruach* refers to the "spirit" of life in man from the first.' (*The Holy Spirit and Modern Thought*, New York: Harper & Brothers 1959, p. 3.)

3. Genesis 1:2. The New English Bible renders *ruach* here as 'a mighty wind.'

4. Jeremiah 1:10.

5. Harvey Cox has advanced the thesis that it is not so much the sin of pride as the sin of sloth that is depicted in the story of the fall. The fatal mistake committed by Eve was to leave to the snake to decide for herself. In his own words, 'we do not defy the gods by courageously stealing the fire from the celestial hearth, thus bringing benefit to man. Nothing so heroic. We fritter away our destiny by letting some snake tell us what to do.' (*On Not Leaving it to the Snake*, New York: Macmillan Company, 1964, p. XIV.)

6. Quoted by James Cone in *Black Theology and Black Power*, p. 28.

7. Nikolai Berdyaev, *op. cit.*, pp. 61-62.

8. See *Life*, April 30, 1971.

9. *Liberation, Justice and Development*, Workshops, Reports and Recommendations, Tokyo, Japan, July, 1970, p. 55.

10. Rubem A. Alves, *A Theology of Human Hope*, Washington/Cleveland: Corpus Books, 1969, p. 123.

11. Luke 4:18.

12. Jürgen Moltmann, 'Toward a Political Hermeuentics of the Gospel,' in *New Theology, No. 6*, edited by Martin E. Marty and Dean G. Peerman, London: The Macmillan Company, 1969, p. 88.

13. Alan Richardson summarizes the biblical concept of 'deliverance' as follows: 'The principal theme of the Bible is God's deliverance of mankind from the power of sin, death and Satan through his action in Jesus Christ; and this mighty deliverance is foreshadowed in the history of God's people Israel by his deliverance of them from such disasters as Egyptian bondage or Babylonian exile.' (*The Interpreter's Dictionary of the Bible*, A-D, p. 814.)

14. Exodus 2:14.

15. Jacques Ellul, *Autopsy of Revolution*, translated by Patricia Wolf, New York: Alfred A. Knopf, 1971, p. 247.

16. From the Campaign Journal of Nestor Paz Zamora, 1970.

17. Amos 3:8. R.S.V.

18. Amos 5:24. R.S.V.

19. Reinhold Niebuhr, *Love and Justice*, Philadelphia: The Westminster Press, 1957, p. 28.

20. Martin Luther King, *Strength to Love*, New York: Harper & Row, 1963, pp. 39-40.

21. In an autobiographical account of his own experience reminiscent of Paul's own account of himself in II Corinthians 11:25-28, Martin Luther King writes as follows: 'Due to my involvement in the struggle for the freedom of my people, I have known very few quiet days in the last few years. I have been imprisoned in Alabama and Georgia jails twelve times; my home has been bombed twice. A day seldom passes that my family and I are not the recipients of threats of death. I have been the victim of a near-fatal stabbing. So in a real sense I have been battered by the storms of persecution. I must admit that at times I have felt that I could no longer bear such a heavy burden, and have been tempted to retreat to a more quiet and serene life. But every time such a temptation appeared, something came to strengthen and sustain my determination. I have learned now that the Master's burden is light precisely when we take his yoke upon us.' (*Strength to Love*, pp. 140-141.)

22. The Watergate Affair which undermined the Nixon government indicates that concentration of power in the name of national security can also be possible in a Western democratic society, and can easily lead to abuse of power.

23. Ignazio Silone, *Bread and Wine*, p. 43. Quoted by James Cone in *A Black Theology of Liberation*, pp. 254f.

24. Nikolai Berdyaev, *Slavery and Freedom*, p. 85.

25. Nikolai Berdyaev, *ibid*. It is interesting to note that Berdyaev speaks of the humanity of God (1939) long before Barth uses it in the publication of his book which bears this phrase.

26. I am here referring to the proclamation of Martial Law in the Philippines in September of 1972 and in Korea in October, 1972.

27. There are two different views regarding the institution of monarchy in Israel: (1) I Samuel 8:1-22; 10:17-27 and 12 contain a criticism of monarchy from the standpoint of religion; (2) I Samuel 9:1-10 and 16 favour the institution of monarchy.

28. II Corinthians 9:22.

29. Matthew 19:21.

30. Matthew 6:24.

31. F. Skladny, 'Christian Existence in a Socialist Society,' in *Aikya*, a national student monthly published by the Student Christian Movement of India, March 1973, Vol. 19, No. 3 (pp. 6-7).

CHAPTER SEVEN

Man's Search for Absolutes

... the religion and religions must be treated with
a tolerance which is informed by the forbearance of
Christ, which derives therefore from the knowledge
that by grace God has reconciled to Himself godless
man and his religion.[1]

—KARL BARTH

1. Beyond Dogmatism and Syncretism

ANOTHER gigantic problem which Christian mission has had to
face is that of religions. The church in the West did not enter
Asia as a religious vacuum. On the contrary, Western missionaries encountered in Asia deeply religious people, who either saw
no need for a religion from the Western land or expressed
antagonism towards the new religion the foreigners had brought
to them. If the struggle for liberation we discussed in the previous
chapters is a relatively recent phenomenon, the problem of religions
has been an old phenomenon which greeted Christian mission
right from the beginning.

But bent on converting and evangelizing the pagans, Western
missionaries had, on the whole, little patience for Asian religions.
They were the self-styled crusaders who had come out to conquer
and not to reason, to convert and not to listen. It was not until
1928 at Jerusalem and 1938 at Tambaram that the theological
and missiological implications of Christian encounter with other
religions were taken up with a seriousness.[2] Religions beside
Christianity ceased to be the subject of special interest and study
only for the historians of religions. They began haunting Christian theologians, missiologists and missionaries. This is no place
to give an historical account of and a theological critique of the
conferences held at Jerusalem and Tambaram and the discussions
and conversations which these conferences provoked in the years
that followed. Suffice it to say that little new ground was broken
with respect to the subject matter of theological understanding of
Asian religions. This was due largely to the fact that there was

little attempt to get at the deep meaning of these Asian religions. in the cultural contexts of Asia. Armed with the formidable theological and philosophical systems of the West, Western missiologists and missionaries aflame with the zeal for the evangelization of Asia subjected Asian religions and religiosity to the analysis and criticism that promised from the outset to yield very little constructive results.

It is no wonder that the Christian churches in Asia either became excessively militant or grew hopelessly impotent as a minority. religion surrounded by these historical Asian religions and the deep-rooted Asian religiosity. There was no theological encouragement to establish the channels of communication, no ecclesiastical sanction to build a bridge between the church and other religions. Consequently, Asian religions, though being such an objective reality existing so closely to the Christian church, became so remote to most Christians that they tended to be regarded as witness to the distortion of human nature and as disservice to the love of God. But, of course, this situation was not allowed to continue forever. Asian nationalism and revitalization of Asian religions after World War II thrust upon the church in Asia the urgent need for self-criticism of her theological assumptions and re-evaluation of the place and the meaning of Asian religions in God's creation and redemption. Although the old attitude of detachment on one hand and hostility on the other still dominates among Asian Christians, there is already a new spirit of tolerance and dialogue beginning to create a new atmosphere in the relation between Christianity and other religions.[3] Needless to say, this calls for serious theological reflection on the meaning of religion and religions and especially the latter's place and role in what we understand as God's revelation. As the old missionary enterprise was premised on the understanding of Christianity as exclusively representing the divine revelation, so any new concept and practice of Christian mission must be premised on a fresh biblical and theological insight into the acts of God in the whole of His creation. It is to this problem that we hope to address ourselves in this chapter.

Our discussion must begin with the understanding of religions as man's search for absolutes. To be sure, the pursuit of absolutes is not limited to religions. It takes different forms in practically

every aspect of man's life. Perhaps this results from man's awareness of his finiteness and relative nature. Not only this, this must
also be due to his perception that there must be something absolute,
that is, something that transcends finiteness and relativity or something that sustains temporal and transient things. According to
Paul Tillich, absolutes

> appear in the most ordinary talk of daily life as well as in
> literature and philosophy, and they appear even in most
> antimetaphysical philosophy. We live in the structures
> they gave us. They provide us with the ontological safety
> without which neither thinking nor acting would be
> possible.[4]

If this analysis is correct, we may describe man as 'being towards
absolutes' on the analogy of what Heidegger calls 'being-towards-
death.' In politics the ruler, especially the dictator in a totalitarian
country, wants to be in possession of absolute power. In a traditional Asian family the master of the house assumed that he had
absolute power to dominate the members of his family.

However, it is in religion that the search for absolutes reaches
the height of intensity. Those who are supposed to have an access
to the realm of absolutes begin to be looked upon as endowed
with special spiritual power. The priests in the Old Testament
religion, the Brahmins in Hinduism or medicinemen in African
religions, constituted the power that evoked both reverence and
fear in the minds of the people. Their influence went beyond the
strictly religious realms and was felt in almost every aspect of
society. Frequently, the political ruling power had to succumb
to the spiritual power possessed by the religious authorities. And
more often than not, it was the latter that conferred the right to
rule on kings or political rulers.

Since, in religions, man's search for absolutes is concentrated,
it is also in religions that dogmatism often prevails. The reason
is simple. Those who affirm that it is only through their religion
that man can gain access to and have communion with the reality
which is absolute and universal will not be able to see in other
forms of religious experiences expression of the same absolute and
universal reality. This is the logical consequence of having gained
entry into what is believed to be absolute. For to give recognition

to other claims to other absolutes is to invalidate somehow my own religion as the reflection of that which is absolute. My religion must be the sole custodian of the truth with regard to the absolute reality man seeks. Therefore, other religions cannot be acknowledged as reflecting the true image of the absolute reality.

It goes without saying that this is an *a priori* claim, that is, a claim made without asking questions as to whether other religions too could be the bearers of the truth. Furthermore, this is a dogmatic claim because it is based on the assumption that my religion can be identified with the whole truth of what is supposed to be absolute. Of course, those who make such a claim refuse to submit it to the test of an objective study of religions. Phenomenology of religion or what is called the history of religions has no place in the *a priori* claim they make on behalf of their religion. They cannot accept the possibility that that which is absolute may manifest itself in religious expressions, be they liturgical or doctrinal, other than their own. Their minds are closed to any possible expressions of religious truth not originated in their limited experience.

Such dogmatism fosters a militant attitude towards other religions. Christianity brought to Asia by Western missionaries, for example, was a militant religion. It was the religion *sui generis.* It tried to establish its place in Asian culture by rejecting the validity of other Asian religions. No credit was given to the spirituality that was part and parcel of being Asian. Consequently, it was stressed that only by making a clean break with other religions and becoming thoroughly converted to Christianity one could hope to gain salvation. This is a familiar story, and one can find various versions of it in the history of Western Christian mission in Asia and elsewhere. Needless to say, such dogmatism and militancy exhibited by missionary Christianity have made the Gospel of Jesus Christ appear to be negative and exclusive not only with regard to other religious beliefs but also to Asian cultural expressions as a whole. Thus, to become Christian is to become uprooted from Asian culture, as well as to dissociate oneself entirely from Asian religions.

Unfortunately, the strength of Christian mission has been derived from the strength of dogmatism. It seems that the more dogmatic a Christian is, the better missionary or evangelist he would become. And it is true to say that the form and content of evangelism has largely been shaped by this dogmatic and militant understanding of the nature of the truth of God. Salvation is identified with the expansion of Christianity and with numerical growth of Christians and the church. The vitality of Christian faith is thus supposed to be found in the validity of the structures of mission which make it possible for missionaries and evangelists to reach out and conquer those whose religious allegiance lies elsewhere. The question is: Does this concept and practice of evangelism do justice to the divine revelation? Will a more objective understanding of God's acts in the world not call for a different approach to the people of other religions? We shall deal with questions such as these in the latter part of this chapter.

On the opposite side of dogmatism there is the so-called syncretism. Curiously, both syncretism and dogmatism begin with the same premise but later they part with each other's company entirely. The premise for syncretism, as well as for dogmatism, is that religion is man's search for the reality which is absolute. However, for dogmatism, that which is absolute can be thought of only in the singular, whereas for syncretism it is conceived in plural. Thus, syncretism operates with the principle of pluralism. Ultimately, the absolute may be one, but it manifests itself in different religions in such a way, that no single religion has a monopoly on the truth. All religions, primitive or sophisticated, partake of the nature of the absolute. Thus, we have what we call syncretistic religion, religion which consists of supposedly true elements gleaned from various religious beliefs, teachings and practices. Buddha, Brahman, Tao or Christ are all thrown into one basket giving the believers the benefit of all religions.

Syncretism is not entirely mistaken in its presupposition that the absolute reality has its manifestations in different religions and cultural contexts. But the practice of syncretistic religion becomes questionable when what is considered to be true and good in a particular religion is taken out of its contexts and made to blend with other religious elements abstracted from their respective *Sitz im Leben*. This cannot be done without causing serious damage to the integrity of the religions in question. For strictly speaking, a religious truth is not an abstract entity constructed out of the blue, as it were. In so far as it has to do with man as well as the truth he seeks, it cannot be rightly grasped unless it is seen in the historical and cultural contexts to which he belongs. To put it in a different way, a religious truth reflects and communicates the meaning of the absolute reality through particular situations in which the reflecting and communicating take place. It follows that if it is forcefully and arbitrarily taken out of its existential contexts, its power to reflect and communicate the meaning of the absolute reality is seriously weakened and even becomes lost. What it now reflects and communicates may be an entirely different thing.

For historical religions such as Judaism, Christianity, or Islam this is a serious matter indeed. As is well known, history plays a crucial role in these religions—history not in a general sense but in the sense of having .to do concretely with particular place, time and people. In these religions, the meaning of revelation is comprehended in a particular temporal-spatial framework. That is why the Christian faith, for example, is not interested in general truths about life and the world or concerned with general religious propositions. The Christian faith has to do with events in the life of man and in the course of history—events which result from interactions between the divine calling and the human response. Therefore, when the historical and existential contexts are disregarded and put aside to make room for the formulation of general propositions, faith loses its inner dynamic and becomes abstract statements concerning faith and morals. This is particularly important for the theological interpretation of the nature of the Christian faith which has its root in the history of the people of God both in the Old Testament and in the New Testament.

Our conclusion, therefore, is that the problems that arise out of the plurality of religions cannot be solved syncretistically. I mentioned earlier that dogmatic assertions on matters concerning faith have contributed to the alienation of other religions from Christianity. But it does not mean that syncretism should now be the answer. Syncretism is no more acceptable than dogmatism. It simply will not do just to incorporate into the body of the Christian faith similar teachings and beliefs that happen to be found in other religions. Of course, there is much to be gained from comparative study of religions. Aside from gaining more accurate knowledge of what other religions teach and propagate through such study, one is bound to be led to a deeper understanding of both the particular and the universal nature of God's revelation. One can no longer restrict the divine revelation to a particular religion without seriously violating the universal nature of God's revelation. The truth of the matter is that one particular religion cannot make a sole claim on revelation.

What we have just said must be supplemented by the following observation: the ways in which the divine revelation is accepted in different religions are distinctively varied. Thus, it is often the case that teachings and beliefs which appear to be similar in different religions belong to the superficial rather than substantial observation. And when they are removed from their original contexts, they will most likely fail to convey the meaning of revelation in the latter's historical and religious situations. We must, therefore, emphasize that exercise in syncretism will serve the truth of God no constructive purpose. If we as Christians adopt a syncretistic approach to religions, we will be denying the historical nature of revelation not only to Christianity but also to other religions. Syncretism is thus no answer to the questions posed for Christianity and especially the Christian mission in relation to the plurality of religion.

We must go beyond dogmatism and syncretism. Dogmatism as the product of the age of Western religious absolutism and syncretism as the outcome of the era of liberalism should be superseded. For Christian mission armed with dogmatic attitude, religions with the exception of Christianity have no positive place in the divine revelation. Nor do religions fare any better under syncretistic treatment. This is due to the fact that religions are treated as if they are not endowed with inherent meaning in the life of believers, as if what they assert as true has only an accidental relation to the total structure of man's spirituality. It goes without saying that neither of these attitudes is tenable. It has to be stressed that the problem of religions cannot be treated in a cavalier fashion. Christians, and especially those who are engaged actively in Christian mission, must realize that Asian religions will continue to play an important role in the life and history of Asia in the years to come. The problem of religions is, therefore, a theological problem. Accordingly, it must be treated theologically. It must find its place in a theological system which purports to give an account to the content of the Christian faith. This may sound self-contradictory, but the fact is that the presence of other religions challenges Christians to a deeper understanding of Christian faith from a much more fundamental perspective. As Kenneth Cragg has put it in particular reference to Islam:

> Islam is particularly calculated to put the Christian interpreter on his mettle since it forces him to a radical and patient expression of his faith. By the very vigour and cruciability of its objections, Islam compels the Christian to delineate Christ more deeply.[5]

More and more Christian mission must expect creative impact from other religions. It is in the context of mutual impacts that the truth of God in Jesus Christ will be rendered with more clarity. Exegesis of Christian faith in Asia must, therefore, take place in multi-religious contexts. The work of Christian theologians cannot be said to be sound until its results are tested by other religions. To be sure, there is a great risk involved here—a risk of having to acknowledge the misrepresentation of God's truth prior to a reference to other religious contexts. But this risk must be taken in order for Christians to see the truth of God from a much wider perspective. It is, therefore, essential that we engage ourselves in theological reflections on the meaning of religions in the divine-human relationships.

2. Theological Meaning of Religions

We have stressed that the problem of religions must be treated and apprehended theologically. We can no longer dismiss religions other than Christianity as negative witness to the revelation of God. From the Christian standpoint, we must admit that

> the other religions play exactly the same part in the lives of others that Christianity plays in ours. Wherever people take religion seriously it determines their life, gives them the rules to which they submit themselves, and in particular it stamps their thought and action and moral behaviour during the times of crisis in life—birth, maturity, marriage, illness and death—and above and beyond this it is a refuge, a source of comfort and of hope.[6]

Walter Freytag, a very perceptive missiologist, has put his finger on what religion is when he made the above observation. Religion has to do with the totality of life. This is true of primitive religions as well as highly developed religions. This is also true of mystic religions and very intellectual religions such as Confucianism. Religion thus demands total commitment of the whole person. That is why conversion from one religion to another always entails a radical change in the life of the convert. It is a radical spiritual change, of course, but not only that. The change also has to do with his human and social relationships and the physical aspect of his life. Conversion is, therefore, a radical change from one total commitment to another total commitment.

And Christian mission has demanded no less than a total change. When one repents and accepts Jesus Christ as one's Saviour, one is also expected to accept cultural values that accompany Christianity from the West. Conversion to Christ is not regarded as complete until one disavows one's cultural heritages and embraces the so-called Christian value systems developed in entirely different historical and cultural contexts. It is no wonder that early Christian converts in Asia were taught to deny their past and to seek refuge in the fellowship of the Christian community.

Someone may say there is nothing wrong in this. In fact, he may stress that a complete break with your own past is the most logical thing to do on the premise that religion has to do with the totality of man's life. You surely cannot serve two masters. You cannot embrace Jesus Christ and at the same time remain Buddhist, Hindu or Muslim or whatever you happened to be before conversion. But this seemingly logical and consistent course of action demanded from a Christian convert is, in fact, not without theological difficulties. This somewhat innocent attitude will actually give rise to at least the following two situations: either validity of other religions must be categorically and dogmatically rejected or the universal claim of the Gospel must be qualified or even seriously impaired.

Let me explain what this means. As has been pointed out, religious conversion as a spiritual event is accompanied by a total reorientation in one's value systems. Thus, to deny the validity of other religions will result in also denying the values that have constituted the essential part of the structure of being and meaning. This will undoubtedly present difficulties. First, there is a danger of iconoclasm without discrimination. Idols are thrown out, burnt and destroyed. But iconoclasm tends to go further. There also will be a denial of the possible expressions of truth, goodness and beauty in non-Christian philosophical systems and cultural activities. It is true that such a radical iconoclasm belongs largely to the early days of Western Christian mission, but some permanent damage has been wrought in the relationship between the church and her cultural environments. Even though those Christians in Asia who are more liberally minded have been doing their best to end the social, cultural and religious isolation of the Christian church, they have barely scratched the surface of the problem. For Christians to be able to recognize and accept without murmurings manifestations of what is true in Asian cultural and religious milieus, a theology that restates the contents of Christian faith in the Asian contexts is a *sine qua non*.

There is, moreover, another important consideration. We have to realize that the Christian contention to belittle non-Christian value systems will call into question the Christian claim to the universality of the truth embraced by the church. If the universality of Christ is identified with the church as we experience her, it is a very limited universality. Limited universality is already a contradiction in terms. Strictly, it is no universality at all. For us to get out of such a self-contradiction, we have to admit that there are manifestations of the universality of Christ in other cultures and religions. Of course, the central assertion of the church is that Christ as the embodiment of God's truth and love is most directly and explicitly manifested in the traditions built on the biblical faith. But this assertion must not lead to the negation of other manifestations of God's truth and love outside the Christian church. At this point, we do not need to go into the problem of the church as both visible and invisible, the church as patent and latent. It would only lead to confusion if we were to regard the possible interactions between God and man outside the Christian church as the latent or invisible church. The church as is used and understood by Christians has become a technical term with definite reference to the community of those who profess to be Christians. It is, therefore, highly questionable to extend the use of the term church beyond the Christian communities and try to apply it to those who do not profess to be Christians.

Thus, the point of departure in our reconstruction of Christian theology and the reconception of Christian mission is not the church. The place to begin is revelation, or to be more specific from the standpoint of Christian theology, revelation in and through Jesus Christ. The claims by the Christian church for the universality of the Gospel must be made, defended and fought here. And as we will try to show in the following pages, it is in facing the implications of the concept of revelation and the event of revelation in Jesus Christ for the whole of creation that we begin to understand the profound divine-human dimension of religions as man's search for absolutes.

As is well known, Paul Tillich has a working definition of religion as ultimate concern. The definition enables him to take account of both religions and what he calls quasi-religions such as communism and fascism. This undoubtedly broadens the area of religious concerns and discussions. Religion, according to Tillich,

> is the state of being grasped by an ultimate concern, a concern which qualifies all other concerns as preliminary and which itself contains the answer to the question of the meaning of our life.[7]

It may be asked whether this definition will do justice to the intensely inter-personal aspect of revelatory situations. But it points out the fact that in religion we are dealing with man's ultimate situation.

What is this ultimate situation? It is the situation beyond which man cannot go any further. It is the situation in which man becomes aware that he is encountered by that which transcends him. This affects him in two entirely opposite ways. On one hand he is elated because he realizes that he is in touch with that which cannot be described by any human language. He is in the presence of the eternity which seems to give the assurance of permanence of life in the midst of the temporal existence. On the other hand, however, he also becomes conscious of his limitation, weakness and finiteness as a human being. He is afraid he is not able to hold on to the eternal and transcendent. He fears that he will be thrown back to his finiteness.

Religion is man's response to the ultimate situation he has thus encountered. From this observation, we can infer several theological meanings of religion. First of all, religion is a witness to the fact that man is not a self-sufficient being. Strictly speaking, man cannot achieve self-fulfilment on his own. This is essentially true in our daily lives. The fulfilment of ourselves as human beings depends in no small measure on the relationships we have with others. That is why family and society have so much to do with the process of our maturity. It is thus true to say that culture is no creation of unrelated solitary individuals. No doubt there are men and women who play much more prominent roles than others in the course of history, but they are able to do what they have done as the result of the inter-play of human relationships. They are no isolated individuals carving out the path of history entirely alone. How true, therefore, it is to say, 'the individual cut off from all contact with his fellowmen and with the very sources of existence, has thus lost his creative powers'.[8]

It is in religion that man's dependency on others, especially on that which transcends himself, that is, on what is normally called God, becomes most evident. Without this God, man is not sufficient. Man without God is thus essentially defective. That which is divine, namely, that which transcends man, is the ontological part of human nature. That is why man must seek absolutes. He knows he is empty and becomes helpless when he tries to become self-reliant. To deny God is to deny man himself. To be cut off from Him is to be cut off from the source of life and creativity. What genuine work of art is not the result of the inspiration from the source of life and being? What true cultural achievement by man is not the expression of his deep indebtedness to the divine reality that surrounds and upholds him? 'The creation of genuine culture', says Joachim Wach, whom we have just quoted, 'is only possible for man when communion with the deity, the primary ground of all things, can serve as a source for his creativity'.[9] Is this an overstatement? Not at all. We can go so far as to say the more genuine culture is, the more religious it becomes, religious being the state describing man's intense communion with God. Man is essentially a religious being—being in need of God for self-fulfilment.

On the basis of what has been discussed, Paul Tillich's definition of religion as ultimate concern becomes intelligible. We have
said that such a definition of religion does not do justice to the
inter-personal relationship which should constitute the essence of
the communion between God and man. This essential personal
characteristic is strikingly absent in it. Granted, one can argue
that one can develop a personal relationship even with an impersonal object. For a poet, a stone, an iron bar or a table can turn
into vivid objects alive with his emotions and feelings. But these
objects remain impersonal outside the poet's momentary imagination. The meaning of Tillich's definition of religion as ultimate
concern does not lie here. His definition substantiates, in our
opinion, our argument here that religion is a witness to man as
being essentially not self-sufficient. This comes out particularly
clear in his stress on the quasi-religious nature of Communism
or Fascism. An atheistic ideology or social system seems to have
dealt a deadly blow to man's need for religion, or his need to be
dependent on a being higher than himself. Man is the highest
being conceivable. He does not need what is called God for his
self-fulfilment. But this is not entirely true. The fact that in a
Communist state an absolute commitment to communist political
philosophy is demanded from the people testifies that man cannot
be self-sufficient, especially when such a demand is made and
accepted with religious fervour. In other words, when the demand
becomes the ultimate concern of the people, the ultimate concern
takes the place of God. Both the rulers and the people are clearly
in a religious situation seeking self-fulfilment not in terms of themselves but in terms of that particular ultimate concern.

It is, however, in the Christian faith that self-insufficiency of
man is stressed with great consistency. The creation of man and
woman conveys, among other things, the idea that man cannot
find his or her fulfilment without mutual inter-dependence of one
on the other. And above all, the divine intervention which calls
man into being demonstrates beyond any doubt that without God
man's self-sufficiency is an illusion. There are some passages
which eloquently express the utter dependency of man on God for
his self-fulfilment. Psalm 8 immediately comes to our mind:

> When I look up at thy heavens, the work of thy fingers, the
> moon and the stars set in their place by thee, What is

man that thou shouldst remember him, mortal man that
thou shouldst care for him?[10]

Left alone, man is a fragile creature in this vast mysterious
universe. The meaning of life is, therefore, not self-derivative.
It is given by God who cares for man. This constitutes also the
New Testament understanding of man. Jesus Christ exhorts
people not to worry for tomorrows. He emphasizes the futility of
contriving all sorts of means through which man may become self-
sufficient. He teaches the uselessness of devising ways on which
one may rest one's security. Hence, his admonition: 'Set your
mind on God's kingdom and his justice before everything else,
and all the rest will come to you as well.'[11] Jesus Christ thus
tries to break man's illusion of self-sufficiency. If the illusion
persists, man will continue to be trapped in false security.

But an ironical thing often happens to religion. Religion,
which is a witness to man's self-insufficiency, turns into an instrument through which man gains the illusion of self-sufficiency and
security. Thus, something turns full circle here. The Biblical
critique of religion is primarily directed against this self-contradictory aspect of religion. The prophets in the Old Testament
are never tired of warning that the religiosity of the people of
Israel will prove to be their downfall. Their religion has successfully shut them off from the God of love and justice in whom
their hope lies. It misleads them into taking the penultimate for
the ultimate, false security for true security. This is also the
main burden of Christ's attack on Judaism. Legalistic religion
such as Judaism blocks the truly meaningful communication
between God and man. Laws and regulations take the place of
love and justice. And man is led to believe that he is sufficient
unto himself as long as he abides by these laws prescribed by his
religion.

This dual character of religion seen in the Bible is common
to all religions, including, of course, Christianity. If we are to
get at the true essence of religion, this biblical critique of religion
has to be applied to religions with discernment. Needless to say,
Christianity cannot be exempted from this biblical critique. In
doing so, we are not advocating that religions be done away with.
Our effort consists in going beyond religions to the ultimate or to
God to which all religions point.[12]

The second thing that must be said about religion as the ultimate situation brought into existence by the divine-human encounter is this: the phenomenon of man cannot be explained completely out of man himself. In other words, man is not a self-explanatory being. That is why through religion man searches absolutes, that is, something that can be self-explanatory and, therefore, can undertake the task of explaining beings other than itself. In fact, it is the non-self-explanatory character of the experiential world that drives ancient thinkers such as Aristotle to conceive of the First Cause that is uncaused but causes all things into being, or the First Mover who, though entirely and absolutely unmoved, moves all things in a series of chain movements. For the same reason, almost every nation has its own version of how the universe comes into being through a maker(s) of heaven and earth. All these versions of creation are mythological and cosmogonic in nature. And in the creation story of the Old Testament, we have a successfully demythologized account of how God is the Lord of His creation. It is the persistent emphasis of the biblical faith that man is nothing or non-entity apart from this Creator God. The phenomenon of man is to be explained in terms of God and not in terms of man himself.

Is it, therefore, not true to say that in religion man endeavours to deal with the mystery of his being on the basis of the reality which, he believes, transcends him? The 'Declaration on the Relationship of the Church to Non-Christian Religions' made by the Second Vatican Council has well said:

> Men look to the various religions for answers to those profound mysteries of the human condition which, today even as in olden times, deeply stir the human heart: What is a man? What is the meaning and the purpose of our life? What is goodness and what is sin? What gives rise to our sorrows and to what intent? Where lies the path to true happiness? What is the truth about death, judgment and retribution beyond the grave? What, finally, is that ultimate and unutterable mystery which engulfs our being, and whence we take our rise, and whither our journey leads us?[13]

All these are the questions fundamentally related to man. And it is in the contexts of religions that man seeks answers in terms of some ultimate reality, that is, in terms of a reality to which questions such as in the above quotation do not occur.

In a sense, it is true to say that religion is anthropological, that it strives to deal with the basic spiritual needs and aspirations of man. But it is wrong to conclude from this that religion is nothing but anthropological. There has been a strong tendency for Christians to assert categorically that with the exception of Christianity all other religions are anthropological. In so far as religions are regarded as anthropological, they cannot but be idolatrous. Thus, Christian mission is supposed to be engaged in warfare with idolatry. Such a judgment on religions by Christians is correct only in so far as they are not able to see something basic to the being of man beyond idolatry. True, idolatry presents a poor and distorted image of something ultimate to man's being, but it deserves all sympathy and understanding because it represents man's yearning for the ultimate reality which may shed light on what man is, what the meaning of life is and what his ultimate destiny will be.

What has been said above does not only apply to the so-called world religions, but also to religions and beliefs which to the more civilized world represent primitive religiosity. The following observation made by the great phenomenologist of religion, G. Van der Leeuw, deserves our attention. He writes:

> It is not man himself who is the active agent in the situation, but, in one mode or another, God. A divine activity sustains all phenomena alike, from their more primitive types to their culmination in Christianity as well as those religious movements which are now concealed by our largely secularized civilization.[14]

A statement such as this must be taken seriously by any theologian who wishes to formulate a theological understanding of religions. It is no longer possible for him to ignore the vast amount of research undertaken by the phenomenologists of religion or historians of religions. But the phenomenology of religion or the history of religions is important not only to Christian theology but also to the Christian mission. Joachim Wach, another very perceptive historian of religions, for example, believes that the more the insight into religions deepens, the more in all Christian missions one motive must stand decisively in the foreground: that behind the religious motive all other motives must retreat to the background, and that the people whom we missionize ought to be led to a religiosity appropriate to themselves and to their uniqueness. So the thorough study of their uniqueness becomes an increasingly important task; to this, too, *Religions-wissenschaft* can contribute its share.[15]

Christian theology cannot be conducted in an ivory tower of so-called Christendom, for the truth it seeks to expound is also present in other religions and quasi-religions.

We cannot, therefore, dismiss religions, be it world religions or primitive religions, as nothing but the product of man's own imagination or his sinful nature. As Tillich has stressed, man 'is given a revelation, a particular kind of experience which always implies saving powers. One never can separate revelation and salvation. There are revealing and saving powers in all religions. God has not left himself unwitnessed'.[16] A realization such as this should make Christians at once humble and joyful—humble because Christianity is not the sole custodian of the truth of God, and joyful because the love of God in Jesus Christ also embraces those outside the Christian church in a way that has to do with salvation.

Our discussion in the foregoing pages leads us to say that religions, Christianity included, have much in common not only in matters of liturgy and institutional structure, but also in the views and beliefs they hold towards the life and destiny of man. This is the third point we would like to treat here. We must be, therefore, very wary of calling one particular religion unique as over against other religions. We want to stress that the word uniqueness, when applied to a particular religion, often expresses the spirit of exclusiveness on one hand and at the same time shows one's lack of deep experience with other religions. In fact, the constant use of it by Christians has successfully immunized many Christians in Asia from understanding the religiosity expressed in other Asian religions. As has been mentioned, there is no religion without the revelation which comes from the ultimate reality or God, or whatever way one may call it. Unless one is to advocate plurality of the ultimate reality or God, which is an untenable position anyway, one must admit all religions are ultimately related to that ultimate reality or God. Due to cultural and historical differences, there are different ways in which response to the ultimate reality or God is made. That is why we have to deal with the pluralism of religions. At the same time, there will be no proper understanding and experience of a religion outside the particular cultural and historical situations in which that religion came into being and is practised. Furthermore, due to human weakness and finiteness discussed earlier, there are bound to be misunderstandings and distortions of the nature of the ultimate reality and work of God. Therefore, no religion can do without criticism and no religion can escape judgment. But again we must not allow ourselves the mistake of rejecting a particular religion *in toto* on the basis of distortions we find in it. Especially when such rejection is made on the grounds of what we hold to be true in our own religion, we can no longer perceive the universal nature of God's presence and acts in the world.

In this connection, we would like to refer to what Barth has said about a branch of Japanese Buddhism called Yodoism which lays great emphasis on grace as the way of salvation. After calling it 'the Japanese Protestantism' Barth goes on to say:

> Only one thing is really decisive for the distinction of truth and error. And we call the existence of Yodoism a providential disposition because with what is relatively the greatest possible force it makes it so clear that one thing is decisive. That one thing is the name of Jesus Christ. Methodologically, it is to be remembered that in face of Yodoism, and at the bottom, of all other religions, our first task is to concentrate wholly upon this distinction, provisionally setting aside whatever other difference we think we recognize.[17]

This is a great concession on the part of theologians such as Barth. His theology is uncompromisingly a theo-christo-centric theology. And it is for the Christian church that he conducted his massive theological adventure. Moreover, he never visited the non-Western world during his lifetime. Consequently, he never had first hand contact with or personal experience of Asian religions such as Buddhism. But he was perceptive enough to urge his fellow Christians to be tolerant to other religions. And in the statement just quoted, he admitted that the concept of grace taught in Yodoism was so similar to that emphasized in Christianity that it was difficult to distinguish one from the other. In the final analysis, that which counts most is Jesus Christ. Jesus Christ is the decisive factor which makes Christianity different from other religions.

Barth's theological discourse on the controversial subject of religions stops here. But, if there is so much similarity in the understanding of the divine grace between Yodoism and Christianity, would it not be logical to suppose that Jesus Christ is also related to Yodoism in some way? To be sure, the name of Jesus Christ is not present in Yodoism. His name is not confessed by its believers. But the substance of the grace of God revealed in Jesus Christ and to which the confessing Christians respond openly cannot be absent in and alien to Yodoism. In my opinion, Barth's theo-christo-centric theology presents real possibility for the church and the Christian mission to come to grips with the phenomenon of religions in a new way.

3. Christ is All and in All

For the Christian church in Asia and her mission to deal with religions in a new way, one of the most crucial elements which needs to be emphasized is the universality of Jesus Christ. Paul seems to have this in mind when he, in writing to the Colossians, points out that 'Christ is all and is in all.'[18] By the universality of Christ we do not only mean that all things have access to Him. We also mean that he is present in all things. His presence in all things may be or may not be recognized, but the reality of his presence is not dependent on man's recognition of it. We can, therefore, say that Paul's statement, namely, Christ is all and in all, is an ontological statement.

Christ's presence cannot but affect all things, including religions. That is why I argued at the end of the last section that the grace manifested by Yodoism cannot but have something to do with the grace of God in Jesus Christ. In Jesus Christ God is near to His creation. God has never given up His ownership of His creation, in spite of the fact that the creation has been invaded by corruption and sin. This is still His creation. And in so far as the creation remains to be His, there are bound to be reflec-

tions of His truth in it. Since religions are man's conscious effort
to search for absolutes or for the divine reality, it is in religions
that we may encounter the truth of God, although in fragmentary
and often distorted ways. It follows that if we deny any positive
relationship between religions and the divine truth concerning
the nature of man and his salvation, we will have to admit either
that God is less than universal or that His presence in all things
through Jesus Christ has no redemptive meaning at all for those
in the cultural and religious settings outside Christianity. Neither
of these propositions can be accepted without misrepresenting the
nature of God and His saving love. We cannot put God in the
strait-jacket of our theology which tends to delimit God and
what He does.

We agree, therefore, with Hans Küng who, in his essay
entitled 'The World Religions in God's Plan of Salvation,' says:

> . . . in its summons to conversion the Gospel of Jesus Christ
> does not require the renunciation of whatever in the world
> religions 'is true, whatever is honourable, whatever is just,
> whatever is pure, whatever is lovely, whatever is gracious'
> (Phil. 4:8).[19]

Such recognition of the truth and grace of God in other religions
will not diminish the critically important place which the Christian faith plays in the history of God's salvation. On the contrary,
it adds to the richness of the truth apprehended in the Christian
faith.

What then is the special contribution which the Christian
church can make in the world of religions? What approach ought
the Christian mission take in communicating God's salvation in
Jesus Christ? Is there still sense in speaking about Christian
mission at all? Would it not be better for those religions to be
left alone to pursue their search for absolutes? In answering these
questions, I would like to refer ourselves once again to Tillich's
observation which provides us, in our judgment, with a basic
understanding of religion. He says:

> In the depth of every living religion there is a point at which
> the religion itself loses its importance, and that to which it
> points breaks through its particularity, elevating it to
> spiritual freedom and with it a vision of the spiritual pre-

sence in other expressions of the ultimate meaning of man's existence.[20]

And then he adds: 'This is what Christianity must see in the present encounter of the world religions.'

The first thing that needs to be said here is this: Jesus Christ is the new spiritual freedom which, to use Tillich's expression, breaks through the particularity of religions. As has been mentioned, each religion represents particular ways in which people in particular existential situations respond to the ultimate reality. This simply means that revelation does not take place in a vacuum. It comes to man through his cultural and historical associations. Thus, particularity is part and parcel of religions. But the chief problem we often encounter in religions is that this particularity tends to be endowed with absolute character. When this happens, a particular religion is absolutized as the sole guardian and interpreter of the truth. The particularity of a religion is taken for the universality of the absolute reality to which a particular religion is, in fact, a merely partial response. This is the tendency to which all religions are too prone to fall.

In striking contrast, Jesus Christ exhibited the spirit of radical freedom towards his own religion. For him, Judaism to which he had been born was a partial response of his own race to the saving love of God. But the corruption of Judaism began when its particularity was thought to embody entirely the absolute and universal nature of the ultimate divine reality. Consequently, it had to resort to laws and regulations meant to be applicable in each and every living situation. The course was thus set for Judaism to become a legalistic religion. The salvation of God was thought to be captured in the law and the way to salvation was naturally considered to consist in the strict observation of the law. In this way God's salvation was institutionalized.

In each and every religion, there is something of Judaism present. That is why religions tend to become mutually exclusive, although absoluteness and universality which each religion claims is of pseudo-character. But just because of this, there seems no way for religions to be free from the impasse of their pseudo-claim to absoluteness and universality. In this way, the particularity of religion, instead of becoming an enriching element in man's diverse and varied ways of responding to God's revelation, proves to be an obstacle not to be easily overcome.

Jesus Christ broke out of the particularity of Judaism decisively. Judaism became a stagnant religion precisely because it misinterpreted its own particularity in the history of God's salvation. As Jesus saw it, it was stifling the truth and the saving love of God. In thus breaking out of the Jewish particularism, he was not only able to restore the universal dimension to the prophetic faith of the Old Testament, but also to give due recognition to the expressions of faith in God, surfaced in his contacts with those outside the religious and cultural milieus of Judaism. He even actually commended the faith demonstrated by the Roman centurion[21] and the Syro-Phoenician woman.[22] The particularism of Judaism, instead of being à particular focal expression of God's love towards all mankind, was proving detrimental to the mission and ministry of Jesus Christ. It lost the ability to see in the people of other religions and nationalities the fellow creatures of God whom Christ came to save. There was no alternative but for Christ to challenge it, break out of it and to emphasize the prophetic message of God's salvation.

This kind of religious particularism has, unfortunately, persisted throughout the history of Christianity. It was even one of the thorny problems which the apostles had to deal with as they began gathering around themselves those who confessed their faith in Jesus Christ. The First Christian council convened in Jerusalem by the apostles had to zero in on the problem presented by the Judaizers in the new community of Christians. The Judaizers asserted that the Gentile Christians must undergo circumcision and obey the law of Moses. Peter and James disagreed. It is the grace of Jesus Christ that saves and not the observance of the law practised in the Jewish religious community. As the author of the Book of Acts tells us in the fifteenth chapter, the contention of the Judaizers was refuted. And on James' proposal, the Council decided to send a letter to the church in Antioch, Syria and Cilicia, announcing that the yoke of the Jewish law would not be imposed on the Gentile Christians. Throughout this Council it was Peter who played the most prominent role. It should be noted that the Council at Jerusalem took place after Peter's traumatic experience at Joppa in connection with the

Roman centurion, Cornelius. We already had occasion to discuss this episode earlier. It is evident that that experience proved to be a turning point in Peter's career, and it enabled him to hold a vigorous position against the Judaizers.

But even this Peter was unable to shed the particularism of Judaism completely. It was after the Council in Jerusalem that Paul had a sharp clash with Peter over the question of eating with the Gentile Christians. According to Paul in his letter to the Galatians, Peter, during his visit with Paul in Antioch, ate with the Gentile Christians initially. But he quickly withdrew from the table fellowship when 'certain men from James'[23] appeared on the scene from Jerusalem. Highly enraged by this inconsistency of Peter, Paul challenged him, declaring that a man is justified through faith in Jesus Christ and not by the works of the law.

It was Paul who proved to be the one who was able to over-come the particularism of Judaism completely. Not only this, in launching into the mission to the Gentiles, the conviction seemed to grow in Paul that 'the full salvation of the Gentiles is to usher in the full salvation of Israel.'[24] Can we call this 'salvation in reverse-flow'? In a sense, can it not be said that the salvation of Israel is dependent on the salvation of the Gentiles? We, too, seem to be witnessing this 'salvation in reverse-flow' in the con-temporary world. After the period of vigorous missionary opera-tion outside the Western world, the church in the West seems now to be besieged by her own problems at home, losing leader-ship in the missionary activity of the total church. It is now the churches in the Third World that are taking upon themselves the responsibility of Christian mission and making efforts to come up with relevant expressions of Christian faith in their own living situations. Is it not now generally agreed that perhaps the churches in the Third World will play an important role in the re-vitalization of the churches in the West? Is it also not true to say that the effort of Third World theologians in re-interpreting the contents of the Christian faith in their cultural and social contexts may provide Western theology with some fresh inputs and throw some new lights on the formulation of viable theological alternatives?

This leads me to stress that just as Christ broke away from the particularism of Judaism and just as Paul set himself free from the particularism of the early Jewish Christian community, so the Christian mission must now be emancipated from the particularism of Christianity imposed on the people in Asia by Western Christian mission. It is my contention that particularism pertaining to all religions must be broken. This is the particularism of elevating particular experience and perception of the divine truth to the ultimate authority. I have tried to show that in Jesus Christ we are confronted with the power to break this particularism of religions. And quite logically, the place to begin the de-particularizing of religions is Christianity. As this de-particularizing process is carried out in Christianity, the Christians in Asia will be enabled to take a fresh look at the religions and cultural world around them. Then a new call to men and women of other faiths and different religious persuasions may be issued by the Christians to venture into the joint mission of finding in Jesus Christ the fulfilment of their spiritual search for the ultimate reality· that constitutes the meaning of life here and now and in the course of eternity.

The approach which we are advocating here is not that of a *praeparatio evangelica* or a *preparatio incarnationis*. According to this view, religions, not including Christianity, have no intrinsic value. They exist for the moment of the incarnation, after which they are to be set aside entirely. Rather, we hold that the Word of God which was present in the beginning of the creation and has now become present in Jesus Christ has always constituted the very basis of man's spirituality. Thus, the Word of God is also present in other religions, even though too frequently in distorted ways.

Walter Freytag, from whom we have quoted earlier in this chapter, seems to disagree with this. He gives an account of the experience he once had in Indonesia as follows. During his visit to a theological seminary in Java, he saw a picture on a blackboard which

> consisted of two flights of steps, each with seven stairs, the one going up to the right and the other to the left, and between them a cross, its base level with and very near the lowest step of each stairway. Its cross-beam, however, was at the same height as the two topmost steps. I asked for the drawing to be explained to me and was told: 'We

were just talking of the relationship between Javanese mysticism and the message of the Bible. And that is it, you see'. The higher mysticism ascends, the more it departs from the cross, although it reaches the same height, and the deeper is the cleft separating the Bible message and mysticism.[25]

If the explanation of this picture—it is very imaginative, we must admit—is accepted as an adequate description of the relation between the cross and other religions, the conclusion that can be drawn from it is very disturbing indeed.

For one thing, to put religions on an ascending scale, characterizing them as higher and lower is already a value judgment on the basis of one's subjective religious standpoint. This will only raise a host of questions and further confuse the issue of religions. Obviously, the value judgment of religions in terms of higher and lower cannot but be a relative judgment. What are the criteria to be used in determining which elements in a religion are higher and which ones are lower? And would a religion which possesses more higher elements than another religion be necessarily superior? The situation can become so confusing that the whole effort of evaluation becomes meaningless. Each religion should be evaluated on the basis of its intrinsic value in given situations. That is why it is often the case that existential experience of a religion will make a far greater contribution to our understanding of that religion than a theoretical knowledge of it.

But there is a far more serious criticism of the picture and the explanation of it in Freytag's story. The picture seems to express the view that the cross has much more in common with lower or primitive religions than higher or more sophisticated religions. We do not think this is true. As has been said, religions, high or low, developed or less developed, have one common essential concern, namely, the search for absolutes. Furthermore, the understanding of the biblical concept of revelation in terms of universality indicates that religions represent different responses to the revelation received in different human situations. We can infer from this that the cross is related to all religions, regardless of the various stages in development, in judgment and redemption.

In his very perceptive study on faith and its practice in Islam and Christianity, Kenneth Cragg substantiates what we have just said. In his own words, as the Christian who seeks to meet Islam in the fullest sense and listens earnestly to the call to prayer,

> he can hardly fail to relate the good in Christ, salvation and God's saving health, the transforming forgiveness and newness of life, to the good of the call to prayer. He cannot escape the relation of his own coming to God through Christ to the Muslim call to surrender. His convictions about the Apostles of the New Testament must bear upon his attitudes to the Apostle of Islam. Prophethood as he has known it in Isaiah and Jeremiah must shape him as a reader when he comes to the Quran.[26]

Short of such an effort to relate to other religions, Christians will not be able to discover the remarkable depth of spirituality in other faiths not being entirely alien to the Christian faith. In my opinion, Western Christian mission has not only failed to give due credit to this underlying spirituality in other religions, but also alienated Christian converts from it. This is now proving to be unfortunate to the Christian church as well as to other religions. Christianity and other religions have come to view each other in the spirit and practice of mutual exclusiveness. With the world situation being what it is now, it is imperative that the attitude of mutual exclusiveness must give way to the acknowledgement of the depth of spiritual meaning which sustains and inspires man's search for the ultimate reality in which the mystery of life lies.

Does this mean that Christians must suspend what they hold to be true? Do they now have to dim out the light of the truth of Jesus Christ, if not to extinguish it? Our answer is definitely No. We are well aware that we cannot avoid the question of truth in religious situations. But we must also have a clear idea of what we mean by truth. By truth we do not mean a dogma, a religious proposition, or a doctrinal presupposition to be pressed for acceptance without further ado. Our own commitment to truth and the commitment we expect of others, cannot be a commitment to a dogma or creed. It is unfortunate that a commitment to a dogma or creed is always viewed as a criterion of one's acceptance of a certain religious faith. This has the beauty of black-white clarity, of neatness with which enthusiastic believers can conveniently process people into the realm of light and the realm of darkness. Such a practice is as dangerous as it is absurd, for it reduces the spiritual matter to something objectifiable and measurable. In so doing, it does disservice to the truth which is beyond adequate explanation by any dogma or creed.

By truth here we mean Jesus Christ who comes to man in his situation not as a dogma or an axiom but as personal truth. He is the truth which operates primarily in personal contexts. He is, therefore, the truth which will not permit itself to be formulated into laws and regulations. Jesus Christ as the truth is to be encountered as a person and not to be held in reverence as the impersonal object of worship. In other words, he is the personal truth which comes to man in the latter's deep spiritual need.

The task of the Christian mission is to confront men and women of other religions, or for that matter in whatever contexts they may be, with this Jesus Christ, the personal truth. What should emerge out of such confrontation, at least from the standpoint of Christian mission, are not religious traditions and institutions posing as barriers defying the interference of Christians. In the course of such encounter, Christians ought to be able to realize that Jesus Christ the personal truth penetrates the facade of religions and stands face to face with men and women behind the religious facade. These are the men and women deeply involved in their religious and cultural traditions and ethos. Personally encountered by Christ the truth, they will undergo change in their own person; and through this change they will be prompted to re-evaluate their religious beliefs, cultural traditions and the socio-political contexts which have constituted the framework of their life and activities.

The Christian church is, therefore, entrusted with this task of presenting Christ to those who have not openly confessed their faith in him, to those who have not publicly acknowledged their relationship to him or to those who have no conscious knowledge of him. This is Christian mission. For this reason Christian mission will not consider it its task to denounce other religions. It is primarily concerned with the proclamation that Christ is the way, the truth and the life. And it proclaims in such a way that it at the same time is engaged in the task of interpreting what this means in the biblical contexts and what it means for the world as Christians see it and experience it. This is how the authors of the Gospels set about recording the Gospel narratives. Luke, for example, addressing himself to Theophilus, decided to write an account of Christ as he knew it, so as to give him 'authentic knowledge' about the matters related to Christ.[27] In defining the Christian mission in terms of interpretation, Kenneth Cragg aptly says:

> The amazing reality behind and within the Christian mission in the world is this task of interpretation. Our duty is to carry over the Word which God has uttered, to be the translators of His speech into the language, the idiom, and the minds of ordinary men.[28]

This implies that Christian mission cannot interpret the Word of God meaningfully without making an effort to understand the language and the minds of ordinary people—people with their religio-cultural traditions and social-political conditions.

In response to Jesus Christ as the personal truth presented to them by Christians, he who holds other religious beliefs will have to give account of the change that has taken place in him. Here conversion does not necessarily mean a clean break from his religious and cultural associations. Since there is something in the depth of his religiosity related to the universal nature of God's truth and love, to deny his religion would also mean denial of that which is of God, namely the ultimate reality he seeks. It is, therefore, theologically not far fetched to suggest as A. C. Bouquet does that

> it might not be improper for believers to exist who called themselves Christian Buddhists or Christian Confucians, and even perhaps Christian Vedantists or Christian Moslems, without in the least abating their adherence to the Catholic faith, and while paying a respectful tribute to the religious insights of their forefathers, and to their enlightenment by the One Logos. There are already some who dare to call themselves Christian Communists.[29]

In Jesus Christ we find the fulfilment of the prophetic message of the Old Testament. For lack of a better term, let us call it 'selective fulfilment.' Not everything said and done and projected found its way into the fulfilment in the person of Jesus Christ. As we discussed before, some elements in the Old Testament had to be rejected and some had to be radically transformed. Since such selective fulfilment took place between the Old Testament and the New Testament, why could it not also take place between Jesus Christ and the religions outside the Judeo-Christian traditions? Granted that there is something special about the relationship between the Old and the New Testaments. But the special nature of this relationship should not be viewed as serving the function of excluding other religions from the dispensation of God's salvation.

True, God's salvation is not co-extensive with world history. But God's salvation for the whole world is progressively revealed as its impact on world history is both intensified and extensified. And it is Jesus Christ who brings into sharp relief the impacts that have been going on between God's salvation and the history of mankind. In this process it is man with his religious beliefs and socio-cultural structures who is brought to trial. Jesus Christ is, therefore, man's trial. In him man is tried, judged and sentenced to death. But this is not the end. It is only the end of the beginning. For in him man is promised the fulfilment of life. Man rises with him from death. Christian mission is to bear witness to this drama of death and life. It urges men and women to find their fulfilment of their search for the ultimate reality in Jesus Christ. It is, therefore, conversion to Christ and not to Christianity that ought to be the supreme concern of Christian mission; for in Jesus Christ the particularities of religions are overcome, and through him men and women are united in the universal love of God.

REFERENCES

1. Karl Barth, *Church Dogmatics* I/2, translated by G. T. Thompson H. Knight, Edinburgh: T. and T. Clark, 1956, p. 299.

2. We may quote here the observation made by Hans W. Frey in his article entitled ' Religion: Natural and Revealed ' in' *A Handbook of Christian Theology*, edited by Marvin Halverson and Arthur A. Cohen, New York: The World Publishing Company, 1958 (pp. 310-320): ' . . . the growth of the ecumenical movement and the rising tide of independence among the "younger" churches beyond Western culture have contributed to the urgent necessity for a theological understanding of the cultural, including the religious matrix of civilizations, both those of the West and of the East . . . One must add here the growing conviction among theologians that the culture of the West is in large degree secular . . . . and is therefore, in its own way, fresh missionary territory ' (pp. 319-320).

3. Cf., *International Review of Mission*, Vol. 79, No. 236, October, 1970, devoted to the subject ' Faithful Dialogue.' For some Asian reactions to dialogues with other religions, see James Pan, 'Dialogue—Some Reflections,' and Ng Lee-ming, ' Dialogue—A Reappraisal of Priorities,' in *Ching Feng*, Quarterly Notes on Christianity and Chinese Religion and Culture, Vol. XIV, No. 3, 1971.

4. Paul Tillich, *My Search for Absolutes*, New York: Simon and Schuster, 1967, p. 77.

5. Kenneth Cragg, *The Call of the Minaret*, New York: Oxford University Press, 1956, p. 274.

6. Walter Freytag, *The Gospel and the Religions*, London: SCM Press, 1957, p. 14.

7. Paul Tillich, *Christianity and the Encounter of the World Religions*, New York: Columbia University Press, 1963, p. 4.

8. Joachim Wach, *Understanding and Believing*, edited by Joseph M. Kitagawa, New York: Harper and Row, 1968, p. 9.

9. Joachim Wach, *ibid*.

10. Psalm 8:3-4.

11. Matthew 6:33.

12. Philip H. Ashby, *History and Future of Religious Thought*, Englewood Cliffs, N. J. : Prentice-Hall, Inc. 1963, p. 90.

13. *The Documents of Vatican II*, edited by Walter M. Abbott, S. J., New York: The America Press, 1966, p. 17. In this Declaration, the Roman Catholic Church has initiated an important step towards the problem of religions. The following comment on this initiative is well made: ' This positive methodological approach . . . . is an extraordinary step, and one can easily wager that not just a single chapter but the all-embracing character of the entire document is the sign by which future scholars will mark its commanding import in conciliar history. Nevertheless, the Declaration, understood along with other documents, has not answered but only presented anew old theological questions ' (*Vatican II An Interfaith Appraisal*, edited by John H. Miller, CSC, Notre Dame and London: University of Notre Dame Press, 1966, pp. 340-341). It has to be noted that the General Assembly of the World Council of Churches in Uppsala, 1968, did not take up the problem of

religions in any seriousness. It was a big lacuna in the Assembly. Since then subunit on Dialogue with People of Living Faiths and Ideologies has been created in the World Council to deal with this particular concern.

14. The quotation is taken from van der Leeuw's *Religion in Essence and Manifestation* (London: George Allen and Unwin, 1938). Its exact location in the book is lost to me. In the same book, van der Leeuw also says that ' For religion, then, God is the active Agent in relation to man . . . . ' (p. 23).

15. Joachim Wach, *Understanding and Believing*, New York: Harper Torch-books, Harper and Row, 1968, p. 140. Among the contemporary theologians it is Paul Tillich who has taken most seriously the History of Religions in his theological work. See, for example, his article ' The Significance of the History of Religions for the Systematic Theologian,' in his book, *The Future of Religions*, New York: Harper and Row, 1966.

16. Tillich, *The Future of Religions*, p. 81.

17. Barth, *Church Dogmatics* I/2, translated by G. T. Thomson and L. H. Knight, Edinburgh: T. and T. Clark, 1956, p. 343.

18. Colossians 3:11.

19. Hans Küng's article appears in a symposium, *Christian Revelation and World Religions*, edited by Joseph Neuner, London: Burns and Oates, 1967, pp. 25-66. The quotation in the text is from p. 51.

20. Tillich, *Christianity and the Encounter of the World Religions*, p. 97.

21. Matthew 8:5-13.

22. Mark 7:24-30.

23. Galatians 2:11-13. There is a question as to whether the clash between Paul and Peter in Antioch took place after or before the Council at Jerusalem. Johannes Munck, for instance, remarks: ' . . . it is overlooked that the text (Gal. 2:11 ff.) leaves open the question of whether the clash in Antioch took place before or after the conference in Jerusalem. And what is still more important, people have shut their eyes to the fact that such an assumption, that the episode in Antioch invalidated the Jerusalem agreement, is not consistent with the text of Galatians ' (*Paul and the Salvation of Mankind*, Richmond: John Knox Press, 1957, p. 106). At any rate Peter's experience in Antioch must have proved to be another important landmark in Peter's deepening awareness of the love of Christ surpassing the laws of religion.

24. Johannes Munk, *op. cit.*, p. 276. For example in Rom. 15:17-24, 'Paul is speaking here of the fullness of the Gentiles, which is to end Israel's unbelief and lead to all Israel's salvation. It is above all on the shoulders of Paul, the apostle to the Gentiles, that the task is laid of bringing about the fullness of the Gentiles, and of thereby preparing the salvation of Israel . . .' *ibid*, p. 277.

25. Walter Freytag, *The Gospel and the Religions*, pp. 20-21.

26. Kenneth Cragg, *The Call of the Minaret*, New York: Oxford University Press, 1964, p. 177.

27. Luke 1:4.

28. Kenneth Cragg, *op. cit.*, p. 273.

29. A. C. Bouquet, *The Christian Faith and Non-Christian Religions*, New York: Harper and Brothers, 1958, p. 424.

CHAPTER EIGHT

Man's Quest for Humanity

An echo of Childhood stalks before me
Like evening shadows on the earth,
Rolling back into piquant memory
The anguished cry of my birth;

Out of the Caverns of nativity
A voice, I little knew as my own
And thought to have shed with infancy,
Returns with a sharpness before unknown.

Poor castaways to this darkling shore,
Void out of the sea of eternity
And blind, we catch by reflex horror
And instant glimpse, the guilt of our see:

The souls of men are steeped in stupor
Who, tenants upon this wild isle unblest,
Sleep on, oblivious of its loud nightmare
With wanton motions bedevilling our breast.[1]

—JOHN PEPPER CLARK, NIGERIA

1. Loss of Creatureliness

MAN's search for absolutes which we discussed in the preceding chapter is in fact his quest for humanity. What man is, namely his essential nature, is exposed to the extent that he exposes himself to the ultimate reality. To put it differently, in order to know man, we have to know God. This statement cannot be reversed. We cannot say, in order to know God we must first know man. That is why the quest for humanity can properly begin only after the quest for the ultimate reality. That is why what we are going to discuss in this chapter must be preceded by what we had to say in the last chapter. To reverse this order is to invite disaster. The cosmos would be reduced to microcosms. The world would be internalized as reflections of man's consciousness. The ultimate reality which man seeks would become subjectivized as the projection of man's feeling. We would have to agree with Feuerbach who defines God in terms of man's feeling. This is what he has to tell us about what is known as God:

> God is pure, unlimited, free feeling. Every other God, whom
> thou supposest, is a God thrust upon thy feeling from with-
> out. Feeling is atheistic in the sense of the orthodox belief,
> which attaches religion to an external object; it denies an
> objective God—it is itself God. In this point of view only
> the negation of feeling is the negation of God.[2]

We cannot reduce God to our subjective feeling. There is nothing ultimate in our feeling. It is transitory and thus subject to
decay.

If Feuerbach's treatment of feeling is illegitimate, do we have
to give glory to God at the cost of man? Will we have to praise
the divinity of God at the expense of the humanity of man? Not
at all. If we cannot go back to the theology of feeling which
flourished in nineteenth century Europe, neither can we return
to the excessive theo-centric theology of neo-orthodoxy which
dominated the Western theology in the early decades of the
twentieth century. What then is the proper treatment of the
humanity of man?

Here Barth can give us a clue as to how to go about dealing
with man theologically. In his *The Humanity of God* he wrestles
with the problem of the relationship between God and man in
such a way that humanity is given a legitimate theological place.
He writes:

> Who God is and what He is in His deity He proves and reveals
> not in a vacuum as a divine being-for-Himself, but precisely
> and authentically in the fact that He exists, speaks, and acts
> as the *partner* of man, though of course as the absolutely
> superior partner. He who does *that* is the living God.
> And the freedom in which He does *that* is His deity. It
> is the deity which as such also has the character of
> humanity. . . It is precisely God's *deity* which, rightly
> understood, includes his humanity.[3]

One may at first be puzzled as to what this humanity in God's
deity means. But surely it must mean that man cannot do without God, that man's self-understanding is essentially related to his
understanding of God. It follows that man's quest for humanity
must be the corollary of his search for absolutes. For this reason
it is our purpose in this chapter to discuss the Christian mission
with reference to humanization.

The place to begin our discussion is the third chapter of the book of Genesis in the Old Testament. In this what is known as the story of the Fall, what is the basic human problem that is brought out into the light? Is the chief purpose of the story to accuse man of rebelling against God? Does it try to portray an angry God like an angry father whose son has rebelled against him? Or is the story of the Fall a rationalization on the transciency of man's life? Does it express the chagrin of man who is forbidden access to the tree of eternal life? None of these can be the central concern of the religious genius which was instrumental in the construction of the story of the Fall. The story is mainly concerned with the disruption which has invaded man— the disruption between man's existential nature and his essential nature. It tries to answer the question why man is not what he should be.

Thus, the main theme of the story of the Fall can be called 'the loss of creatureliness'. One theological commentator says:

> Man is *sicut deus*. Now he lives out of himself, now he creates his own life, he is his own creator. He no longer needs the Creator, he has become a creator himself, to the extent that he creates his own life. With this, his creatureliness is finished and destroyed for him. Adam is no longer creature. He has torn himself away from his creature-liness—Together with the *limit* Adam has lost his creature-liness. Limitless Adam can no longer be addressed in his creatureliness.[4]

With the Fall man has lost his creatureliness, the basis on which his relationships with God, his Creator and with other creatures were constructed. Thus, the loss of creatureliness is the loss of humanity. This is the root of all tragedies that accompany the life of man.

One immediate result of man's loss of creatureliness or humanity is related to the serious problem of his identity. He can no longer take for granted his identity as the creature of God. He has to find his place in the order of the creation. He is forced to establish his own identity. But however hard he may try, he has to realize that it all ends up in adding to his identity problem. In a sense, we can say that the history of mankind is the history of man seeking wrong identities. He seeks his identity in the civilization he is able to build. But as soon as his cultural identity seems established, it comes into clash with other cultural identities. He may seek his identity in the supremacy of race. Then he becomes the victim of a racial superiority complex. Some may establish his identity in political power, but his effort, if successful, often ends up in political dictatorship. One may find his identity in economic power, but it will not take long for him to realize that his economic power has made him exercise exploitation on other people. Or finally, one will seek his identity in a religion. Here again he is not entirely on safe ground, for he may become so sure of what he believes that he becomes an advocate of religious absolutism denying validity to other forms of religious expressions and practices. Wrong searches for human identity thus bring about chaos to the created order.

In the contemporary world we have all been experiencing the identity problem in its intensity. We call it identity crisis. We find ourselves in the midst of the crisis either individually or collectively. We are not sure any more where we belong in this on-going passage of time. The crisis of identity is intensified as social and political changes rapidly take place. These changes have impersonal character. True, man is still the agent in all these changes. But, he is no longer an active agent. There seem to be gigantic forces at work to push man into the stream of change. He has to obey the command of these impersonal forces behind all changes. This makes man extremely restless and unhappy. He is aware of his potentiality to create. That is why he attempted to be *sicut deus* in the first place. But once the change is set in motion, he can no longer be the master of it. This highly developed and still ceaselessly developing world has become a huge machine demanding his service and dictating his *modus vivendi*. Man is no longer a free agent. He is in the grip of fate which decides what his future will be.

Closely related to this loss of identity is the problem of dehumanization. This problem of dehumanization becomes more and more acute as human society makes a transition from being agricultural to industrial, from rural to urban, from person-oriented to system-centered, and from communal life-style to individualistic life-style. We thus cannot help viewing industrialization and urbanization as a mixed blessing. Industrialization has succeeded in uncovering both human and physical resources for the development of technology. It has rendered the physical distance between man and man of little significance. Through efficient and elaborate systems of management, 'the affairs of man and the world are managed effectively. At last man seems to be able to sit back and enjoy the fruits of industrialization.

But there seems to be a stern law of good and evil at work in the world. Every good achieved always seems to be accompanied by evil. Not only this, good tends to be overshadowed by evil in the long run. Thus, the success of industrialization is tarnished by the evil it has brought with it. For one thing, industrialization has caused great imbalance in the demographic picture of the world. The great concentration of manpower in urban centers where industrialization is developed by leaps and bounds has made the rural area seriously short of manpower. But a large number of those who have come to urban centers in search of opportunities and better life do not fare any better. They are quickly assimilated into the systems of industrialized society and become part of the process of production. Man is no longer judged by what he is as the creature of God but by the product he has had a part in bringing into existence. Man has become a part of the complex machines that keep the industrial society moving.

Another result of loss of creatureliness is what Tillich calls estrangement. According to him,

> the state of existence is the state of estrangement. Man is estranged from the ground of his being, from other beings and from himself.[5]

This enables Tillich to say that 'today man experiences his present situation in terms of disruption, conflict, self-destruction, meaninglessness, and despair in all realms of life. This experience is expressed in the arts and in literature, conceptualized in existential philosophy, actualized in political cleavages of all kinds, and analysed in the psychology of the unconscious'.[6] This is a pretty grim picture of the state of man and the world. But it does call our attention to the extent to which the loss of creatureliness has led man.

Estrangement has affected the relationship between God and man. For man to be estranged from God amounts to cutting himself off from the *fons et origo* of his being. He denies that his humanity is derived from the divinity of God. To be completely estranged from God thus means to become completely atheistic. It follows that a man who holds a completely atheistic view, who will absolutely have nothing to do with God, must face the possibility of losing his humanity completely. But so long as one still holds on to some kind of ultimate or absolute, be it religious, social, cultural or political, one cannot be an atheist in the sense we described above. As long as one still retains respect of reverence for a power that somehow transcends man, one has not completely separated oneself from the root of one's being. We can, therefore, argue that religions, from primitive religions to sophisticated ones, are evidence that man, though estranged from God, is not completely severed from the origin of his being. That is why we tried to look at religions as man's search for absolutes in the preceding chapter. In the context of our reasoning here, religions are signs that man is not left entirely to his own resources, that man's ultimate hope is not in man himself but in God. In our opinion this is another theological meaning of the phenomenon of religions.

Man's estrangement from God has profoundly tragic effects on his relationships with his fellow man. Human relationships are now vitiated with suspicion, hatred and jealousy. Cain's answer to God's question about the whereabouts of his brother Abel puts this disrupted human relationship in a nutshell: 'Am I my brother's keeper?' This denial of his responsibility towards his brother shows man as a self-seeking being. That is why the human society has turned into an arena of ruthless competitions. In every competition there will be both winners and losers, victors and victims. This is particularly true when a society becomes more and more industrialized. Small industries are absorbed by big industries; less imaginative and adventurous business men tend to yield to the pressures from hard-driving and aggressive ones. You have to become tough-hearted to survive in this kind of competitive world.

After a long period of trial and error, people in the world have on the whole adjusted themselves to this reality of life. They first emerged out of a collective society and worked out an individualistic form of life. Human relationships based on individualism were redefined in terms of contract. Western society in particular is thus a contractual society. Each person, in order to avoid unnecessary conflicts and in order to safeguard order and justice, is expected to act and behave according to the rules of the game. This accommodation to estranged human relationships has given the Western society a semblance of order. But this device to regulate disrupted and broken human relationships on a contractual basis is on trial now, for it has become increasingly clear that there is no guarantee that everybody will play according to the rules of the game. And when the power play enters into the game, rules and contracts are thrown overboard, and one begins to pursue one's political and social objectives with such an intensity that one threatens to destroy any vestiges of respectability in human relationships. That is why in the political structure of Western democracy we have a most noble and at the same time a most vulnerable system of government.[7]

Estrangement, when it has invaded the personhood of man, results in the disruption of man within himself. This is another point which must be mentioned here. As has been pointed out, the humanity shaken loose from the divinity of God is the most tragic expression of man's estrangement not only from God but also from his own true humanity. By becoming estranged from God, man becomes estranged from himself; by becoming independent of God, man becomes independent of himself, of his true nature. This is the very source of the existential predicament of man. The being of man is now infected with disorder. He is affected physically, mentally and psychologically. The story of the fall to which we have been referring in our discussion here expresses this existential condition of man by describing how man comes to be aware of his nakedness and to become ashamed of it. In other words, 'shame' is used to express our more sophisticated term 'disorder of being'. Thus, according to von Rad,

> Shame, for our narrator, is the most elementary emotion of a guilty feeling at the deepest root of human existence, the sign of a breach that reaches to the lowest level of our physical being. We must conclude, therefore, that because he grasped for what was forbidden, man has experienced a longing . . . which again and again makes itself independent and tears apart from the unity of body and spirit;

and man reaches to this innermost disturbance with a feeling of shame.[8]

It is, therefore, mistaken to interpret the story of the Fall as man's waking out of his innocent state. It is not the problem of a transition from innocence to puberty that is involved here. To interpret it this way is to miss the fundamental truth of man's nature estranged from God. It was not innocence but harmony that ruled the relation of man to God. But this harmony is broken because he has denied his dependence on God. His humanity has now been divorced from the divinity of God. This is what sin essentially means in the biblical and theological sense of the word. Sin, therefore, has to do with the essential nature of man.

From the above analysis it is clear that what Christian mission must deal with is this man whose being is deeply disturbed. He has to be brought out of his isolation and set once again in the relational contexts with God, his fellowman and himself. This is no other than the restoration of the whole humanity of man. That is why Jesus' discourse with Nicodemus was focused on the theme of being born again. 'In truth, in very truth' I tell you,' says Jesus to Nicodemus, 'unless a man has been born over again he cannot see the Kingdom of God'.[9] To be born again means to regain man's creatureliness, to be fully man again, in other words to become human again. It is in this sense that we must speak of Christian mission as having to do with humanization.

2. The Humanization of God

Humanization begins at the very heart of God. It is the movement that starts with God and moves towards man. Man by himself is not capable of humanization. As has been shown in the last section, man is driven more and more to dehumanization, the very opposite of humanization. He puts himself in the situation of being incapable of becoming what he should be without outside help. On account of this God has to move in and becomes engaged in the creation of the new humanity. This, in essence, is what the incarnation means. The incarnation, the Word become flesh, is no other than the humanization of God. It is the act of God which makes Himself available to man in human terms. It is the operation of God to make it possible for man to become once again His partner by becoming a man. This man is Jesus Christ. Jesus Christ, therefore, is the humanization of God. In him we see God. Through him we come to have knowledge of God, and through him God has shown us what man should be. And since to regain true humanity means for man to regain his wholeness as a human being, the humanization of God in Jesus Christ results in man's salvation. That is why Jesus Christ is our salvation. In him man is healed, saved and becomes human. Christ is thus our Saviour. My thesis here, therefore, is this: the humanization of God is the salvation of man. To use the traditional theological language, Christology fulfils itself in soteriology. Salvation in terms of humanization is part and parcel of what God is in Jesus Christ. Immanuel; God with us—this is the fundamental meaning of salvation.

It is unfortunate that this basic theological meaning of the concept of humanization tends to be badly misunderstood and misinterpreted when transported to and employed in missiology. A good illustration can be found in the sharp and heated debate on the report of Section II (Renewal in Mission) at the General Assembly of the World Council of Churches at Uppsala in 1968. The report, under the first section entitled 'A Mandate for Mission,' begins with these provocative words:

> We belong to a humanity that cries passionately and articulately for a fully human life. Yet the very humanity of man and his societies is threatened by a greater variety of destructive forces than ever. And the acutest moral problems all hinge upon the question: What is man? ... There is a burning relevance today in describing the mission of God, in which we participate, as the gift of a new creation which is a radical renewal of the old and the invitation to men to grow up into their full humanity in the new man, Jesus Christ.[10]

The emphasis of the report is unmistakably on man and his humanity. But on the whole it is a balanced theological statement without by-passing the centrality of the biblical teaching on the incarnation. 'Jesus Christ', says the report, 'incarnate, crucified and risen, is the new man'.[11] However, the concept of evangelism as aggressively converting millions of unbelievers to Christianity is replaced by that of 'bringing about the occasions for men's response to Jesus Christ'.[12] This change of tone is in fact long overdue, especially from the standpoint of the Third World people who have been the object of Western missionary zeal and evangelistic fervour.

For missiologists notably such as Beyerhaus and those at the Institute of Church Growth in California, this almost amounts to the betrayal of the cause of Christian mission. For them the emphasis on the new humanity which enables man 'to break through racial, national, religious and other barriers that divide the unity of mankind'[13] has seriously compromised the Christian faith. In the words of Beyerhaus, for the evangelicals 'the present ecumenical attempts to redefine the goal of mission in terms of humanizing the social structure reveal a decisive theological deviation at the very heart of the Christian faith'.[14] This is a gross misunderstanding of what humanization means theologically. Humanization, understood in the sense I described, is not to be equated with the humanizing of the social structure. The humanizing of the social structure is not the whole of Christian mission. But when the social structure becomes oppressive, when it obstructs the development of man, the Christian mission which proclaims God's love and His justice cannot avoid the responsibility of performing some vital role in bringing about the change. The primary concern of Christian mission is, therefore, man, man for whom Christ came, died and rose again, and not the social structure as such.

But Beyerhaus not only has misgivings about the Christian involvement in the change of social structure. He is fundamentally sceptical about the role and place of man in God's saving act. After pointing out the atheistic tendency in the secular humanism which has replaced God with man and transferred the center of history from God to man, Beyerhaus is

> shocked to see how naively current ecumenical missiology can take up the concept of humanization and put it one-sidedly into the motivation and goal. True enough, the New Testament does describe Jesus as the New Man and the beginner of a new humanity. But this is a complementary exposition to the other, more central concept, that in Jesus Christ we are meeting the pre-existent Son of God. . . Separating these two concepts and putting his human nature into the foreground will always create the risk of

perverting the Christian faith into a humanistic syncretism which at the same time removes the ontological diastasis between biblical faith and non-Christian religions and ideologies.[15]

In this way, Beyerhaus rules out any place for humanization in Christian theology and in Christian mission. As man is forcefully pushed out of the perimeter of God's saving act, one begins to wonder what salvation is for, or for whom it is carried out. Does Beyerhaus mean to say, in the good tradition of the Reformation theology, God saves man for His own glory? Then, is man to be considered as a means to God's self-glorification? Why do theologians with Beyerhaus' theological inclination always have to be so suspicious of man that man is brought to the presence of God's saving love through the back door?

We are by no means unaware of the humanistic attempt, both in its Western version and in its Eastern form, to stress the self affirmation of man at the expense of God. But this is no reason to relegate man to an insignificant place in God's salvation. It has to be said with the utmost clarity that salvation is not the drama in which God is the sole actor. On the contrary, man is right at the center of the drama, playing his role. There will be those who accept the saving love whole-heartedly. There will be some who accept it only half-heartedly. Still others will adopt the attitude of a passive onlooker. There will, of course, be some who oppose it. And there will be those who are unaware that they are drawn into the drama of God's salvation. No matter what role a man may play in the drama, he is right there in the midst of it, not because he has chosen to be there but because God in Christ has placed him there. That man is in the very center of God's salvation is the fact which must be strongly affirmed. If we deny or doubt it, we would be seriously compromising the full intention of God to be fully with man in Jesus Christ.

This is not merely a matter of theological emphasis. We want to contend that this is very basic to our experience and understanding of what God has done for man in Jesus Christ. Man cannot be made the easy target of theological castigation. Western Christian mission would have been a much happier affair if it had been more sparing of such theological castigation of man. We, therefore, agree with Barth when he says:

It is when we look at Jesus Christ that we know decisively that God's deity does not exclude, but includes His humanity.[16]

Then with characteristic humour he says of Calvin: 'Would that Calvin had energetically pushed ahead on this point in his Christology, his doctrine of God, his teaching about predestination, and then logically in his ethics! His Geneva would then not have become such a gloomy affair.'[17]

God affirms humanity! That is why theology, for Barth, is a happy science. There is no reason for theologians to sound pessimistic when it comes to the matter of humanity. This is not making light of the sin of man or his estrangement from God. But his existential predicament has not made God give up on man. On the contrary, God claims man back in Jesus Christ. And in this Jesus Christ 'the fact is once and for all established that God does not exist without man'.[18] With a stroke of theological boldness, Barth declares: 'God is human.'[19] Man has certainly won a place in Barth's theological system. Can we thus not say that theology is not so much the science of God as the science of man? By this we do not mean to reduce theology to pure anthropology. Rather, theology is the study of man on the basis of the humanization of God in Jesus Christ.

Humanization, far from being a deviation from the Christian faith, is integral to the proclamation of salvation. In other words, humanization must be the central concern of Christian mission. We do not preach God in abstraction. It is not God in Himself that constitutes the content of the Christian proclamation. God in Himself is the subject of metaphysical speculation and not the Person with whom we can enter into a personal relationship. God in Himself is out of human contexts and, therefore, irrelevant to the men and women who daily struggle and toil for their existence. He would be indifferent to the sufferings and miseries of this world and detached from the destiny of man. He would be the God of the arm-chair philosopher, the God of the classroom theologian, and the God of the well-provided evangelist. For those of us who have the fortune or perhaps the misfortune to live in the twentieth century, the terrible holocausts of the World Wars, the meaninglessness of the Vietnam War, and the hunger and death that mercilessly strike those who are destined to the so-called

famine belt stretching across the tropical zone from the Sahara
desert eastward to India— for us all these cannot but raise questions regarding the meaning of our life and destiny. Unable
to find an answer to ultimate questions of life, there are men and
women who cry like Average Woman in a play called *The Sign
of Jonah:*

> God is guilty! That is true! True! True! I speak for all
> the mothers of the twentieth century! I speak in the name
> of all those innocent children who died in the last two
> wars. I speak in the name of those who froze to death
> while fleeing for their lives. . .[20]

In answering this maddening accusation against God, Jonah says:
'That's the raving mad twentieth century.'

From the standpoint of the Christian faith, it is precisely into
this raving and mad world that God came in Jesus Christ. God
humanized Himself to bring humanization into the world. Thus,
the humanization of God is the salvation of the world. Humanization is not merely the goal of the mission of God. It is also the
starting point of His mission. The mission of God begins with
humanization and achieves its purpose in humanization. In short,
salvation is humanization.

In our judgment, the phrase 'the humanization of God' expresses more adequately what the time-honoured theological term
'incarnation' intends to convey. This is especially true in today's
Asia, and for that matter in the Third World. Although the
term incarnation has its biblical origin in John 1:14 where it is
said that the Word became flesh, it has a certain metaphysical
overtone. Consequently, the dynamic of the Greek verb *egeneto*
in *ho logos sarx egeneto* tends to get lost sight of in the use of
the term incarnation. It is true that most churches in Asia subscribe to the Nicene Creed and confess that Jesus Christ is fully
God and fully man. But without taking into serious account the
verb *egeneto*, how is it possible for us to comprehend the mystery
of God and man becoming one in Jesus Christ? It is no wonder
that one can detect a curious dichotomy in the Christological thinking of the church in Asia. On one hand, a great stress is laid
on Jesus Christ as the Son of God. He is no other than God and
worshipped as such so much so that the humanity he assumed
is almost regarded as sham humanity. On the other hand, there

does not seem to be hesitation in viewing Jesus Christ as a great moral teacher. That is why faith tends to be reduced to moralism in the churches in Asia, especially in the Chinese churches in which the strong influence of Confucianism prevails.

The theological thought of T. C. Chao, a Chinese theologian of considerable stature active in the church in China during the first half of this century, can be cited as an example of viewing Jesus Christ mainly from a moralistic point of view. In his study of T. C. Chao's thought, Lee-ming Ng made the remarks that for T. C. Chao

> the fact that Jesus Christ was our saviour did not mean that there was any special relationships between him and God. It was true that Jesus was sometimes called the 'Son of God', but this was due only to the 'moral excellence' that he had himself attained to. In other words, it was as a result of the perfect life that he lived that Jesus was called the 'Son of God', and it was not because he was the 'Son of God' that he had lived a life of perfection.[21]

It must be noted that T. C. Chao finds no reason to relate Jesus Christ to God in any substantial way. It is through his moral perfection that Jesus Christ attains a divine quality. Thus, in the Chinese church moralism is placed at the center of discipleship. To be saved is to become morally perfect. Salvation is detached from God and attached to the moral quality of the believers. Salvation is the upward movement of man and not the downward movement of God. It has more to do with the divinization of man than with the humanization of God. In this way, moralism which has to do with the day-to-day living in the mundane world gets related to the other-worldly religious thought. Moralism, practised with a view to one's salvation, becomes divorced from one's responsibility for the world.

It is due to this divinization of man, or the spiritualization of the message of salvation that the church in Asia, and notably the church in China, was not able to come to grips with the role of the church in society. On the whole, the church was content to save the soul of man, leaving Christians with no answer as to what Christian responsibility was in the face of momentous social and political changes. Again the case of T. C. Chao is a good illustration of the mind and attitude of the church in China in the first half of the twentieth century.

'As we search the writings of Chao', says Lee-ming Ng, 'we can find neither any concrete programme of political and social reform nor even a clear direction that an individual Christian should take in relation to society.'[22] He does speak of social reconstruction, but as far as the church is concerned, it means a spiritual reconstruction. He thus stresses that 'the mission of Christianity in China is to build for China a new spirit . . . that is to preach the gospel and to save souls. In other words, it is to build a new spirit in man'[23] After the church in China came under the impact of Communism, T. C. Chao seemed to make some re-adjustment in his thinking towards Christian responsibility for society, but the verdict is that he failed to come up with any vigorous change significant enough to chart a new course for the church which found herself in a society under a radically different political ideology.[24]

What is the problem that we have to take seriously here? Why has it been so difficult, if not impossible, for the church in China to see the relationship between the spiritual reconstruction of man and the reconstruction of society? Why is the gulf between these two so wide? In my judgment, one of the basic reasons lies in the fact that the theology of the incarnation did not become incarnate in the Chinese soil, that the Word did not become *flesh* in the Chinese mind. If this is true, we must reinforce the theology of the incarnation with the theology of humanization. God, to use Barth's expression, is human. But He is not human only in Himself. He lets His humanity become a reality in the world. In other words, He becomes humanized. He comes to meet us in the very depth of humanity. The incarnation is, therefore, not the meeting of divinity and humanity as is traditionally understood. The incarnation is the meeting of God's humanity with man's humanity. In this meeting, in this confrontation, man's humanity which becomes distorted on account of sin, is judged and saved. This humanity is the humanity that constitutes individual men and women, society and the world. In other words, it is the humanity God created to manage, sustain and develop the world as part of the total creation of God. That is why the coming of God in Jesus Christ proves to be a revolutionary event.

The humanization of God in Christ is a revolutionary mission. Confronted with God's revolution, we can no longer take our own humanity for granted. Our society cannot remain unaffected. And the world cannot carry on business as usual.

This theology of humanization which we have tried to develop above should constitute the basis of Christian mission. Christian mission is no other than participation in the humanization of God. It does not have its own separate purpose and programmes. Its purpose and programmes are entirely defined by the humanization of God. It cannot pose itself as a rival to what God has done in Jesus Christ. Nor can it by-pass the God who is not content to be human in Himself but wills to reveal His humanity. The Christian mission, if it is to be truly the mission derived from the mission of God, cannot regard humanization in the sense we have defined as something contrary to its main purpose. The servant cannot be greater than his master. Christian mission cannot behave and act as if it knows better than God what the mission of God should be. It cannot pretend as if it is better informed than God Himself as to the shape of God's relation to man. The Christian mission exists to serve God and not what it considers to be important for the salvation of man. In fact what God has done for mankind takes man completely by surprise. Who would have thought it possible for God to take such a lowly and humble manner when He decided to be one with man? The manger was the least likely place to which the God of glory was to come. But it was in the manger that Christ was born. Who could, furthermore, have suspected that in this poor carpenter the humanity of God was to reside?

The humanization of God in Jesus Christ has gone the whole way! It is in this humanization that Jesus Christ becomes one with man. This explains why he has a profound insight into the human nature even in its distorted and corrupt form. His penetration into the inner sanctuary of man's heart is of both judgmental and redemptive nature. Man is exposed to him completely. There is nothing that can be hidden from Him. Jesus Christ is the crisis of man and at the same time his hope. In the humanization of God in Jesus Christ, therefore, we are dealing with something ultimate to man, his culture and his religions.

The Christian mission of humanization must be viewed with special reference to what has just been mentioned. Any missiological critique of Christian mission as humanization will become out of focus and irrelevant if it is conducted without due consideration of our preceding argument. We must emphasize once again that the concept of Christian mission as humanization is not contradictory to the concept of God as the Creator and Saviour. In fact the concept of humanization sums up very vividly what God has been doing through creation and salvation. If God treats man with such importance, how could Christian mission regard man as if he is already condemned? How could theology speak of man as if he has no right to be there?

Writing from the suffering of the Nazi prison cell, the place where one might have least hope in the humanity of man, Bonhoeffer has this to say:

> . . . to be a Christian does not mean to be religious in a particular way . . . but to be a man.[25]

A Christian is someone who has discovered the truth that to be in relation with God is to be a man because God is human and becomes a man. For man to aspire to some divine quality is, therefore, to put himself in enmity with God. We have seen this when we discussed the story of the Fall earlier. In this sense, mysticism, whether in Western form or Eastern, risks far greater danger than humanism does in becoming the enemy of God. To be sure, mysticism is full of religiosity. Through elaborate cultic or ritual expressions, or through the simplicity of ascetic life, mysticism has all the appearance of reverence towards God. But its ultimate purpose is to deny man's humanity in order to be merged with the divinity of God. In such religious aspiration and endeavour, humanity becomes a great hindrance. Consequently, humanity is belittled and has to be overcome. In so doing, mysticism, knowingly or unknowingly, poses itself as a challenge to the God who is the author of humanity and whose love is poured out for the humanity He has created.

In contrast, humanism seems to have all the qualities related to impiety and godlessness. It is viewed as a philosophy of life and the world in which man is the measure of all things. Naturally, God does not seem to have a place in such a philosophy. What happens in humanism is that 'contemporary man is *in toto* his own Lord, both in setting his own standards according to his own capacities and enacting them by his own powers rather than, in this case, receiving these transcendent and ultimate standards from outside—but finding from outside no help to enact them'.[26] It is no wonder that the theologians who identify the humanization we discussed earlier with humanism regard humanization as a perversion of theology because it seems to dispose of God altogether. It is true that in humanism God does not have a part to play. But it will be too hasty to give it up as entirely atheistic and, therefore, lost from the point of view of the Christian faith. What humanism is after is essentially the authentic being of man. When it plunges into the search for the authenticity of man's being, it may not be entirely impossible for it to realize that man's being cannot be self-authenticated. Ultimately speaking, man cannot transcend himself. In reality he is heading for the termination of his being. It is when man reaches the critical point at which his being is threatened or is shaken from its root that he is likely to encounter God, the source of his being.

The chief concern of Christian mission is, therefore, man—man who has derived his humanity from the humanity of God. In Jesus Christ this man is reconciled to God and to his brothers and sisters in Jesus Christ. That is why the humanization of God results in the reconciliation of man with God and with his fellowman. Man becomes human once again because of reconciliation. It is this reconciliation that constitutes the goal of Christian mission. Christian mission is the mission of reconciliation. Thus, humanization and reconciliation are inter-dependent. Let us, therefore, further examine the meaning of reconciliation in the total context of humanization.

3. The Imperative of Reconciliation

Paul has a firm and clear understanding of the essence of the Christian mission as reconciliation. In his second letter to the Corinthian church he made the strong affirmation

> that God was in Christ reconciling the world to himself, no longer holding men's misdeeds against them, and that he has entrusted us with the message of reconciliation.[27]

In other words, reconciliation is the heart of the humanization of God in Jesus Christ. This means that reconciliation must constitute the imperative of the mission undertakings of the church. It is in reconciliation that man rediscovers the meaning of being truly human. Through acts of reconciliation man finds it possible to live authentically again. The man reconciled to God and his fellowman regains his humanity which became inauthentic on account of his estranged situation. It is this central message of reconciliation that the Christian mission is entrusted to share with the world.

The remarkable story of Esau and Jacob in the Old Testament especially with regard to their reconciliation is one of the examples in the Bible giving us a picture of the restored relationships between the two estranged brothers. If we read the story in Genesis 33 carefully, we will realize that Jacob, in his usual shrewdness and calculation, was taking no chances. He re-arranged the procession of his entire entourage in such a way that he might win the pleasure of his brother, Esau. And since Jacob had terribly wronged Esau, he was getting prepared for any harm that might be inflicted on him. In contrast, Esau, the wronged party, conducted himself in an entirely different way. According to von Rad, the author of the story

> draws a noble picture of Esau, who is simply overcome with the joy of reunion. In clear contrast to the deliberate Jacob, Esau expresses himself quite impulsively at the meeting. Not a word is said about the past, the embrace expressed forgiveness clearly enough.[28]

We wonder if the narrator of the story had in mind, among other things, to restore the image of Esau marred by his carelessness with regard to his birthright. But this is not an important point. What interests us here most is the fact that it is Esau who accepted Jacob back into his own life without harking back to the past. Injustice had been done to Esau and the estrangement that followed between Jacob and Esau made them into enemies. But by forgiving Jacob and becoming reconciled to him, Esau was able to have the human relationship restored between them.

This is a striking reflection of the reconciliation which God brought about in Jesus Christ. It is God who is the wronged party. And it is this God who came to man in His humanity in Jesus Christ in order that He might reconcile man to Himself. As the event of salvation unfolded itself, we see that this act of reconciliation involves Jesus Christ in the suffering of the cross. Reconciliation thus means the cross for God. This just does not follow our logic. It does not fit our ethic. It surely goes against the grain of our common sense. The famous German poet, Heine, is reported to have said on his death bed: 'Forgiveness? It is God's business.' It is God's business to forgive, but it is the business which, whether you like it or not, concerns you deeply, personally and eternally. Without the forgiveness of God, we remain in enmity with Him and our humanity remains impaired.

It is on the basis of what God has done in Jesus Christ that we are confronted with the imperative of reconciliation. Reconciliation, no matter whether it takes place between man and God or between man and man, cannot be anything but an imperative. It is the power that compels man to forsake his inhumanity and accept the humanity which God has shown in Jesus Christ. This is the imperative of love. This compelling power of God is the dynamic of the divine love. The imperative of the divine love has nothing to do with sentimentality. The love that has to face and bear the cross cannot be sentimental. It is the power that constitutes what God is. And it is also the power that makes man what he should be. No less than this power of love is required to set the God-man relationship on the right footing once more. By the same token, it is no less than this power that effects reconciliation between man and man. And the Christian mission is the focal point at which this power of love is to be embodied in a particular place at a particular time.

This power of love which must be translated into the imperative of reconciliation overcomes by allowing itself to be defeated; it heals by letting itself be wounded; it creates by submitting itself to the power of destruction; it gives forth new life by tasting the sting of death; and it brings about heaven by descending into hell. This love, therefore, is the exact opposite of non-participation or non-involvement. And involvement means suffering and the cross. That is why Jesus Christ appropriated for himself the role of the Suffering Servant in the Second Isaiah. Suffering in the context of God's imperative of love in reconciliation is not passive endurance of the wrongs, injustices or evils committed against us and our society. It has nothing to do with the attitude of resignation. It is not the same thing as submitting oneself to the tyranny of evil social or political power. Nor is it to submit oneself to the dictate of fate. From the biblical and theological point of view, suffering is the power of love which fulfils itself by fulfilling others. Suffering is, therefore, not defensive. It is a positive action with redemptive quality. It heals and redeems by bearing the pain and agony contingent with healing and redemption. The humanization of God is thus painful. But it is through the pain of humanization that God has reconciled man to Himself.

In Jesus Christ reconciliation between man and man has also become a reality. He makes it possible for us to be reconciled to our brothers and sisters from whom we are estranged. The removal of estrangement on the human level without the passion of God in Jesus Christ is difficult. The reason is that everyone of us is so self-defensive. This is the opposite of what we just said about suffering. The wrongs we have received, the injustice rendered to us, the shameful way in which we are used, the cruel way in which the dignity of man is trodden under the feet of the mighty, all these make us at once very defensive and offensive— defensive because that which pertains to our interests, to our very being, is threatened to be destroyed, and offensive because we must do something in our power to make sure the same thing will not happen to us and to our children again. We cannot, of course, minimize the forces of social evil which turn the world into hell. There are diabolic powers at work in the world which work to widen the gulf between the privileged and the underprivileged. But from the Christian point of view, we are saying that self-defence does not and cannot heal the disrupted relationship among men and women. Self-defence, in fact, perpetuates that disruption. It continues to serve as a barrier between man and man and thus constitutes a hindrance to the actualization of humanization. Humanity remains crippled and human conflicts in every stratum of our lives continue.

There is no manifestation of liberation and freedom in such human relationships built on self-defence. As Helmut Gollwitzer puts it:

> Self-defence is solely in one's own interest. . . It is clearly a
> false, unchristian reaction, the reaction of one who is already

defeated, who is subject to the situation, not master of it, and who is afraid.[29]

The Christian mission as the mission of reconciliation is not the mission of self-defence. Its task is not to defend Christianity. Self-defence of Christianity not only puts itself in hostility with other religions but also makes itself into an isolated religious body. This automatically rules out or at least restricts the expression of love as the power to heal and redeem the broken humanity.

The nature of love demands that those who are engaged in mission cannot make Christianity into an isolated religion. Love, by its very nature, does not deal with man in isolation. It refuses to see a man in separation from other human beings. A man in isolation can neither be the subject nor the object of love. Love has no meaning for such an abstract human being. Furthermore, he would be personifying in himself the denial of love. Strictly speaking, therefore, he could not be regarded as a *human* being. To be human is to love, and to love is to be in the community in which he could become at the same time the subject and the object of love. Simply put, he should be in the situation in which he can love and can be loved.

For Christian mission to become the mission of reconciliation with integrity is to throw away whatever self-defence it may have. It will not defend Christianity over against other religions. It will not serve as the spokesman for the so-called Christian culture in opposition to other cultures. It will not even hold out ethical standards developed out of the Christian backgrounds as the norms to be accepted by those with different cultural and religious backgrounds. We have to remember one thing, namely, the truth of God is self-authenticating. That is, the truth of God authenticates itself as love. God's work of healing and redemption consists in the fulfilment of the humanity created in the image of the humanity of God.

It is, therefore, true to say that Christian mission which is carried out on an exclusively denominational basis or on the doctrinal presuppositions which allow no compromise or flexibility cannot be regarded as the Christian mission engaged in the mission of reconciliation inspired by the love of God. It is no wonder that an Old Testament scholar such as Ernest Wright is prompted to say:

Modern Christianity in the multiplicity of its missionary forms is an enemy to itself, and more important, to the achievement of one world.[30]

Is this an overstatement? Certainly not. The history of the modern Christian mission substantiates the statement.

The Western Christian missions during the past century were almost invariably denominational missions. And these missions were further entrenched with the spirit of antagonism chiefly due to doctrinal rigidity. When the ecumenical movement became the thing of the day, it was already too late to make substantial and fundamental impacts on denominational and sectarian missions to cause any radical change in the denominational structure of the Christian church established in Asia and elsewhere in the Third World. The church was already too strongly planted in denominational and sectarian soil. The question is whether the richness of the Gospel has to be expressed denominationally with different creeds, confessions of faith and liturgy complete with different clerical attires. Even with due respect to the achievements of Western Christian missions during the last hundred years or so, it has to be admitted that denominationally conditioned Christians still find it somewhat difficult to feel at home with one another. It may sound ironical, but what the ecumenically-minded Christian leaders were doing could have been described as a war of attrition. They became alarmed at the harm which the divisiveness of Western Christianity was doing to the 'younger' churches in the non-Western world. But the time factor seemed to be working against their good intentions. In some cases, it was now national Christians who had become far more denominationally minded than more progressive and ecumenically conscious Western colleagues. In this sense, the established churches in Asia or in the Third World are more like Jacob than Esau. Like Jacob the Third World churches have too much at stake. They have too much to lose. They are not in the position to run out with passion and with risk to embrace one another and be reconciled. And as we discussed before, with their heavy doctrinal and historical inheritance from the past, they are even further from the position to meet the genuine spiritual needs of those in other religious and ideological camps.

In a situation such as this, we can almost cry out from the bottom of our hearts saying: Never mind your Westminster Confession of Faith or your Thirty-nine Articles. Put away your clerical collar. Drop the words like altar or missa. Never mind standing or kneeling when praying. For all this, in the last analysis, has nothing to do with the God of love and mercy who discarded His divine glory to lie naked and defenceless in the manger. Can you come to this manger with rich and colourful vestments and regalia? Can you worship this Jesus Christ with your denominational creeds and sectarian theology? Can you offer your service to this Saviour with your imported traditions and rubrics? Obviously, you cannot! You cannot treat the God of incarnation like that. You cannot pretend to be in the presence of the divine being when your worship and confession of faith will not enable you personally to be confronted with the humanity of God. In the presence of the God who is human, you should rather strip yourself naked, literally naked, of all the ornaments and set-assumptions in order that you may be truly reconciled to God in Jesus Christ and to your fellowman whom Christ comes to save. And together with them you can begin to wrestle with the questions of how to confess Jesus Christ, how to follow him, how to become the community in which the redeeming love of God becomes manifest, and how to direct the longing for the ultimate reality in the depth of man's spirituality to God. You can help other people find their humanity in the humanity of God only when you are willing to be confronted by God in His humiliation.

This criticism of Western Christian missions in the past must become a warning to what is now called Mission on Six Continents. This concept of the Christian mission is new in the sense that Christian mission is no longer the expansion of the Christian church from the West to the East. The Christian mission must now be conceived as the sharing of the experience of God's love in Jesus Christ on the global basis. For the first time in history, Christian mission will become a global movement. And as the impact of the church in the West on the non-Western world diminishes, there will be significant increase in the impact in the reverse way. It is, therefore, important for those who will be directly involved in Six-Continent Mission to remember what Stephen Neil has once said:

> It seems to me that a missionary ceases to be a missionary on the day on which he sets foot on the shores of the land

in which he has been called to work. From that moment on, he is a servant of the church in that place and nothing else.[31]

Does this statement come out of his experience as a missionary in India? He has to answer this for himself. But one thing is clear: the imperative of reconciliation cannot be translated into real action unless we are prepared to meet each other humbly in Jesus Christ.

What has been discussed above seems to be a diversion from our subject of Christian mission as imperative of reconciliation. In fact, it is not a diversion. The fact is that Christian mission is in need of reconciliation at its very heart. Reconciliation has to begin with the Christian church and her missions. In other words, the church and her mission must experience the agony and joy of reconciliation in the midst of believers divided on the ground of creeds, confessions and liturgical expressions. It is only when Christian mission does not bear in vain the cross of reconciliation that it can become engaged in the ministry of reconciliation. There is a danger for different denominational missions to forget this. But the fact is that not only for the Third World but also for the Western world, the church badly divided has the effectiveness of her witness to the reconciling love in Christ seriously reduced. And the church beset with divisions appears to be an anomaly and loses her appeal to those outside the church. No wonder such a church is left alone to pursue her own interests by this fast secularizing world. God's mission of reconciliation, therefore, makes it imperative that the church is the place in which reconciliation is not only preached but also put into practice. The church which is not intensely concerned about reconciliation within her cannot become engaged in the ministry of reconciliation beyond her domain.

4. End of Morphological Fundamentalism

The imperative of reconciliation not only calls for a reconciled church but also for the structures of Christian mission that conform to the ministry of reconciliation. But how far we are from new mission structures can be seen from a report which says:

> The form (*morphe*) of the ancient Western world view belongs to the past. The structures of Western Christendom are no longer capable of helping the congregations to fulfil

their task. Even worse, in a time when the churches of Jesus Christ, for the sake of their calling, must once more involve themselves in this world, these structures support a 'morphological fundamentalism' which not only makes difficult any acceptance of responsibility in the world, but also threatens to enclose the churches in an ecclesiastical world of make-believe.[32]

The report explains that the term 'morphological fundamentalism' indicates a rigid and inflexible attitude toward the *morphe* (structure, 'Gestalt') of the congregation similar to the attitude prevalent in 'biblical fundamentalism'.[33]

It must be stressed that morphological fundamentalism makes a complete mockery of the humanization of God in Jesus Christ. For the sake of man's salvation the humanity of God in its divine *morphe* became the humanity in the human *morphe*. Humanization of God is therefore the change of the divine *morphe* to the human *morphe*. Without such a change Jesus Christ would not be recognized as the Saviour of the world. The fact that such a morphological change with God is possible shows that God would have little to do with rigidity and inflexibility in carrying out His mission of salvation. The God whom we see in Christ is a 'changeable or flexible' God. It is in God's morphological change that man encounters the presence of God in Jesus Christ.

The concept of change is, therefore, essential to our understanding of God and His dealings with the world. It is not change for the sake of change. Nor is it a change for the sake of novelty. The change in the *morphe* of God's humanity is dictated by the saving love of God. God will have nothing to do with morphological fundamentalism.

Besides this theological nature of the concept of change, there are existential considerations too, which are pertinent here. Change has been the most spectacular phenomenon in this era of modernization and secularization. This does not mean that there was no change before this new era. History, viewed from one perspective, is a movement, a series of changes. And underlying the movements of history is the change of time. Time brings change to history, making it a process rather than a fixed amount of unchangeable data. Of course, history understood in terms of the past does no longer change. As the records of the past, history belongs to libraries, archives and museums. History in this case is not a process. It is arrested at a certain point in time.

On the whole, however, history is a movement. It moves into the future. That is why change is a concept closely related to history. But the pace of change differs from one period to another. It also varies from one sector of life to another. Granted that this is true, it is correct to say that the pace of change in the pre-modern periods is slow. Sometimes it is so slow that change becomes imperceptible. Changes take place unnoticed. But with the dawn of this new era of secularization, change bursts upon us. It is like water breaking loose from a dam, roaring forward without restraint. The force of change thus bursts into us and infiltrates every aspect of our lives. That is why we have been witnessing radical changes in our physical and spiritual lives. Our environments are subject to change in such a way that we are now faced with ecological problems of one kind or another. Our ethical and spiritual value concepts too have been undergoing fundamental changes. And we are left with widening gaps between the old values and the new ones.

All this affirms that change is a fact of life. We are not saying that all changes are necessarily good. But the force of change has brought about this new era of secularization enabling us to gain far deeper insight into the mystery of the creation.

The church's response to change is rather slow and half-hearted. This is especially the case with the church in Asia. In all fairness, it must be said that this is not typical of Christianity. Religions tend to represent conservative forces resisting the force of change, and Christianity is no exception to the rule. But in the case of Christianity there is no excuse for its negative attitude toward change simply because, as we have argued above, change constitutes the very center of the Christian faith, namely, the incarnation, or as we prefer to call it, the humanization of God. This resistance to change takes different forms, but in my view morphological fundamentalism is one of the basic forms that proves to be most difficult to deal with.

Unlike biblical fundamentalism which is characteristically limited to some theological trends, morphological fundamentalism seems to cut across all theological leanings and ecclesiastical backgrounds. Although emphasis on morphological fundamentalism differs from one group to another, it can be detected in all. It appears in denominational structures of the church, in theological formulations of the contents of the Christian faith, in conceptualization of the relation of the church to religions and culture and also in working out approaches of Christian mission to the contemporary world. Thus, morphological fundamentalism is the bastion that has to be demolished in order for the mission of reconciliation to be carried out effectively especially in a changing Asia.

First of all, the mission of reconciliation makes it imperative that the churches in Asia must make a hard attempt at crossing denominational barriers. A lot has, of course, already been done, but not enough to initiate a new *morphe* of the Christian communities embodying in themselves the reality of reconciliation. Moreover, the attempts that have been made to bring the churches in Asia together have happened mostly at ecumenical levels, for instance, at the level of the National Council of Churches or at the level of the East Asia Christian Conference (now called Christian Conference of Asia, after the 5th General Assembly in Singapore, May-June, 1973). The contributions of these ecumenical bodies have been inestimable, but it must be conceded that local churches have not been sufficiently challenged to cross their denominational frontiers. Fundamental questions still need to be directed to the church polity and liturgy that have been inherited from the Western denominations. Denominational theology too must undergo critical examination in the light of new understanding of the Gospel in Asian contexts. Active steps must be taken to eliminate those archaic expressions that originated from Western culture rather than from the Bible. And more thought and energy must be spent on bringing into existence Asian liturgy and Asian confessions of faith. And as the churches in Asia begin to act in this way, the churches in the West must make every effort to erase their denominational vestiges in Asia.

Secondly, the imperative of reconciliation not only demands that the denominational barriers be demolished, but also requires that the frontiers of the church be crossed. This means that the ministry of reconciliation should take the place of evangelism, especially evangelism in its militant forms and in the form of proselytism. Accordingly, Christian mission can no longer be regarded as the expansion of the boundaries of the Christian church just as it was regarded and practised as the expansion of the boundaries of 'Christendom'. In essence, the church has no boundary. It is Christianity as a religion in the course of its history that has created the boundary to distinguish itself from the rest of the world. It has thus given the false impression that to be reconciled to God means to be reconciled to the church. This notion was particularly strong in the Middle Ages in which the church in Europe dominated practically every aspect of life. A similar pattern is introduced to the non-Western world. To become Christian is to get admitted to the church not only in the sense of fellowship but also in the sense of organization or institution. To serve God is to serve the church. To follow Christ is to follow the teachings of the church. In a word, to become converted to the Christian faith is to step inside the boundary of the church.

As has been stressed before, the church in the New Testament sense of the word *happens*. It is an event. It is not an institution for those confessing Christ to join. Whenever and wherever reconciliation of man to God takes place, there is 'church'. The church is the people reconciled to God. And their ministry is to let church happen to other people. Does this mean that we have no use for the church in the institutional sense? Not exactly. The church as an institution is the place where Christians are trained to let church in the sense of reconciliation between man and God happen in the world. What is the difference, then, between the church in the institutional sense and the church in the sense of event or happening? The church as an institution exists to serve the church as an event. She should not become a normative force controlling and prescribing the life and faith of those converted to and confessing Jesus Christ as their Lord and Saviour. The church has, since the post-apostolic age, been doing just this. She has the last word to say about the faith and morals of her members. She even goes to the extent of pretending to have authority over the salvation of mankind. This is expressed in the biblically unfounded and theologically untenable position that outside the church there is no salvation. Hans Küng correctly remarks that 'this axiom, in its negative, exclusive formulation . . . continues to give rise today to innumerable misunderstandings both inside and outside the Catholic church. While it may have helped the church and her mission in the past, it is most certainly damaging them today.'[34]   He then advises that 'this statement should be as far as possible set aside and not used, because it causes more misunderstanding than understanding.'[35]

If we put primary emphasis on the church as event and regard the church as institution as secondary, it follows that the hierarchical and sacerdotal structure of the church must go.   Since the sacramental acts of the church, namely baptism and the Lord's Supper especially, should take place through the confessing Christians where church as an event comes into existence, there will be no need for the church as institution to be the channel of the divine grace.   The church as an institution will become a place where fellowship of Christians and their training to be the witness to the love of God are held as her main functions. This re-conception of church and re-structuring of it accordingly will enable Christians to become more effectively engaged in the ministry of reconciliation.

Thirdly, Christian mission as the ministry of reconciliation should render obsolete the practice of singling out some men and women as missionaries.   Missionaries are those Christians who bear witness to God's reconciling love in Jesus Christ.   To use the New Testament terms they are 'apostles', namely, messengers of the Gospel of salvation.   That is why the noun *apostole* means not only apostleship but also mission.

At the time of the Reformation, one of Luther's famous assertions is expressed in the phrase 'the priesthood of all believers'. Quoting I Peter 2:9 which says: 'But you are a chosen race, a royal priesthood, a dedicated nation, and a people claimed by God for his own, to proclaim the triumphs of him who has called you out of darkness into his marvellous light', Luther asserts that 'our baptism consecrates us all without exception, and makes us all priests'.[36]   It is true to say that in Luther we have the first advocate of what is now known as the lay movement.

In the same way, we should give more serious emphasis to the apostolate of all Christians.   All Christians are missionaries in the original sense of the term.   To be Christian means to be in mission.   It is thus unfortunate that the term 'missionaries' has come to be reserved for those sent abroad by their churches to be engaged in mission.   And as time goes on, very elaborate and complicated mission systems have been developed to cater to the needs of the so-called missionaries. 'Missionaries' thus becomes a professional term. Perhaps this has been necessary. But certainly there is no need now to perpetuate this wrong use of the term, just as the continuing existence of elaborate missionary support systems has become anachronistic. It is true that mission systems developed by the churches in the West have much to do with the churches in the Third World as well as missionaries. But at this day and age when the churches in the Third World should be and can be on their own, there is no justification for the continuing presence of Western mission systems in the person of mission executives and missionaries. Therefore, the use of the term missionaries, particularly for Christian workers from the West, must be discontinued. It is one of the remnants that lingers on to remind people of special privileges and status enjoyed by Western missionaries.

By the apostolate of all Christians we stress the fact that all Christians, by virtue of their calling to follow Jesus Christ, are called and sent to be the witnesses of God's love. In their person God's reconciliation has taken place. They are now entrusted with the task to let reconciliation happen in other people as well. No Christian can escape this responsibility. Christian mission, under the prevalent ecclesiastical structures consolidated in the course of the history of Christianity, tends to be regarded as the business for ministers, priests or evangelists. Needless to say, this makes the apostolate of all Christians an abstract concept.

The ministry of reconciliation makes it imperative that such ecclesiastical barriers to the apostolate of all Christians be removed. This is no easy task as can be seen in the following observation made by D. T. Niles:

> A . . . direction in which one must look for the strengthening of the missionary cause is that of a development in unofficial initiative in forwarding the Christian mission. One of the weaknesses, particularly among the younger churches, is to be too dependent on the official courts of the church. In this connection such organizations as the Y.M.C.A., Y.W.C.A. and the W.S.C.F. have an important part to play.[37]

Development of Christian mission in such a direction is in itself to be commended. But the question is: if this is the direction that we must take, why let it remain an 'unofficial' approach to be taken outside the normal boundary of the church? Does the fact that such an approach has to be regarded as 'unofficial' not point to the unhealthy state of the 'official' church? If the church fails to let her members become aware of the part they have to play in mission, she has no reason to exist any more. The church, as the fellowship of those called to follow Jesus Christ, should be the place where they are mobilized for and commissioned to the Christian mission of reconciliation.

What has been said implies that the Christian mission as the mission of reconciliation should determine what the church should be and do. The shape, structure and order of the church are by themselves not sacrosanct. An unchanging church is, therefore, a disobedient church, or even a rebellious church, for she refuses to listen to what the mission of reconciliation demands and dictates. She elevates the secondary elements such as traditions, liturgy and so on to the primary place. This is the danger of the church falling into idolatry. She becomes the object of worship. She is viewed as the goal of Christian piety. That is why the church needs reformation. In order to be the church witnessing to God's love, she needs to be stripped of all her pretensions and become the instrument of God's reconciliation. It is through the church reformed and reforming, reconciled and reconciling, that Christian mission gains integrity. It becomes a glorious and joyous undertaking. And primarily on account of such church, we are not people 'having no hope and without God'.[38] The Christian mission must, therefore, be the mission of hope. This will be the theme of our next and last chapter.

REFERENCES

1. John Pepper Clark, 'Cry of Birth' in *Modern Poetry from Africa*, edited by Gerald Moore and Ulli Beier, Penguin Books, 1968, p. 116.

2. Ludwig Feuerbach, *The Essence of Christianity*, translated by George Elliot, New York: Harper and Row, Harper Torchbooks, 1957, pp. 10-11. To speak of God in terms of feeling can be very misleading. In his introductory essay to Feuerbach's book, Karl Barth rightly says: 'In fact, anyone who knew that we men are evil from head to foot and anyone who reflected that we must die, would recognize it to be the most illusory of all illusions to suppose that the essence of God is the essence of man. He certainly would not disturb "the good Lord" by such a confusion of Him with the likes of us, even if he thought Him to be a dream' (*ibid.*, p. xxviii). Barth's strong reaction here is understandable especially in view of the predominantly theo-centric trend in his early theology. He maintains the irreversible order of God and man even when he comes later to speak of the humanity of God.

3. Barth, *The Humanity of God*, translated by Thomas Wieser, Richmond, Virginia: John Knox Press, 1960, pp. 45-46.

4. Dietrich Bonhoeffer, *Creation and Fall*, a Theological Interpretation of Genesis 1-3, London: SCM Press, 1959, p. 73.

5. Tillich, *Systematic Theology*, Vol. II, Chicago: The University of Chicago Press, 1957, p. 44. In using the word estrangement Tillich emphasizes the *state* in which man finds himself existentially. Thus, he has not intended to replace the term 'sin' by estrangement. Sin, according to him, points to the personal responsibility which brings into existence the state of estrangement (Cf. *ibid*, p. 46).

6. Tillich, *Systematic Theology*, Vol. I, Chicago: The University of Chicago Press, 1951, p. 49.

7. At the time of writing this chapter, the Nixon administration was shaken to its root by what is known as the Watergate Affair. Those who worked for Nixon's re-election resorted, without scruples, to espionage to ensure the re-election of Nixon in 1972. By these men in power, the democratic system of the American government was threatened to turn into a totalitarian system.

8. Gerhard von Rad, *Genesis*, A Commentary, translated by John H. Marks, Philadelphia: Westminster Press, 1961, p. 88.

9. John 3:3.

10. *The Uppsala 68 Report*, Geneva: World Council of Churches, pp. 27-28.

11. *The Uppsala Report*, p. 28.

12. *ibid.*

13. *ibid.*

14. Peter Beyerhaus, 'Mission and Humanization,' in *International Review of Mission*, Vol. LX, No. 237, January, 1971 (pp. 11-24), p. 16.

15. Beyerhaus, *ibid.*, pp. 20-21.

16. Barth, *The Humanity of God*, p. 49.

17. Barth, *ibid.*

18. Barth, *ibid.*, p. 50.

19. Barth, *ibid.*, p. 51.

20. Guenter Rutenborn, *The Sign of Jonah.*

21. Lee-ming Ng, 'An Evaluation of T. C. Chao's thought,' in *Ching Feng*, Quarterly Notes on Christianity and Chinese Religion and Culture, Vol. XIV, No. 1 and 2, 1971, (pp. 5-59), p. 12. According to the author, T. C. Chao's view of Christ changed substantially in the 1940's. Perhaps greatly influenced by Paul, he now writes in 1947 in his *Life of Paul*: 'Now I deeply believe that Jesus is the Saviour the Christ, and the only Son of the ever living God' (Lee-ming Ng, *op. cit.*, p. 54).

22. Lee-ming Ng, *op. cit.*, p. 14.

23. Quoted by Lee-ming Ng in *op. cit.*, p. 40.

24. Cf. Lee-ming Ng, *op. cit.*, p. 59.

25. Bonhoeffer, *Letters and Papers from Prison*, p. 154.

26. Langdon Gilkey, *Naming the Whirlwind, the Renewal of God-Language*, New York: The Bobbs-Merrill Company, 1969, p. 162.

27. II Corinthians 5:19.

28. von Rad, *Genesis*, A Commentary, p. 322.

29. Quoted by Hans-Werner Bartsch in 'The Foundation and Meaning of Christian Pacifism,' in *New Theology*, No. 6, on Revolution and Non-revolution, Violence and Non-Violence, Peace and War, edited by Martin E. Marty and Dean G. Peerman, London: The Macmillan Company, 1969, p. 188.

30. Ernest Wright, 'The Old Testament Basis for the Christian Mission,' in *Theology of the Christian Mission*, edited by G. H. Anderson, p. 29.

31. Stephen Neil, *Creative Tension*, London: Edinburgh House, 1959, p. 92.

32. *Planning for Mission*, edited by Thomas Wieser, p. 137.

33. *Ibid.*, p. 134.

34. Hans Küng, 'The World Religions in God's Plan of Salvation,' in *Christian Revelation and World Religions*, edited by Joseph Neuner, p. 34.

35. Hans Küng, *ibid.*, p. 37.

36. John Dillenberger, *Martin Luther*, Selections from his Writings, New York: Doubleday & Company, Anchor Books, 1961, p. 408.

37. D. T. Niles, *Upon the Earth*, p. 174.

38. Ephesians 2:12.

CHAPTER NINE

Mission of Hope

Lord,
make us instruments of thy peace.
Where therer is hatred, let us sow love;
Where there is injury, pardon;
Where there is doubt, faith;
Where there is darkness, light;
Where there is sadness, joy.

ST. FRANCIS OF ASSISI

1. No Exit?

HOPE has always been the integral part of the Christian faith. Christianity is the religion of hope. Hope is a very dynamic concept. It is related to the future in such a way that the past is not considered lost and the present is not regarded as meaningless. Indeed, hope is the power that brings meaning to a man's life. This power of hope works in the totality of his being, and through him it makes its influence felt on society and the world. Hope has, therefore, as much to do with the past and the present as with the future. Hope makes it possible for us to view our life as a totality and not as fragments of time. Hope is not merely promise in relation to the future but also the reality that redeems the past and puts meaning into the present. In a word, hope is the meaningfulness of life taken as a whole. Later we will further discuss the nature of hope, especially in relation to time.

The Christian understanding of hope poses a striking contrast to expressions of despair found in some literature. Sartre's play, *No Exit* is a case in point. It typifies the prevailing spirit of the age during the two decades after World War II. It was the spirit of despair and the loss of a sense of direction that especially prompted existentialist writers to describe man as trapped in the confusion and conflict of the present. In the play, Sartre's three main characters found themselves accidentally shut up in a small room without exit. They were total strangers to one another. They had little in common. They became so irritated and intolerable to one another that they had to conclude in utter despair: 'Hell is—other people.'[1]

Hell signifies condemnation, despair and death. It is the dark side of human nature. It is the situation in which the worst in man is brought out into the open. When a man lets his dark and base nature loose, chaos and tragedy ensue. Consequently, he will be debased; his high aspirations will be put to an end; and he will be enchained to destructive forces such as hatred, jealousy and ill will. In a situation which is thus described as hell, every man lives for himself. There is little consideration for others. Selfishness becomes the order of the day. Each person harbours his own secret over against other people. He rejects intrusion into his privacy. He is thus closed to others. Meaningful and constructive communication between person to person is impossible under such circumstances. He faces other people and the outside world with suspicion and hostility. This is what we call hell.

Furthermore, there is no room for God in hell. God is regarded as an intruder and an enemy. He, therefore, is to be rejected. Man may be afraid of God, but he will try to put Him away from his mind. In hell man wants to be his own master and thus free from God. But he will discover that as he does this, his misery is aggravated, for man without God is man without hope. There is no promise in his life. Future ceases to exist for him. He lives in the eternal past of unfulfilled desires. His life will become a battle with his own past, namely, with his own self.

Dante, with a stroke of genius, wrote at the entrance of hell in his *Divine Comedy*: 'Abandon hope, all ye who enter here'. Of course, hell, from what has been said above, is not a geographically identifiable place depicted in crude folk religions and primitive beliefs. Hell is man who, without God, has become hopeless. As he has done away with God, he has also done away with hope. That is why he has to give up hope at the gate of hell. In this sense, the death-of-God theologians have not only rendered theology impossible, but also pronounced the dead-end of human existence.[2] The words such as future, possibility, newness, and so on, become, of necessity, superfluous. History becomes a closed book. Man is reduced to a mathematical point without vertical and horizontal dimensions. The death of God is, in fact, the death of man.

But God cannot die. Even hell cannot do away with God. What happens is that the more man tries to keep God away, the more real God's presence becomes. Where conscious struggle goes on to do without God, there God's presence is felt all the more. It is, therefore, not without significance that in the Apostles' Creed Jesus Christ is mentioned as descending to hell. All literalism apart, this essentially means that God simply does not allow any place in the whole of His creation to be without His presence. There is simply no place in the whole universe where man can hide from God's presence. This is the confession of the psalmist who wrote Psalm 139. In utter amazement he has to confess and say:

> Where can I escape from thy spirit?
> Where can I flee from thy presence?
> If I climb to heaven, thou art there;
> If I make my bed in Sheol, again I find thee.
> If I take my flight to the frontiers of the morning
>   or dwell at the limit of the Western sea,
> Even there thy hand will meet me
>   and thy right hand will hold me fast.

It is this kind of faith that sustains us through the turmoil of our lives.

Christ's descent to hell is a pictorial way of saying that God's love simply does not let anybody go. For every man without exception, there is hope and future because God is with him. Despair and death are not the final words. Suffering cannot be all that constitutes and determines the life of man. That is why the cross is not the last destination of Jesus Christ. The cross has to be borne, but it is borne for the sake of the resurrection. It is for the glory of the resurrection that the agony of the cross is suffered. It is by the affirmation of life through the resurrection that the suffering and death on the cross takes on a positive and redemptive meaning. On account of the resurrection we can begin to celebrate the cross.

Jesus Christ embodies in himself God's hope for all mankind. His descent to hell declares that God will never give up anybody for any reason. Hell is, therefore, not the last verdict on man. God's hope for man in Jesus Christ extends even to hell. God's salvation is thus for all, even for those who reject Him and try to do without Him. Perhaps this can be stated more positively. God's hope is precisely made available in Jesus Christ for those who rebel against Him. The mission of God in Jesus Christ is, therefore, the mission of hope. Christian mission, derived from God's mission, must thus also be the mission of hope, of universal hope.

The Christian faith which confesses that Christ descends into hell cannot exclude anyone from the sphere of influence of God's saving love. There has been a strong tendency in Asia and elsewhere for some Christians to turn Christianity into an elite religion, namely the religion of the few elected men and women. This spiritual elitism, inherited from conservative Western missionaries, has been one of the principal reasons for the exclusive claim to salvation only in the context of Christianity. It has done much to isolate Christians from cultural activities that are going on around them. They have lost the freedom to enjoy their historical heritages, cultural accomplishments and at times personal contacts with non-Christian friends. Christianity has thus not been seen in Asia as dynamic faith which transforms not only man but also society and the world.

It follows that the theology of hope must be translated into the mission of hope. To put it differently, the theology of hope and the mission of hope must be supplementary to each other. The theology of hope without the mission of hope is a metaphysical theology dealing with God in an abstraction. It is hope without content. Hope without the content of hope is simply an illusion. Illusion can be described as the degeneration of hope. Those who hold degenerated hope will sooner or later, pass into the realm of the unreal. They are thus heading for the empty future. The message of the Christian mission is chiefly this: God has come in person in Jesus Christ to declare that God has the future full of promise. It is this Jesus Christ who makes God's hope for us concrete. He thus fulfils our life with the promise of God. And as he does this, he also fulfils our future with meaning and content. He is our future.

This, in essence, is the chief content of Christian proclamation. The world in which we live is not without exit. The humanization of God we discussed in the preceding chapter breaks open our self-contained world full of inner struggles. It is through this exit that we can see the future of promise unfolding before our eyes. Jesus Christ is this exit through which we shall arrive at our future. Christian mission exists to assert this fact and to point out for the people where the exit into God's future is.

2. The Impact of the Future on the Present

Christianity has been rightly regarded as a religion deeply rooted in the movement of time and the process of history. Ever since it parted company with Judaism and moved into the Greek world and the Roman empire, it has had a crucial role to play in the formation of the cultural history in the Western world. It has also made deep and lasting impressions on almost every phase of Western life and society. The Christian faith is essentially historical in nature so that it has much to do with the movement of time from the past, through the present and finally to the future.

History can be viewed as the activity of man in response to the challenge of time. It is the frontier where man struggles to gain mastery over the past and the present in such a way that he may create the future for himself and for the world in which he lives. But history is not merely a horizontal affair. It can be also viewed as the arena of the interactions between God and man. Or to put it differently, history becomes a human reality because it is first of all the divine possibility. Just as God calls man into being, so He calls history into being by inspiring man to respond to Him and His creation. That is why history cannot be separated from revelation. Revelation, for whatever worth, is revelation in history.

From the standpoint of the Christian faith, Jesus Christ is this revelation in history. In Christ God reveals Himself and His will. And at the same time in Christ man makes response to God's self-revelation. Jesus Christ is, therefore, the focus of the divine-human meeting. In him that which is transcendent becomes immanent. He embodies in himself the history of revelation. That is why the past and especially the Old Testament can only be properly understood through him. In the same way, the future and particularly the New Testament can be created out of his involvement in the aspiration of man.

On account of God's self-revealing acts, history is open-ended. This is why history can be a fascinating subject of study. Since

God's revelation in Jesus Christ, viewed from the human side, takes place always in our existential situations, it cannot be grasped in terms of axiom, principle or proposition. Likewise, history called into being by revelation cannot be static. That is why a new interpretation of past history is always a possibility. On the contrary, literalism, especially when applied to the Bible, proves to be negation of newness in relation to the history of revelation. What biblical literalism does is to seal revelation in the Book, so that revelation is to be read out of the Book literally. History becomes a ready-made thing, a dead record. It ceases to be existential responses to God's self-revealing acts. Literalism claims finality for a particular outlook on life and the world. In the area of morals, it turns into absolute legalism. Life can only be built on the basis of certain fixed moral codes supposed to have universal validity. In the case of faith literalism turns into dogmatism which allows no room for new interpretation of the Christian faith.

This amounts to the captivity of God. God is imprisoned in the Bible. He even ceases to be the master of His own words. He loses His freedom to do something new. God is thus determined completely by the past. He becomes the God of the past and not of the future. In other words, He is the God of fate and not of promise. It is this kind of Christianity that dominated the Christians in Asia. Under the influence of such dogmatism of faith, Christians adopted a passive attitude towards the present. Their involvement in society with a view to bringing about change and reform was discouraged. It is only recently that the church in Asia has come to realize more and more the mistake of the literalism of faith. And as the impact of secularization becomes greater and greater, the church in Asia will have to have a total re-orientation of faith in order that she may be able to read the meaning of the changes that are taking place in practically every sphere of our life.

If biblical literalism imprisons the Christian faith in the past and thus empties the promise of its meaning, what about the stress on the present as the point of departure for our understanding of the Christian faith? What about interpreting the Bible in terms of here and now? No doubt there is great validity in approaching matters related to faith in relation to my present situation. After all, without my personal involvement, faith loses its challenge and excitement. But the sole emphasis on the present, the complete focus on here and now, is not without its danger. In this case, the present becomes isolated from the past and the future. History becomes localized in the present. It becomes detached from the past and ceases to move towards the future. The historical present thus is no more than historical subjectivism. The Bible has meaning in so far as it is relevant to me personally here and now. The Christian faith as an historical faith is in this way in danger of becoming a religion of subjectivism. The sole stress on the present leads the Christian faith on the road to historical subjectivism.

If the biblical literalism stresses the importance of the past and if the subjective interpretation of the Christian faith lays particular emphasis on the present, oriental religions, generally speaking, have the tendency to isolate the future from the process of history. The future constitutes in fact a very important factor in oriental religions. This has been largely overlooked by Western philosophers of religion and theologians. But the future in oriental religions does not constitute a link in the chain of time with its past, present and future. It can stand by itself by breaking out of the chain of time. It is a completely self-subsisting and self-sustaining state of bliss. The concept of time ceases to have meaning for it. Therefore, the word future is almost inadequate for a state such as this. It is the future arrived at by tearing oneself away from the agony of the past and from the suffering of the present. The future thus attained transcends the time sequence in which the consciousness of time, together with the consciousness of space, vanishes. And here is a crucial point— inasmuch as the self constitutes the center of consciousness in time and space, it must be transcended. Thus, with the attainment of the state called future, the self is eliminated as the center of a man's consciousness. Obviously, this kind of future is not the future as we understand it. It is the future which has no relation to the past and the present. It has nothing to do with time and history. It is an a-historical future. Apparently this kind of future has no impact on the present. It is in reality a flight from the present. On the whole, oriental religions, like those Christians with conservative trends, hold negative and passive attitudes toward the present. In my opinion, such future detached from the present and history, loses its meaning for a person who tries to make sense out of life in the midst of the turmoil of this world.[3]

Contrary to the various views discussed above, I want to emphasize that only the future pregnant with historical meaning can set us free from the tyranny of the past, the despair of the present and the illusion of the future. In other words, we do not leap into the future, for the meaning of the future is already contained in both the frustration and the fulfilment of the past and the present. This is particularly evident in the failure and success of a revolution. Failure of a revolution in the present is the unfulfilment of the meaning which the revolutionaries cherish for the future. On the contrary, the success of a revolution results in the realization of the meaning they held for the future. For such future countless men and women have given their lives. The celebration of revolution in our present day is the celebration, on the one hand, of the sacrifices of these men and women, and on the other, the celebration of the realization of the future in the present. Revolution is, therefore, conceivable only for those people who take the future seriously as part of the process of time. For those who hold the future in detachment from the present and for those who have no concept of future in their perception of time, revolution will not be a possibility. This shows why revolution is the socio-political phenomenon which is very much related to the influence of the Judeo-Christian understanding of time. It is interesting to observe that the revolutionaries in Asia and Africa have often been those people who came under the influence of the Christian faith in one way or another.

The future is, therefore, a definitive reality in our search for the meaning of life and history. Without the promise of the future, the past and the present will be deprived of intrinsic value. They will not have the dynamic to move out of their own sphere. The dynamic of our life is the dynamic of the future pregnant with meaning and promise. It is this future which gives us strength and courage to continue our pilgrimage of life. This is one of the main contributions of the Christian faith to the spiritual welfare of mankind.

The biblical faith is essentially the faith which inspires and transforms the present with the power of the future. Perhaps this is one of the major points which distinguish the Christian faith from other faiths. As has been mentioned, what oriental faiths lack is not the future as such, but the future that can give meaning and strength to the present. The future of oriental faiths has no special interest in, and thus no significant impact on, the present. One can only call such future an illusion. Maybe this is one of the reasons why Mao Tze-tung and his fellow revolutionaries had to do away with religions, Christianity included. Communism, with its future filled with the idea of a classless society constituting the chief driving force in the struggle of the present, is basically incompatible with religions which attempt flight into the illusion of the future. Religion, in its broad sense including idolatrous expressions, will have no chance of survival. As early as 1972 Mao wrote:

> The idols were set up by peasants, and in time they will pull down the idols with their own hands; there is no need for anybody else to throw away prematurely the idols for them. The agitational line of the Communist Party in such matters should be: 'Draw the bow full without letting go the arrow, and be on the alert'.[4]

Communism, with its zeal to transform the present fate of masses of people on the verge of starvation, cannot tolerate religions which regard the future as refuge from the present. Any thought of bringing Christian mission back to China needs to take this point seriously. The kind of crude eschatology prevailing in the Chinese churches in Asia will absolutely have no place in China in which the present constitutes the chief concern of the people. Except in their weak moments the people in China are not permitted to turn to the illusion of the future.

In the light of what has been said above, perhaps it may not be facetious to suggest that Mao Tze-tung and his comrades read the mind of the Chinese more accurately and saw their needs more realistically than the propagators of religious faiths. As van Leeuwen has observed, Chinese Communism:

> has evinced a dynamic openness to the essential needs of Chinese society, as Western Christianity in general has obviously failed to do.[5]

This means that careful and critical study of how Chinese Communism fulfils both the physical and spiritual needs of the Chinese is an absolute requisite to any consideration for future Christian mission in China.

In this connection, it may be further pointed out that perhaps it is by no accident that Moltmann finds in Ernst Bloch, a Marxist, his chief mentor for the development of his theology of hope.[6] This is suggestive of the future direction which Asian theology, and particularly Chinese theology, should be taking. A future Asian theology perhaps will have to emerge out of serious confrontation between the Christian faith and Communist faith. The following statement made by Roger Garaudy, the French Communist Party's leading theoretician, seems to substantiate our view. He says:

> The future of mankind cannot be built on opposition to those with a religious faith, nor even without them; the future of mankind cannot be built in opposition to the Communists, nor even without them.[7]

If this is true, mutual accommodation will have to take place between Christian theology and Communist ideology. From the standpoint of the Christian church in Asia, this is a path which perhaps is full of both anticipated risks and unexpected surprises. But one thing is certain: the confrontation envisaged here will force Christians in Asia to come to grips with the meaning and demand of the Gospel in an honest and rigorous way. And in my judgment, one of the unavoidable questions will be related to the concept of future. It will be the future which fulfils the needs and aspirations of the present that will have to receive a thorough study and consideration. There will be sharp contrasts as well as some superficial similarities. Out of such effort a living Asian theology may emerge to mark a certain stage in its development.

The little digression above is meant to reinforce our emphasis on the function and meaning of the future for the present. As a religion of hope and future, the biblical faith always stakes its present on the promise of the future. Without this integral relationship between the present and the future, it is difficult to understand the special meaning of salvation in the Old and the New Testament. It is true to say that in no period of the history of Israel and of the church is God's promise to His people ever fully realized. There have always been unfulfilled promises which

cause frustration among the believers. This has prompted Bultmann to say that Old Testament history 'is fulfilled in its inner
contradiction, its miscarriage'.[8] In the eyes of ordinary men and
women, the history of Israel in particular was the history of frus-
trations and failures. The people of Israel never won complete
mastery over the promised land. Even the great reign of David
and Solomon was no exception. And when the tragic debacle
finally came in 586 B.C. and the Jews were taken into captivity,
the divine promise for the future seemed to have been dealt a
death blow. Indeed, the writer of Hebrews is right when he says:

> By faith Abraham obeyed when he was called to go out to a
> place which he was to receive as an inheritance; and he
> went out, not knowing where he was going.[9]

In a very true sense, the biblical faith is the faith 'in spite of'.
Despite the fact that he did not know where he was going, still
Abraham obeyed the divine call, and went out in search of the
land of promise.

Is it, in retrospect, for this reason that the writer of Hebrews
defines faith as 'the assurance of things hoped for, the convictions
of things not seen'?[10] Is Paul thinking along the same lines when
he writes to the Christians in Rome as follows?

> Now hope that is seen is not hope. For who hopes for what
> he sees? But if we hope for what we do not see, we wait
> for it with patience.[11]

Is Paul here engaged in rationalizing the seeming impossibility to
attain the future goal? Is he at pains to explain that the faith
in Jesus Christ is not an illusion? As we know, the early church
expected that Jesus Christ would return speedily and his prolonged
absence became a source of anxiety for them. Is Paul then trying
to justify the absence of any sign of Christ's return in glory and
majesty? Are his words merely an expression of comfort to those
threatened with death or deprived by it? Or does Paul mean to
say that hope has nothing to do with the reality of the present?
Is hope related to a future unseen world detached from the present which can be seen and experienced? Would this not amount
to denying the validity of the present?

Our answer to these questions is as follows. The future which
can be assimilated into the present is not the future in the true

sense of the word. Our future, namely, the future which, we believe, has come within our grasp, is usually not capable of resisting such assimilation. Our future is always threatened by the present. It is devoured by the present to become part of the latter. Our future is, thus, constantly passing into the present. But the process does not stop there. Through the present it further passes into the past and eventually becomes what is past. What we see here is the regression of the future. Instead of pulling us out of the pressure of the present and bringing us into the future which is ahead of us, our future recedes into the past and eventually becomes part of what is behind us. This kind of future, that is, the future which submits to the tyranny of the past, offers no hope to us. In order to have hope, we need to press forward by conquering the past, overcoming the present and creating the future. The future that would redeem the past and have impact on the present must stand above the present, superior to it, and capable of resisting the force to assimilate it into the present, What is this future? Where will it come from? Obviously, it cannot come from man himself. It is the future given to us by God. It is God's future. And in so far as it is God's future, it becomes our future. This is the ultimate future capable of bringing ultimate hope and meaning to the present. It is present in our present but not to be absorbed into the present and to pass into the past. It constitutes the dynamic within the present and pushes the latter forward into the future. We may call this the ultimate future. This ultimate future is the power that fulfils the aspirations of the past and the present. It is in this ultimate future and hope that Paul exhorts us to rejoice and have patience in the midst of the tribulations of the present time.[12]

3. The Resurrection as Our Ultimate Future

What then is the content of this ultimate future endowed with the power of fulfilment? What is it that makes it possible for this ultimate future to carry what is true and valid in the past to its fulfilment? What should be the message of the Christian mission when it proclaims a future and a hope for the world?

The content of this ultimate future is the resurrection. This is the reason why we confess and proclaim that Jesus Christ rose from the dead. Why has it got to be the resurrection? Could

God not have used some other way to show us what the ultimate future is? Here we must realize that the ultimate must be met with the ultimate. The ultimate which puts an end to all our futures and hopes is death. Death renders man silent in the present and then crystallizes him into the past. Death is thus the ultimate enemy of the future. It forces the future to become a non-entity. It nullifies the future. As far as death is concerned, future is a meaningless concept. The simple fact is that in death there is no future. Time has come to a stand-still with death and eventually loses its meaning. With death, time forfeits the only quality that makes it be called time, that is, the quality of time. This is a tautology, but that is what happens. Death deprives time of its time quality.

Furthermore, death dehumanizes all relationships which once surrounded man. When death occurs, everything is changed. That is why death cannot but be cruel and tragic. It destroys love—the power that creates, sustains and enriches person-to-person relationships. Once love is gone, memory too fades away. The memory of those loved ones who were once so dear and near to us fades farther and farther back into oblivion. Even God may no longer remember those who have departed into the land of death. For this reason the psalmist of Psalm 88, brought to the threshold of Sheol, is gripped with fear. And he desperately cries to God:

> I am now numbered with those who go down to the abyss,
> And have become like a man beyond help,
>> like a man who lies dead
>> or the slain who sleep in the grave,
> Whom thou rememberest no more
> Because they are cut off from thy care.[13]

Such is the tyranny of death over man. Heidegger calls man 'being-towards-death'. And in so far as man is a being-towards-death, he has no future, no hope, and thus no God. No wonder death for Paul is the last enemy to be conquered.[14]

This ultimate power of death has thus to be negated and over-come by the ultimate power of life which is the resurrection. This is then the meaning of the resurrection: man as a being-towards-death is now transformed into a being-towards-life. That is why the resurrection is the ground of our hope and our future. As Moltmann says:

> The Christian hope for the future comes of observing a specific event—that of the resurrection and appearing of Jesus Christ. Hence to recognize the resurrection of Christ means to recognize in this event the future of God for the world and the future which man finds in this God and his acts.[15]

The centrality of Jesus Christ in the Christian faith is, therefore, the centrality of the resurrection.

From the perspective of the resurrection, everything comes to be seen in a completely new light. The Gospels are written out of the experience of Easter. Christ is risen! This Easter faith dominates the writers of the Gospels when they begin to give an account of the birth, ministry and the cross of Jesus Christ. Christ for them is no longer a rabbi, a mere moral teacher, or a religious leader. He is the risen Lord. The resurrection faith thus constitutes the pivot from which the kerygma of the early church is developed.

It is Paul who is another dramatic illustration of the centrality of the resurrection for the Christian faith. The meeting with the risen Lord compelled this persecutor of the new faith to become the tireless evangelist and eventually the martyr of that faith. Without the resurrection, there would be no Christ, no Christian community, and no Christian mission to the Gentiles. The New Testament is, therefore, the witness in the resurrection. This is the beginning of a journey to the future, a future filled with hope and promise. At the same time, because of the resurrection, the present becomes filled with the meaning of the future. The present is pulled out of the threat to become part of the past and directed to the future. In this way, the present becomes meaningful; now the present is the future.

Because the Easter event makes man free for the future, man can now be free for the present. In a very true sense, man becomes a lord of the present. He will no longer be buried under the pressure of the present. He will become emancipated from petty preoccupation with his own self and from the burden of the present. He will become open for others and begin to live not just for himself but for others. The resurrection life is, therefore, the life enriched by enriching the lives of others.

The Christian involvement in the affairs of man and the world comes, therefore, from the imperative of the resurrection. Anything that is opposed to the new life in the resurrection becomes the object of Christian concern. That is why the Christian cannot be indifferent to injustice in society simply because injustice is the distortion of human relationships made possible by the risen Christ. He feels most painfully the forces of evil that try to deprive men and women of their ultimate meaning in life such as political oppression and loss of freedom. The loss of freedom makes it impossible for man to be open for the future, and to strive towards the promise that is before him. Once a man is deprived of his freedom, he loses his mastery over the present. This is no other than the enslavement of man to the past and thus to the inevitability of death. This is precisely the opposite of the resurrection. For this reason, he cannot but be opposed to the social structures and political systems which attempt to keep people under the yoke of the past. The liberation movements we discussed before have, therefore, profound theological meaning. These movements, viewed from the Christian perspective and conducted and guided by the Christian hope in the future of God, become instrumental in setting man free for the life of the resurrection, namely, the life oriented to the future.

Even during the ministry of Jesus Christ in the world we have the demonstration of how Jesus tried to pull man out of the enslavement of the past and to give him the power to march into the freedom of the future. He dined and stayed with Zaccheus, the tax collector. He had forgiving words to say to the woman caught in adultery. And nothing could prevent him from freely mingling with those despised by society. To them Jesus Christ had the words of promise and hope. In fact, his presence itself was their hope. To come into his presence was to have the fore-taste of the resurrection life, the life primarily oriented towards the future. Jesus Christ was, therefore, the hope of the people without protection from normal religious and social conventions. That is why Christ was their salvation. To be with him was to be under the power of salvation. When John the Baptist sent

two of his disciples to Jesus with the question: 'Are you he who
is to come, or shall we look for another?' Jesus replied:

> Go and tell John what you have seen and heard: the blind
> receive their sight, the lame walk, lepers are cleansed, and
> the deaf hear, the dead are raised up, the poor have good
> news preached to them. And blessed is he who takes no
> offence at me.[16]

In this answer Jesus shows to John's disciples what he as the
Messiah has undertaken to do. The Messiah, as Jesus understands
it, is the bringer of healing to people in all aspects of their lives,
Through him, healing has come to them. In other words, he leads
them into a new life, namely, life directed and open to the future.

We can, therefore, describe the ministry of Jesus Christ as the
ministry of the resurrection. The event of Easter day is the
culmination of his ministry. It is not something that happens
in complete isolation from the whole ministry of Christ. Rather
it is the full manifestation of what is already at work during his
ministry. Can we go so far as to say that not only the brief
period of Christ's ministry but the whole event of the incarnation
is in reality the resurrection? The baby in the manger is the new
life, the new humanity to be given to the world. It is the life
filled with the promise of the future. It embodies in itself the
promise of the life that will be open to the future and therefore
to be dedicated to the salvation of the world from the past and
death. The event of the incarnation and the event of the resurrection are two events. But the event of the resurrection is already
contained in the event of the incarnation.

Life with Christ thus cannot be anything but joy and celebration. It is the celebration of life in the resurrection. On another
occasion when John's disciples asked Jesus why they had to fast
whereas the latter's disciples did not, Jesus replied: 'Can you expect
the bridegroom's friends to go mourning while the bridegroom
is with them?'[17] The implication here is self-evident. Jesus
Christ came to celebrate life because through him the life of the
resurrection had come into the world. For him death has lost
its power. It is already overcome. That is why to Martha, overcome with grief over the death of her brother, Lazarus, Jesus said:

I am the resurrection and I am life. If a man has faith in
me, even though he die, he shall come to life; and no one
who is alive and has faith shall ever die.[18]

Faith in Jesus Christ is faith in the resurrection life. For this
reason, the Christian life should be a life of victory and triumph,
even though it still has to be lived in the harsh realities of this
world. This means that the cross, too, instead of being a sign
of defeat and death, is a sign of victory and life. The cross without the resurrection has no place in the Christian faith. It remains
as the symbol of the pain and agony of God in Jesus Christ. But
the cross as pain and suffering does not stand by itself. It stands
under the shadow of the resurrection. On account of this, the
cross must be borne with the celebration of the resurrection and
life.

'True Christianity', says Moltmann, 'is the "Rose in the Cross
of the Present".'[19] Rose and the cross under normal circumstances do not go together. But viewed in the light of the resurrection, they convey the victorious nature of the Christian faith.
This image of the rose in the cross is supposed to have come 'from
Luther's coat of arms in which a black cross is represented in
the center of a heart surrounded by white roses. Underneath is
the inscription, "The Christian's heart walks upon roses when
it stands beneath the cross." Luther interpreted this in the following manner: "This is a mark of my theology: *Justus enim fide
vivet, sed fide crucifixi."* '[20].

When we apply our discussion here to Christian mission, this
is what has to be said: Christian mission is the celebration of the
resurrection. And in so far as it is the celebration of the resurrection, it is also the celebration of life. Life must be celebrated
neither because it is without pain and suffering nor because it is
free from sin and evil. But seen in the light of the resurrection,
pain and suffering or sin and evil have no ultimate meaning for
us any more. We are given power to endure them cheerfully. We
are endowed with grace to bear them without complaints. And
above all, we are able to overcome them because of the promise
of the future through the resurrection. Christian mission should,
therefore, emphasize the positive meaning of life made manifest
in the resurrection.

Here again the chief emphasis of Christian mission should not be on the effort to convert people to a particular denomination or a particular theological point of view. There has been too much of this in the past. Christian mission should be the demonstration of the power of the resurrection life. It consists in imparting this power to people so that they will have the courage and strength to stand firm despite the adverse powers at work to undermine their existence. It further enables them to see the meaning of life in the midst of the senselessness of death. It also supports those who strive to gain freedom from injustice and oppression.

Christian mission should continue to call upon people to repent of their sin. But sin in this context here is not solely a moral and religious concept. Sin which Christian mission as the herald of the power of the resurrection has to deal with is that irrational force in man urging him to disturb the order of God's creation, to inflict injustice on other people, to gratify the inordinate desires for power at the expense of others, and to work towards self-interest without the slightest respect and concern for interpersonal relationships. The task of Christian mission cannot be less than that of dealing with such sin with the power of the resurrection.

When the Christian engages himself in this kind of Christian mission, he will be the sign of the love of God. He will point to where the Kingdom of God is to be found. He will be instrumental in giving a new future to those bound by the past and to those who are unable to see beyond the present. His ministry is thus the ministry of the sign of the Kingdom of God. The church in Asia is now called to this ministry, to be the sign of the Kingdom of God. And she has to respond to this call in the midst of political and social changes affecting most profoundly the nature of man and the structures of his society.

4. Sign of the Kingdom

At the conclusion of the last section we affirmed that Christian mission as witness to the power of the resurrection must be the sign of the Kingdom of God. As a sign, it cannot pretend to take the place of that of which it is a sign. This is self-evident because it is inherent in the nature of a sign not to identify itself in substance with that which it signifies. We must, therefore, point out that Christian mission loses immediately its sign-character when it pretends to be more than a sign, that is, when it pretends to be the Kingdom of God itself. The Christian church has, at various stages in her history, erred precisely at this point. We have, for example, the Roman church asserting that there was no salvation outside the church. And to enhance the power and authority of the church, the doctrine of the infallibility of the pope was advanced to absolutize the power of the pope. Theoretically, he was still the vicar of Christ, but practically he made Christ superfluous, since it was now through him and the massive machinery of the church over which he presided that the grace of God was transmitted to the believers.[21]

When a sign loses its sign-character, it simultaneously loses its openness to the future. It will develop and consolidate its own authority, and it will harden itself against any challenge to the legitimacy of its self-established authority. Inevitably it becomes a closed entity, resisting change and reform. It will eternalize its present. It will not accept the future as a possibility. By the same token, when Christian mission loses its basic nature as a sign of the Kingdom of God, it becomes a closed mission. It becomes closed to the future. For those engaged in such a closed mission, the present is their ultimate end. They mistakenly believe that they have reached the journey's end while they have hardly gotten started. They live in an absolute present. The contents of the Christian faith, their outlook on life and the world on the basis of their faith, become crystallized and thus unchangeable. They will become involved in the practice of piety which has no redeeming function for the sufferings and evils resulting from human injustice and social inequality. They thus betray the cause of the Kingdom of God.

Christian mission, as the sign of the Kingdom of God, is eschatological in nature. The term eschatology, used theologically, has as much to do with the present as with the future. In contrast to common understanding, eschatology does not deal with 'last things' in some indefinite time in the future when all things come to an end in the temporal process. Theologically, last things are dealt with in the context of the present. They are seen and experienced in the light of here and now.[22] Eschatology has to do with the vision of the future which provides the basic dynamic for the meaning of the present and which pushes the present open towards the future. It is thus clear that the vision and hope of the future is never a substitute for the responsibility in the present. Understood in relation to this concept of eschatology, Christian mission should become the place where the impact of the future and the dynamic of the Kingdom of God are most intensely made on the present. In other words, Christian mission makes eschatological claim on the present. As Oscar Cullman puts it:

> The missionary work of the church is the eschatological fore-taste of the Kingdom of God, and the biblical hope of the 'end' constitutes the keenest incentive to action.[23]

Thus, Christian mission embodies in itself the tension between the present and the future.

Being eschatological in the sense we discussed above, Christian mission cannot take the present for granted. It cannot be satisfied with the present *status quo*. It challenges the present not to become a closed present. It stresses that the present is not the end but the beginning. In this way, Christian mission must be always in search of frontiers where it can become engaged in the eschatological mission of bringing hope to the present situation. The predominant note of Christian mission should, therefore, be the urgency of hope and not the threat of condemnation. Even the wrath of God must be seen in the light of the hope of God. That is why the wrath of God, seen in isolation from hope, becomes demonic and thus destructive. We cannot experience the redeeming nature of God's wrath unless it is experienced in relation to the cross and the resurrection.

The history of the church tells us that when the Christian church parts company with Christian mission which is eschatological in nature, she loses her inner dynamic to become open and creative for the future; she loses her incentive for action. She lives on her past. She becomes more and more a liturgical church. The priestly function of the clergy overshadows the prophetic function. The clergy become preoccupied with the church as an institution, and the activities of the church members are directed to the conservation of the church as an institution. This kind of church has no passion for the world. And with the loss of passion for the world, she loses passion for God. Is it often not the case that when a church is built high and beautiful, the members of that church tend to sit back and slip into a lethargic period of their religious life? It is life without excitement, without future and without hope. They come to the church to meditate on the life to come and not to seek the call of God for the present world. It goes without saying that they are no longer interested in becoming actively and whole-heartedly involved in Christian mission as the sign of the Kingdom of God.

Christian mission as eschatological in nature is furthermore a broken sign of the Kingdom of God. Its brokenness is part of the completeness of the Kingdom of God at the end of time. Christian mission, set out to transform the present with the passion for the future, cannot afford to be too much concerned about the perfection of its form and content. In fact, such perfection does not exist. It has to be content with its brokenness. Only in its brokenness can it point to and serve the beauty of perfection which belongs to the Kingdom of God. For this reason, Christian mission has to pull Christians out of the temptation to get settled in the comfort of church life, in theologically sound creeds and in well-organized ecclesiastical systems. This is the war which Christian mission must wage on the homefront. For it is the church which must exist for Christian mission, and not vice versa. When this irreversible relation between the church and Christian mission is reversed, the integrity of Christian mission will be threatened. Christian mission will no longer be a broken sign of the Kingdom of God. It now identifies itself with the church as the Kingdom of God. When this happens, Christian mission will lose its essential nature of being eschatological. Such church and such Christian mission will resist the Holy Spirit who constantly moves from the present into the future.

It is unfortunate that so much of the so-called Christian art has also tended to make the work of the Spirit of God a captive of the static past. Strictly speaking, the Spirit of God bursting into the world in Jesus Christ cannot be represented in any plastic form. The beauty of artistic forms representing various aspects of the divine-human encounter in Jesus Christ tends to convey a false illusion that Christian faith is to be appreciated aesthetically. The true beauty of God's act in Jesus Christ can be expressed only through the brokenness of artistic forms. As it is said of the Suffering Servant:

He had no form or comeliness that we should look at him,
And no beauty that we should desire him.
He was despised and rejected by men;
A man of sorrows, and acquainted with grief;
And as one from whom men hide their faces
He was despised, and we esteemed him not.[24]

It is sometimes said that crisis of Christian mission comes from the modern world. Industrialization and modernization have secularized the world so much that there is now little room for the fear of God. For fervent Christians the contemporary world is identical with impiety and atheism. But can the modern world, especially the non-Western world, pose as a threat to Christ who comes to feed the hungry, to defend the rights of the oppressed, to comfort the hearts of those torn with grief? If Christian mission has run into crisis, if it becomes discredited, if it does not have as much impact on the people as before, it is mainly because the church has become too respectable, beautiful and rich. When Christian mission comes to represent this kind of church, it ceases to be a sign of the Kingdom of God. It speaks for this church and not for the Kingdom of God. It thus loses its sign-character.

Furthermore, Christian mission as the sign of the Kingdom of God should be the bringer of crisis to the present world. Christian mission is a sign of crisis, for wherever the Kingdom of God becomes manifest what goes on in the world is put into question, challenged and critically examined. Therefore, Christian mission must pose as a crisis to the present. It demands men and women to decide for the past or for the future. It challenges them to opt for life or death, for God or demon. In other words, Christian mission must be conducted in such a way that it disturbs the people and challenges them to ask fundamental questions concerning themselves and the world.

As long as Christian mission does not cease to become the bringer of crisis, the world will be held by hope despite the threat of annihilation. Thus, Christian mission can never adopt the attitude of a spectator in relation to the world. Those engaged in Christian mission are not spectators watching what is happening in the world from a fence. They cannot escape the fact that they are part of this world. That is why Barth says that 'a wide reading of contemporary secular literature—especially of newspapers—is . . . recommended to anyone desirous of understanding the Epistle to the Romans.'[25] We cannot, therefore, treat spiritual matters as if they have nothing to do with the secular world. We cannot turn the preaching of the Word of God into a spiritual exercise bearing little relation to the events and happenings in society. God's entry into history in Jesus Christ is not the subject for meditation. It is an action, an event which has changed the world and turned the tide of history. Since Christian mission is to serve this event of the Word of God, it cannot but find itself addressing social and political issues as well as personal and spiritual problems pertaining to individual men and women.

Christian mission is thus a broken and critical sign pointing to the Kingdom of God. But what does the Kingdom of God mean in contemporary Asia? In other words, what should Christian mission do so that the Kingdom of God will become relevant to the millions and hundreds of millions of people in Asia? What are the signs which Christian mission should consider becoming if the Kingdom of God is not to become a utopia merely filling the spiritual gap of the people?

First of all, Christian mission, in order to be a sign of the Kingdom of God, should take materialism seriously, for the Kingdom of God has to do with the world of matter as well as the world of the spirit. The fact that the Kingdom of God has already broken into our world in Jesus Christ affirms that the dualism of matter and spirit should become an obsolete concept in Christian faith. But much of Christian mission in Asia is still conducted on the basis of such dualism. It still makes its conventional emphasis on spiritual values as over against material values. Such Christian mission cannot but be an anachronism. One cannot help becoming painfully aware of this anachronistic nature of Christian mission especially in the Chinese churches in Asia, especially when one realizes that it is not a hollow expectation in a spiritual realm but the down-to-earth, day-to-day struggle for material welfare that proved to be a powerful force in the life of the people of China. Here is a case of staunch materialism intent on regulating an entire nation and its people on a completely different socio-political system and on an entirely different life style. Thus, what van Leeuwen has said is correct: 'What we need most desperately is a clear theology of materialism.'[26]

A theology of materialism should begin with the affirmation of the spirit not apart from matter but within matter. This does not mean that all matter is automatically imbued with the Spirit of God. This would lead to pantheism. What is affirmed here is that it is through matter or the material world that the Spirit of God works in the world. In other words, the Spirit of God does not work in a matter-less world. Such a world does not exist. Much of the indifference shown by Asian Christians towards society can be traced to this unbiblical and untheological understanding of the world of matter. That the material world is infected with sins, a favourite theme of zealous evangelists, has made it difficult in the past for Christians in Asia to hold positive attitudes towards the development of their own society and nation. Indeed, the exaltation of spiritual life at the expense of the material world has proved costly to the mission of the church in Asia.

The recognition of a spiritual force embedded in matter is of particular importance when secularization has been changing the face of Asia since the end of World War II. In secularization we see a new spiritual force taking the place of the old spiritual force which dominated the old Asia under conventional morality and feudalistic value systems. This old world has largely been secularized. Everywhere people are demanding betterment of their lot by discarding the shackles of fate, striving towards freedom, fighting for justice and making efforts to eliminate poverty. Unless Christian mission is able to come to grips with the spiritual force at work in all this, it will have no message to communicate to contemporary Asia. It can only speak to those who are in search of a spiritual world unrelated to the present world.

Christian mission should affirm that materialism itself is not atheistic. It cannot continue its indiscriminate attack on materialism as arch-enemy of faith in God. The subject matter of debate or dialogue between Christian faith and materialism has not so much to do with the existence of God as to do with man's being. Materialism poses as a threat to man, thus dishonouring God only when it develops into an ideology constituting the basis of a political system demanding unconditional loyalty and obedience from man. In this case man is submitted to a slavery, depriving him of his freedom and integrity. The issue here is, of course, that of dehumanization which we discussed in the previous chapter.

Furthermore, as a sign of the Kingdom of God, Christian mission must point out that the historical destiny of peoples in Asia is not alien to God's salvation. The identification of 'Christendom' with the Kingdom of God tended to encourage Christians both in the West and in the East to think that the history and culture of Asia had no substantial relationship with the Kingdom of God. In fact, Asian history and culture were considered as antagonistic to the purpose of God's salvation. There was, therefore, conscious effort to isolate Asian Christians from their historical and cultural roots and to add them artificially to the history of the church in the West. This misconception of the Kingdom of God has largely been corrected. We now realize that it is wrong to view the Kingdom of God in Asia through the looking-glass of Western Christian culture.

This does not, however, mean that we can identify the historical destiny of Asian peoples with God's salvation. To do so is to commit the same mistake of regarding the entire history of Western Christendom as the Kingdom of God. The Kingdom of God cannot be identified with any history or culture entirely, for it breaks into history and creates redemptive impact on it but will never lose itself into it. The Kingdom of God cannot be immobilized in a particular historical or cultural confinement. It breaks out of history just as it breaks into it. This is a metaphorical way of saying that the Kingdom of God is both immanent in and transcendent from history. It, therefore, can be immanent in and transcendent from the history and culture of Asia just as it has been immanent in and transcendent from the history and culture of the West.

Would what has been said above amount to the denial of the validity inherent in the history of the church in the West? Not at all. The history of the church in the West discloses how the Kingdom of God has been at work in that particular segment of human history. And there is much to be learned from it. But this in no way requires and dictates that those from outside the West be exposed to the Kingdom of God only through the Western experience of God's salvation. In fact it is more important for them to be related to the saving love of God directly in their own historical contexts. For this purpose, those engaged in Christian mission in Asia have to develop insight into the Asian history and culture so that they will be able to discern in them the hidden presence of the Kingdom of God.

The criterion of such discernment is Jesus Christ in whom the Kingdom of God is most intensively manifested. Ultimately it is what conforms to this Jesus Christ and not to the history and tradition of the church that is important. Thus, Jesus Christ as the center of history is freed from the confinement to the framework of Judeo-Christian history. He is the center of history in the sense that historical events and cultural phenomena outside the Judeo-Christian tradition are interpreted and evaluated with reference to Jesus Christ. It is to be expected that uniformity can no longer be maintained in the history of the church. There will be diversity of interpretation with regard to the meaning of Jesus Christ for different histories and cultures. Naturally there will be different expressions in accordance with the ways in which Jesus Christ is perceived to be at work in different historical and cultural contexts. This will contribute to the enrichment of Christian theology. Christian mission is to serve this enrichment of theology by bringing out to the open the Kingdom of God which gets broken into diversified presence in histories and cultures and thus is not at once obvious and perceptible.

There is another point which must be mentioned before bringing this section to a close. Christian mission as a sign of the Kingdom of God must bring the note of urgency to Asia today. The proclamation of the presence of the Kingdom of God is made by Jesus Christ with great urgency. According to Mark's Gospel, Jesus began His ministry by saying: 'The time has come; the Kingdom of God is upon you; repent, and believe the Gospel'.[27] Asia has been witnessing tremendous change and transformation in recent years. It has been brought out of its timeless past and placed in the process of time. In other words, Asia has been contemporalized. Transition from timelessness to time is a momentous change. The result is that more and more Asians have become very time-conscious. They race with time. There is, therefore, urgency in many aspects of life in Asia today. National development is planned and carried out according to a carefully worked out time-table. We have become used to hearing about a three-year plan, five-year plan, and so on. National salvation is thus identified with the successful carrying out of these plans.

However, change itself or development itself is not the Kingdom of God. Christian mission must proclaim that the Kingdom of God impinges upon the change and development that place Asia in more and more of a crucial position in world history. Precisely because of this, the nations and peoples in Asia must open themselves up to the dimension that comes with the Kingdom of God. As the gravity of world history seems to be moving away from the West towards the East, it is inevitable that the East will play an important role vis-à-vis the future of mankind. Christian mission in Asia is thus endowed with the grave responsibility to let the Kingdom of God be manifest in Asia. In so far as Christian mission in Asia is able to fulfil this responsibility, there will be hope for the future of Asia and the world. Thus, Christian mission cannot be less than the mission of hope.

5. Mission of Hope

That which makes a prophet in the Old Testament great is his extraordinary gift to rise above the confusion, lostness and despair of the present and to point towards the future God has in store for His people. Jeremiah is such a prophet. His message of hope to his compatriots in the Babylonian captivity is, therefore, very pertinent to Christian mission today.

Outwardly, Jeremiah's experience suggests little hope. He is personally and tragically related to the fate of his own nation. He sees clearly that Judah is heading for destruction. Her fate is almost sealed. There seems little prospect of reversing that fate. Jeremiah hesitates and even refuses to speak out on behalf of God on account of anticipated misfortunes. Who wants to be a prophet of doom? Who is willing to bear the burden of telling the people of Judah nothing but war and disaster? It is only under a strong divine compulsion that Jeremiah has taken up such an awesome task. But what he anticipated has happened. He is met with derision, threat and persecution. At one point he has to say in desperation:

O Lord, Thou hast seduced me, and I am seduced;
Thou hast raped me, and I am overcome.[28]

The strong language used by Jeremiah here conveys vividly the tremendous pressure under which he has to carry out his ministry. It is over against this background that we are all the more surprised by the message of hope he communicates in his letters to those exiled in Babylonia. Among other things he says:

For I know the plans I have for you, says the Lord, plans for welfare and not for evil, to give you a future and a hope.[29]

The prophet of doom has turned into the prophet of hope. It is clear that for Jeremiah it is hope and not doom that is the last word.

Hope is not something that comes out of the blue. Hope for the future, if it is to be true hope, has to emerge from hardship, confusion and despair. In order for hope not to become illusion, it has to be related to suffering of the present. Jeremiah speaks of hope not by minimizing the traumatic impact which the Babylonian captivity has had on his people and his nation. But he tries to interpret the meaning of their present suffering in the light of the hope which God has for them in the future.

The content of his message of hope is most remarkable. God promises 'a future and a hope' for Israel, but this future and this hope is to be saturated with the welfare of the present. Accordingly, Jeremiah exhorts his compatriots in Babylonia to work for their welfare by building houses, planting gardens and rearing families. In other words, the present must be affirmed for the ushering in of a future. Or to put it differently, the future must be built on the strength of the present. It is only the fully-lived present that can be taken into the hope of the future. Perhaps we can even say that the hope of the future consists in the fulfilment of the meaning of the present. In this way, the mission of hope must begin with the present. It begins when Christians themselves are filled with the affirmation of the present for the sake of the future.[1]

But this is not all Jeremiah has to say. He exhibits the true stature of a prophet when he writes: 'Seek the welfare of any city to which I have carried you off, and pray to the Lord for it; on its welfare your welfare will depend'.[30] This counsel must not be regarded as a shrewd realism based on the realization that the welfare of the people in exile is irrevocably bound with the welfare of their captors. It would be the height of religious dishonesty, if Jeremiah were to exhort them to pray to God on behalf of the Babylonians out of such pragmatic calculation. Furthermore, what makes obnoxious the practice of securing one's own well-being at the expense of others is its immoral character. It degrades others, dehumanizes them and makes them a mere tool of achieving one's goal. There is no hope and no future for a society in which such degradation takes place. It corrupts humanity and thus destroys the basis of human relationships. When this happens, the divine-human relationship too is affected.

The Jews in exile are to pray to God on behalf of the Babylonians and to seek the latter's well-being as well as theirs. The Jews are no longer a separate entity having nothing to do with other nations and peoples. Through the experience of the Babylonian captivity, Jeremiah has come to deep awareness that the history of his own nation is bound up with the history of other nations. Historical isolationism is no longer possible. The hope and future of his nation cannot be envisioned in separation from the hope and future of other nations. Not only this, having been involved in the unfolding of God's saving love through their historical experiences, those in exile should be in a position to be a witness to the hope and promise of God among their new neighbours. Thus, instead of giving themselves away to despair and disappointment, they should re-organize themselves in such a way that they can be a sign of God's saving love for all mankind.

A new understanding of the mission of the people of God as consisting in hope for the future as seen by Jeremiah and others out of their profound Babylonian experience furnishes Christian mission with a central commission to be a mission of hope. Christian mission, as a mission announcing God's hope for the world in Jesus Christ, is carried out in the contexts of world history in which the providence of God is unfolding itself in the midst of human ambiguities. The main task of Christian mission is, therefore, not to Christianize the world, not to make the so-called pagans Christians, but to be the agent of peace. (The Authorized Version aptly renders the word welfare as peace in Jeremiah 29). Christian mission is to engage those it encounters in pursuit of *shalom*, that is, in pursuit of healings of wounds inflicted politically, racially, socially or religiously. In so doing, Christian mission points to the end of time, namely, to God's future for man. As someone has put it:

> The goal of Christian missionary presence is always the presence of Christ, to whom witness is to be borne as the one

who died and was raised again for the love of God to the world. To that extent, 'the basic form of witness is presence—to exist in a situation with a sense of responsibility towards men in it, and with the constant intention of witness to the Christ-event within it. This is the essential form of mission.'[31]

Christ's presence in the world made visible through Christian mission—this is what primarily makes Christian mission a mission of hope.

The crux of the matter here is Christ's presence and not Christian presence. The distinction is made between the two not on the grounds of academic interest nor with the spirit of cynicism. In the course of the history of the church, Christian presence in the world has more often than not obscured the presence of Christ. The presence of Christians in a church, where a certain group of people is excluded on account of race, creed and nationality, is an insult to the presence of Christ. The existence of Christian communities which seek their own internal well-being in entire oblivion of the dire needs of those outside has, of course, ceased to be witness to the presence of Christ. The church, which refuses to cross the boundaries of culture and ideology, grieves the heart of God poured out for men and women, even for atheists, and drives Christ out from her midst. The mission of such a church or Christian community is a mission of despair. In short, Christian presence is often loaded with political, cultural and religious burdens of those engaged in mission.

It may be observed that it is Christian presence rather than Christ's presence that continues to preoccupy Western Christian mission directed outside the boundaries of the Western world. With the gradual military disengagement of the Western powers from Asia, beginning with the British and the French soon after World War II, and now with American retreat from Indochina, Western presence through military personnel and operations has become much less important than before. It has taken almost a century to bring this about since the Western powers forcefully opened the gates of China to the West through the Opium War, 1839-1842. Western Christian mission may have cause to celebrate because the day seems to have arrived when it can now carry on its work without being accused again of having to do with

Western colonial and imperialistic conspiracy. But celebration is too premature. Instead of military offensive, there has been massive economic offensive which exposes the people in Asia helplessly to the economic interests of the affluent West. Undoubtedly, this will perpetuate and deepen the distorted image of the Western presence in Asia. And let us admit that whether they like it or not, Western missionaries are part of this distorted image.

It may be appropriate to add a few remarks here with regard to the church in Japan. The remarks to be made here are prompted by the following consideration: on account of the crucial and influential role which Japan has begun to play not only in Asia but also in the whole world, it is only right that the church in Japan, more than any other churches in Asia, needs to think of her responsibility seriously in relation to the rest of Asia. On the whole, it is accurate to say that the church in Japan is still economically weak, despite the fact that Japan has become one of the great economic powers in the world.[32] Japanese economic invasion of Southeast Asia through investments and personnel is already arousing anxiety among Southeast Asian nations. In the providence of God, the church in Japan is not in the position economically to initiate missionary operations in the rest of Asia to any significant degree. In fact, she was more dependent on her historical ties with the churches in the West than some of the less developed nations in Asia. And there is still a great deal of effort to be made to enable her to become free from the Western influences which have shaped much of her ecclesiology and theology. Undoubtedly, this is not a task which can be accomplished in a short time. But it is clear that no evasion of the task can be justified. It is only fair to add here that the same thing applies equally to the churches in the other parts of Asia. This poses as exciting future for us all. Be that as it may, if the church in Japan had grown affluent like the rest of Japanese society, there is reason to expect that she would have launched out into missionary enterprise largely similar to that of Western churches. That would have been unfortunate both for the church in Japan and the churches in the rest of Asia.

What we should expect fom the church in Japan is, therefore, twofold. Firstly, she should undergo a process of critically evaluating her relationships with the churches in the West. The growing influence of Japan in the politics of Asia is already a cause of concern for the nations in Asia. The continued alliance of the church in Japan with the churches in the West will constitute a double threat to Asian churches.[33] For the sake of the church in Japan and in North America, and especially in the hope of expressing the sense of common responsibility for the future of Asia, there is no question about the fact that the church in Japan has to radically change her West-oriented posture to an Asia-oriented one. This leads to the second point of our concern here. This is the time for the church in Japan to be in full consultation with the churches in Asia for the future course of Christian mission in Asia. This is particularly important in view of the fact that conflicting forces are at work to make it difficult, if not impossible, to visualize a future at hand in which some of the most pressing human issues and socio-political problems will be solved. For better or for worse, we must realize that some of the dramatic changes which have been taking place in some Asian nations challenge the churches in Asia to rethink their role in the shaping of the destiny of millions and hundreds of millions of people in Asia. After all the political turmoils which have shaken and continue to shake Asian nations, we are driven to admit that the destiny of Asia must be shaped by the Asians, that the churches have an inescapable responsibility in this agonizing task. It is from this perspective that the relationship of the church in Japan, and for that matter, any church in Asia, with the churches in the rest of the world must be evaluated and formulated.

After this digression, let us return to our discussion on distinction between Christ's presence and Christian presence. The distinction is important because Christ's presence judges Christian presence. This implies that the church, which is the visible expression of Christian presence in the world, cannot be assumed to hold the keys to heaven and hell. The church, herself under the judgment of Christ's presence, cannot determine who will be saved and who will be damned. Christian presence in the world, therefore, does not judge, nor for that matter can the church act as the judge of the world. The church serves Christ's presence by becoming witness to it. Therefore, Christian presence is a sign to the presence of Christ. It is a sign to the reality of God's judgment and salvation through Jesus Christ. As a sign of Christ's presence, Christian presence also receives the judgment and salvation of God. It is when Christian mission is in service of this Christ that it becomes a mission of hope.

Strictly speaking, Christian mission is not the mission of hope. It *becomes* the mission of hope as Christ's presence is manifested through it. This further implies that neither Christian mission in particular nor man in general can create hope for the future of mankind. Hope is the gift of God. It is when man gives up self-reliance and self-autonomy and gives himself up to God that the hope of God will become a reality to him. Modern man begins to learn this lesson in a hard way. His faith in science is greatly reduced by the fear of a global atomic war. It becomes apparent that an enduring peace for the world cannot be built on the power of destruction. His faith in man's technological ability to conquer the world for the welfare of mankind is increasingly marred by pollution of air, water and environments. The warnings which ecologists are giving are not unfounded. Man's power to explore and make use of resources in nature seems to be in danger of being cancelled out by his power to destroy nature. The on-going process of urbanization, too, continues to disclose man's vulnerability to disorder and vice.

In fact, the problem of the contemporary world is man himself. The world has almost become the projection of man's great genius for both construction and destruction. Man has tried to take the Kingdom of God by violence and enthrone himself as the master of the created world. We have seen enough of this happen in Nazism, in Japanese militarism and in the development of atomic energy for destructive purposes. Indeed, the spirit of the twentieth century is the spirit of man defying the divine authority and of attempting to become the ultimate authority. It is the restless spirit of rebellion against God in the depth of man's being. Man must be saved from his restless spirit. Reinhold Niebuhr has once said:

> It is the business of the Christian church to bear witness not to the righteousness of Christians but to the righteousness of God, which judges all men, and to the grace of Christ which saves all who truly repent of their sins.[34]

This business of the church is also the business of Christian mission. Christian mission is to lead the restless spirit of man to the righteousness of God and to the grace of Christ for man's salvation.

Moreover, Christian mission becomes a mission of hope as it seeks to give witness to Christ's presence in solidarity with the rest of humanity. This thrusts Christian mission right into the world of realities. It seeks the acts of God not inside the church but outside the church. And in its solidarity with humanity in suffering and joy, in hate and love, in death and life, it becomes the real witness to the incarnation which is nothing other than God's oneness with man. Christian mission must be, therefore, incarnational in nature. That is to say, it must be structured in accordance with the nature and intent of the incarnation.

Herein lies the hope of the world. In a very true sense the incarnation goes on in the world through Christian mission. It is perhaps more accurate to say Christian mission continues the incarnation. It proclaims that Christ is in the world and with mankind until the end of time. That is why Christian mission should represent Christ in standing on the side of the oppressed, the under-privileged and the poor. As we have discussed before this is the basic theological reason why Christian mission means involvement in the affairs of the world. And in such involvement, Christian mission becomes a living witness to the hope of man in Jesus Christ. Christians, who are first made to have a foretaste of this hope, are commissioned to explore this hope within historical processes and in existential situations. And biblical faith assures us that through the history of Israel and the events in the early community of the followers of Christ, the future of individual men and women becomes a reality in the present as Christians and their fellow creatures envision hope in their day-to-day struggle for justice, freedom and peace in the world. In this sense, and in this sense alone, man becomes God's co-worker and partner in the creation of a future which leads to the ultimate future, namely, the future which fulfils God's purpose of salvation.

We must remember that Christian mission as the mission of hope fills the time between Easter and the ultimate future. As a post-Easter event and in solidarity with humanity on the grounds of hope in the resurrected Christ, we are assured that no tears are vainly shed, no pain and agony are wasted and no human search for the Reality in religion, culture and especially in the process of secularization at the present time, will pass away un-

judged and unredeemed. Since the Fall of man, man has been
desperately engaged in search for hope for the future. His search
has ever so often turned into despair, destruction and death.
Despite all man's failure, or precisely because of man's failure,
God has entrusted the mission of hope first to Israel and then to
Christianity. The mission of hope is, therefore, the divine commission. Christian mission is the divine imperative which must
be carried out until Christ is found to be 'all, and in all.'[35]

REFERENCES

1. Jean Paul Sartre, *No Exit*, translated by Stuart Gilbert, New York: Alfred A. Kopf, 1954.

2. Thus, according to Harvey Cox, Marxists such as Ernst Bloch, pose a serious challenge to the death-of-God theologians. 'The death of God,' writes Cox, 'cannot become either the content of Christian proclamation or the determinative condition under which theology must now proceed. . . . It cannot define theology's task since the mere disappearance of God does not answer what for Blacks remains the crucial question, i.e., "What holds history open for man and man open for history ?" ' ('Ernst Bloch and "The Pull of the Future",' in *New Theology*, No. 5, edited by Martin E. Marty and Dean G. Peerman, New York: The Macmillan Company, 1968, p. 200).

3. In his study of eschatology in the context of African religions, John S. Mbiti says that the concept of future does not exist for the Akamba and many other African peoples. He writes: 'The most significant factor is that Time is considered as a two-dimensional phenomenon; with a long "past," and a dynamic "present." The "future" as we know it in the linear conception of Time is virtually non-existent in Akimba thinking. My findings from other African peoples have not yielded any radical difference' (*New Testament Eschatology in an African Background*, London: Oxford University Press, 1971, p. 24).

4. Mao Tze-tung, *Report of an Investigation into the Peasant Movement in Hunan* (made in 1927). Quoted by Richard Bush in *Religion in Communist China*, Nashville and New York: Abingdon Press, 1970, p. 30.

5. van Leeuwen, *Christianity in World History*, p. 380.

6. Harvey Cox in *op. cit.*, (p. 203) asks very thought-provoking questions: 'I have often speculated on how different theology would be today if Ernst Bloch, rather than Martin Heidegger, had been our conversation partner for the past twenty years. Would we be as miserably lacking as we are in a theologically grounded ethic ? Would we be as disastrously out of touch with the revolution that is transforming the third world and burning the centers of our American cities ? Would we have needed the catharsis of the death-of-God theology ? Would we have allowed the ecclesiastical furniture shuffling of recent years to pose as a real renewal of the church ? Might we have produced a theology that was truly radical in its impact on the world and not just in its rhetoric ?'

7. Roger Garaudy, 'Communists and Christians in Dialogue,' in *New Theology*, No. 5, edited by Martin E. Marty and Dean G. Peerman, New York: The Macmillan Company, 1968, p. 212.

8. Bultmann, *Essays, Philosophical and Theological*, translated by James C. G. Greig, New York: The Macmillan Company, 1955, p. 205.

9. Hebrews 11:8.

10. Hebrews 11:1.

11. Romans 8:24.

12. Romans 12:12.

13. Psalm 88:4-5.

14. I Corinthians 15:26.

15. Jürgen Moltmann, *Theology of Hôpe*, translated by James W. Leith, London: SCM Press, 1967, p. 194.

16. Luke 7:22-23.

17. Matthew 9:14-15.

18. John 11:25.

19. Jürgen Moltmann, *Hope and Planning*, translated by Margaret Clarkson, New York: Harper and Row, 1971, p. 148.

20. Cf. Karl Lowith, *From Hegel to Nietzsche*, 1964, 14ff. This exposition of the image by Lowith is quoted and expanded by Moltmann in *Hope and Planning*, p. 150.

21. Just prior to the formulation of the dogma on papal infallibility in 1870, so Hans Küng, in his critique of the dogma, points out 'among the council fathers . . . some singular theories about the pope were circulating. Some spoke of the pope as "Vice-God of mankind" and Mermillod, auxiliary bishop of Geneva, spoke of the "three incarnations of the Son of God" in the Virgin's womb, in the Eucharist, and in the old man of the Vatican' (*Infallible ? An Inquiry*, translated by Edward Quinn, New York: Doubleday and Company, 1972, p. 88).

22. For Moltmann eschatology has to do with hope rather than with last things. He says: '. . . . eschatology means the doctrine of the Christian hope, which embraces both the object hoped for and also the hope inspired by it. From first to last, and not merely in epilogue, Christianity is eschatology, is hope, forward looking and forward moving, and therefore also revolutionizing and transforming the present' (*Theology of Hope*, p. 16). Paul Tillich also puts emphasis on the present as well as future when he writes : '. . .the *eschaton* becomes a matter of present experience without losing its futuristic dimension; we stand *now* in face of the eternal, but we do so looking ahead toward the end of history and the end of all which is temporal in the eternal' (*Systematic Theology*, Vol. IV, The University of Chicago Press, 1963, p. 306)

23. Oscar Cullmann, "Eschatology and Missions in the New Testament, in *The Theology of the Christian Mission*, edited by G. H. Anderson, p. 43.

24. Isaiah 53:2-3.

25. Barth, *The Epistle to the Romans*, 6th Edition, London: Oxford University Press, 1933, p. 425.

26. van Leeuwen, *Christianity in World History*, p. 437.

27. Mark 1:14.

28. Jeremiah 20:7. This is Heschel's translation. His comments on this verse are worth quoting : 'The striking feature of the verse is the use of two verbs *patah* and *hatak*. The first term is used in the Bible and in the special sense of wrongfully inducing a woman to consent to pre-nuptial intercourse. . . The second term denotes the violent forcing of a woman to submit to extranuptial intercourse. The first denotes seduction or enticement; the second, rape. . . . The terms used in immediate juxtaposition forcefully convey the complexity of the divine-human relationship: sweetness of enticement as well as violence of rape. . . . The prophet feels both the attraction and the coercion of God, the appeal and the pressure, the charm and the stress. He is conscious of voluntary identification and forced capitulation' (*The Prophets*, New York: Harper and Row, 1962, pp. 113-114).

29. Jeremiah 29:11. Revised Standard Version.

30. Jeremiah 29:7.

31. Gerhard Rosenkranz, 'Christian presence Across the Frontiers,' in *The Church Crossing the Frontiers*, p. 142. The quotation in the text is from R. K. Orchard, *Missions in a Time of Testing*, London, 1964.

32. The following observation made by James M. Phillips, Professor of Church History at the Tokyo Union Theological Seminary, is worth quoting as an accurate description of the church in Japan: 'From the 1970's, almost all of the Japanese Christian denominations, from the extremely conservative Protestant groups to the larger Protestant denominations, and the Roman Catholic and Orthodox Churches, have all felt the ever-growing pressures towards Japanese autonomy . . . But although lip service was often paid to such ideals, there were numerous ways in which foreigners could maintain a measure of control in the immediate post war years, due to the privations which Christians in Japan were then facing. But the nation's astounding economic growth changed these circumstances, even though Christians themselves did not share in the average increase in affluence. Quite apart from economic factors, there was a growing realization that it was unwise for Christian groups in Japan to be beholden to overseas Christians for personnel or directions, especially when the signs of the times seemed to point to unique forms of witness which only Japanese Christians could carry out in relation to their society, and toward people of other nations as well' (See Phillips' monograph entitled 'Ecumenicity's Unsteady Course in Modern Japan, 1945-1972,' published by Oriens, Institute for Religious Research, Tokyo, Japan, June, 1973, pp. 23-24).

33. The new structure inaugurated between the United Church of Christ in Japan and the churches in North America in January, 1973, under the name Japan North-American Commission on Co-operative Mission is supposed to replace the missionary relationship in the past by the church-to-church relationship. But it still remains to be seen whether the new structure will live up to the goal set by its founders. Furthermore, by consolidating the tie between the two sectors of the Christian church on both sides of the Pacific, it is not clear it will have a constructive part to play in relation to the churches in other parts of Asia.

34. Reinhold Niebuhr, *Essays in Applied Christianity*, p. 35.

35. Colossians 3:11.